Praise F
Jewish Spiritual
Wisdom, Activities, Rituals and I
with Spiritual Balance and

"An invaluable resource for parents who are concerned not only with their children's success, but with their souls."

—**Rabbi David Wolpe**, Max Webb Rabbi, Sinai Temple, Los Angeles; best-selling author, *Teaching Your Children about God*

"Engaging and spiritually motivating.... A must-read for clergy, parents, grandparents, teachers and anyone charged with the holy task of nurturing young souls."

—**Rabbi Ilana C. Garber**, Beth El Temple, West Hartford, Connecticut; blogger, ilanagarber.com

"With warmth, candor, Jewish insight and practical wisdom, Paul Kipnes and Michelle November show us all how to be better parents. By reminding us that both childhood and parenting are spiritual journeys, they illuminate a path toward wholeness for us all."

—**David Stern**, senior rabbi, Temple Emanu-El, Dallas

"A wonderful resource for people striving to raise their children with Jewish values and traditions in our materialistic, 'me-centric' society.... A very helpful guide at many levels."

—**Joanne Doades**, author, *Parenting Jewish Teens: A Guide for the Perplexed*

"Gently encourage[s] the reader to explore the myriad ways of infusing parenting with moments of deep meaning."

—**Rebecca Einstein Schorr**, co-editor, *The Sacred Calling: Forty Years of Women in the Rabbinate*; blogger, This Messy Life (rebeccaeinsteinschorr.com)

"A wonderful, idea-packed, practical guide for shaping a spiritually alive Jewish family. The perfect gift for parents and grandparents looking to bring joy and meaning, blessings and kisses into the home."

—**Dr. Ron Wolfson**, Fingerhut Professor of Education, American Jewish University; author, *The Best Boy in the United States of America: A Memoir of Blessings and Kisses*

"Inclusion is a value that the entire Jewish community must practice—in its synagogues, schools, camps and community organizations. Paul Kipnes and Michelle November have been leaders on this issue in their community and we can all learn from their example of acceptance and inclusion."

—**Jay Ruderman**, president, Ruderman Family Foundation

"Paul Kipnes and Michelle November share their decades of wisdom on our most sacred work as parents—raising our children.... They live it, breathe it, teach it. Their children are the greatest testimony."

—**Ruben Arquilevich**, executive director, Newman Center for Year-Round Engagement

"With rare wisdom, gentle love and humor, Paul Kipnes and Michelle November turn parenting into a spiritual adventure. This book is a blessing to a new generation of families. I will joyfully share it with new parents and grandparents."

—**Rabbi Edward Feinstein**, author, *Tough Questions Jews Ask: A Young Adult's Guide to Building a Jewish Life*

"Insightful, uplifting and filled with lots of practical tips.... It should sit right next to Dr. Spock on the nightstand."

—**Dr. Kerry M. Olitzky**, executive director, Big Tent Judaism / Jewish Outreach Institute; author, *Introducing My Faith and My Community: The Jewish Outreach Institute Guide for the Christian in a Jewish Interfaith Relationship*

"This book is a gem. The authors serve as your warm, wise and candid guides to a stunning range of Jewish wisdom for the here and now.... Learn and enjoy."

—**Dr. Wendy Mogel**, author, *The Blessing of a Skinned Knee: Using Jewish Teachings to Raise Self-Reliant Children*

"An invaluable guide for parents seeking to raise spiritually resilient and grounded children."

—**Rabbi Rick Jacobs**, president, Union for Reform Judaism

"There are many how-to books on the market, but few address how to nurture a soul.... A provocative, honest and practical guide for cultivating the soul. It is a gift to all of us who care about the spiritual imagination of children."

—**Rabbi Sandy Eisenberg Sasso**, author of many award-winning children's books, including *God's Paintbrush*

"Offer[s] a powerful blend of useful information, insightful questions and concrete practices that meets each of us where we are and takes us where we want to go."

—**Carla Naumburg, PhD**, author, *Parenting in the Present Moment*

Jewish Spiritual Parenting

Wisdom, Activities, Rituals *and* Prayers *for* Raising Children *with* Spiritual Balance *and* Emotional Wholeness

Rabbi Paul Kipnes and Michelle November, MSSW

For People of All Faiths, All Backgrounds
JEWISH LIGHTS Publishing
Woodstock, Vermont

Jewish Spiritual Parenting:
Wisdom, Activities, Rituals and Prayers for Raising Children with Spiritual Balance and Emotional Wholeness

2016 Quality Paperback Edition, Second Printing

Biblical and Talmudic translations are the authors' unless otherwise indicated.

"A Rebbi's Proverb," from *And God Braided Eve's Hair* by Danny Siegel, modified by and used with permission of the poet. "When Your Mother Says She's Fat" courtesy of Kasey Edwards, www.kaseyedwards.com. *Hashkiveinu*/"Shelter Us," from Mah Tovu's evening liturgy, English lyrics by Larry Jonas, © 1996 Steve Brodsky and Josh Zweibach, published in *The Complete Shireinu: 350 Fully Noted Jewish Songs*, edited by Joel N. Eglash. Used by permission.

Library of Congress Cataloging-in-Publication Data
Kipnes, Paul, 1963– author.
Jewish spiritual parenting : wisdom, activities, rituals and prayers for raising children with spiritual balance and emotional wholeness / Rabbi Paul Kipnes and Michelle November, MSSW.
pages cm
Includes bibliographical references.
ISBN 978-1-58023-821-2 (pbk.)—ISBN 978-1-58023-849-6 (ebook) 1. Parenting—Religious aspects—Judaism. 2. Child rearing—Religious aspects—Judaism. 3. Reform Judaism. I. November, Michelle, 1961– co-author. II. Title.
BM725.4.K57 2015
296.7'4—dc23
2015018671

10 9 8 7 6 5 4 3 2

Manufactured in the United States of America
Cover and interior design: Tim Holtz
Cover art: © art4all / Shutterstock, modified by Tim Holtz

For People of All Faiths, All Backgrounds
Jewish Lights Publishing
A Division of LongHill Partners, Inc.
Sunset Farm Offices, Route 4, P.O. Box 237
Woodstock, VT 05091
Tel: (802) 457-4000 Fax: (802) 457-4004
www.jewishlights.com

To our parents,
Linda and Ken Kipnes
&
Teri and Murray November,

who between them, bequeathed to us:

compassion
authenticity
gratitude, and
a sense of humor.

Your love made us the people and parents we are today.

Contents

Part 2
Practicing Spiritual Living for Spiritual Growth

Introduction

> Children are a heritage of God;
> the fruit of the womb is a precious reward.
>
> —Psalm 127:3

Michelle: "I'm Sorry, Mom"

Each year, Paul and I serve on camp faculty at the Union for Reform Judaism's (URJ) Camp Newman in Santa Rosa, California, our family's summer home since our children were young. At camp, our children flourished as campers and now as counselors.

One day, I walked into the *chadar ochel* (dining hall) just before lunch and saw our son Daniel, a counselor-in-training, with his head in his hands. Just three days after his campers had arrived, he looked exhausted. Our conversation was precious.

Mom: What's up?

Daniel: Mom, I'm really sorry.

Mom: For what?

Daniel: For everything!

I smiled broadly. As counselor for the youngest and most energetic campers, Daniel was exhausted from supervising these wonderful, rambunctious boys. My heart simultaneously broke at his shattered spirit and soared at his newfound understanding. While Daniel quickly bounced back, his words of apology stayed with me long afterward. Daniel's appreciation for the all-encompassing, nonstop responsibilities that we parents carry on our shoulders made me feel genuinely valued.

Children rarely perceive or acknowledge the pervasive nature of parenting. Of course, before we are parents, most adults also cannot truly comprehend how never-ending, draining, and immensely rewarding parenting can be.

While raising our three children, we learned a parenting secret: that bringing up a child transforms us and transforms our world. We discovered that being parents is a spiritual journey that begins in an act of love and continues through intentional actions. The Holy One bequeaths to us minimally formed creatures, all potential, morally neutral. As parents we transform those children into compassionate, loving human beings. We become partners with God.

The Challenge of Parenting: Kids Arrive Without an Instruction Manual

The responsibilities of parenthood are awesome. We aim to keep our children physically safe, emotionally balanced, and spiritually centered. It is a marathon that begins when they enter our lives and has effects long after we are gone.

Whether the child was long planned for or a blessed surprise, few of us are adequately prepared for parenting; we simply dive in. Our initial parental responses to our babies are cyclical: feeding, changing, holding, and hugging. Repeat.

Soon we are confronting novel parenting challenges and we wonder, how do we move forward toward ensuring our children's spiritual wholeness?

And Teach Your Children to Swim

We can turn to Jewish tradition for timeless teachings and values to guide us to be insightful, inspired parents. The classic articulation of parental responsibilities appears in the Talmud, a collection of Jewish law dating back to the fifth century. The ancient Rabbis delineated five (or six) central obligations incumbent on all parents:

> *Brit* [to circumcise him], *pidyon haben* [to redeem the firstborn son], to teach the child Torah, to find the child a spouse, to teach the child a trade; and there are some who say: to teach the child how to swim. (Talmud, *Kiddushin* 29a)

In this concise text, the Rabbis convey four overarching lessons:

1. Responsibility for preparing a child for life rests with the parents. The Hebrew words for parents (*horim*) and teachers (*morim*) are derived from the same Hebrew root word meaning "to teach" and "to instruct." Parents teach values, set limits, take action, and guide the child's experiences through life.[1]
2. Raising children is a journey in Jewish spirituality, with spiritual and secular obligations intertwined. Parents guide children toward intellectual competency and spiritual wholeness.
3. Parenting occurs in specific actions, not amorphous ideals, like "love him" or "nourish her." Jewish tradition conveys transcendent values through concrete actions.
4. Parents must teach children to swim. Why? Perhaps the Rabbis recognized the poignant symbolism that on occasion each of us will be thrown into waters over our head and need to keep ourselves afloat. To prepare our children to navigate the uncharted waters of life, we parents fill their life rafts with a strong enough set of ethics and ideals, skills, and practices so that they can keep their heads above raging torrents. We need to show our children that within each of them are many diverse tools—intellectual, physical, emotional, and spiritual—to help them steer through the currents of life.

To these, we add the expectation of egalitarianism. While the Rabbis focused on the obligations of a father toward his son, reflecting an ancient belief in separating the genders and holding differing role expectations of men and women, we who live in an egalitarian world extend to both mothers and fathers the same obligations and responsibilities for all their children.

Jewish Values for Raising Children in an Internet World

As children's lives increasingly move online, parents struggle with the inevitable challenge: how do we cultivate and stay a part of our children's inner lives, gaining direct insight into their hearts and minds? In an increasingly complex world that influences our children's lives far beyond our control, we parents need to engage more deeply with our children. We want them to be able to make good decisions and navigate through the storms along the way. More than ever, we seek guidance to help them become the people we hope they will be.

We believe that Judaism presents a strong framework of values that can effectively guide our parenting. *Jewish Spiritual Parenting* elucidates the Jewish values we cherish most and illuminates the wisdom, activities, rituals, and prayers that help us impart significant Jewish spiritual values to our children. Its distinctive Jewish spiritual parenting methods enable parents and children to discover gratitude, joy, and meaning. Along the way, we share accessible illustrations from real life that will expose vulnerability and lead us to laugh too.

Lessons from Twenty-Three Years of Parenthood

You might like to know a little more about us. We are blessed with three children. As we write, Rachel, our oldest, is twenty-three and a college graduate. Daniel, our second child, is twenty-one and a third-year college student. Noah, our youngest, is eighteen and graduating high school. Along with the publication of *Jewish Spiritual Parenting*, we are celebrating our twenty-fifth wedding anniversary. We bring together insights discovered through parenting our own children and from our many years of working professionally with young people. We generously draw wisdom from colleagues, family, and friends who have been our role models and have served in the parenting trenches alongside us.

Paul is rabbi of Congregation Or Ami, an innovative, spiritual, musical Jewish community in Calabasas, California. A former camp director, North American Federation of Temple Youth regional advisor, and national award–winning Jewish educator, he lectures regularly on raising ethical, resilient Jewish children. Ordained at Hebrew Union College–Jewish Institute of Religion, where he earned a masters in Jewish education, he later studied with the Institute for Jewish Spirituality. Trained in spiritual counseling for addictions, he also lectures on engaging interfaith families. He serves as rabbinic dean at URJ Camp Newman.

Michelle is senior admissions officer at de Toledo High School (formerly New Community Jewish High School) in West Hills, California. Earning a master's degree in social work from Columbia University in New York, she directed the national college education department of the Union of American Hebrew Congregations (now Union for Reform Judaism). She served as program director of Stephen Wise Temple in Los Angeles, California, and as a supervisor in its Family Support Center. She has guided families as a parenting teacher and through the design of family camp retreats. She founded *N'siah,* a Jewish women's spirituality group. On the URJ Camp Newman *Nefesh* team, she provides support to summer camp counselors and camper parents.

Wisdom for Parents, Grandparents, Rabbis, and Educators

In *Jewish Spiritual Parenting* we affirm all parents, recognizing that family structures are diverse. Each distinct parenting model brings both challenges and opportunities. We are only one particular tile in the mosaic of individuals, couples, and combinations of adults who are raising Jewish children. Still, we write for all who are raising children, whether on their own or in a marriage or partnership. These children might be your biological children, your partner's children, or adopted. You may be biological or adoptive parents sharing responsibilities with stepparents. As single parents—raising a child yourself by choice, divorce, death, or some other reason—some of you are doing the parenting alone; others have the help of an ex-spouse or ex-partner, a significant other, or a grandparent. Some of you are grandparents, foster parents, or relatives of children for whom you are de facto parents. Whenever we speak about "parents" and "parenting," we have each of you in mind.

Some families include one Jewish parent; others two or more. We acknowledge the reality that often the non-Jewish spouse is responsible for creating a Jewish spiritual home life. Some Jewish families are also multicultural or multiracial; some include a mix of parents and/or children who are gay, lesbian, transgender, bisexual, or questioning. We honor the many kinds of families in which children are being raised.

This book is also a resource for professionals who guide parents and their children toward healthy Jewish spirituality. Teachers, rabbis, youth professionals, educators, camp counselors—anyone involved with guiding parents and their children—can easily make use of the book's Jewish wisdom, activities, rituals, and blessings.

Featured within each chapter are "Try This" activities designed to help you practice Jewish spiritual parenting. Since Judaism, a religion of practices and rituals, teaches by doing, we provide a multiplicity of conversations, activities, and blessings for families to experiment with and consider. Some activities are parent-focused, inviting adults to explore their own ideas, behaviors, beliefs, and upbringing. Others are intended to be practiced with their children. The activities also lend themselves to use by professionals to guide Jewish parental growth.

The Jewish Spiritual Parenting Journey

Jewish Spiritual Parenting has two parts: "Building Foundations for Spiritual Parenting" and "Practicing Spiritual Living for Spiritual Growth."

Part 1 focuses on the foundations of spiritual parenting, exploring five abiding Jewish values—spirituality, partnership, parental contraction, family, and truth—and illuminating best practices.

Part 2 delves deeply into the practices of spiritual living for spiritual growth. Six more Jewish values provide the framework through which we can nurture our child's Jewish spirituality—living holy lives; living in God's image; caring for body, mind, and spirit; reframing and deciding; practicing loving-kindness; and celebrating life with joy. This section includes an abundance of child-focused activities and rituals.

In preparing the book, we pulled from many resources to capture the breadth and depth of Jewish wisdom on spiritual parenting. If we inadvertently omitted crediting any resources, we hope to correct that in future printings.

Paul & Michelle: Tears, Smiles, and a Blessing

There are once-in-a-lifetime experiences that mark momentous transitions. Indelibly etched in our hearts, they capture the blessedness of parenthood. They are *Shehecheyanu* moments—moments of holiness and gratitude—that we cherish forever.

We remember consecration. During this celebration of the beginning of their formal Jewish education, energetic kindergartners stand before the *aron kodesh* (holy ark) to receive a mini-Torah. Our own little Rachel sings joyously alongside her friends, feeling proud of herself. Tears roll down our faces as we acknowledge that our firstborn is growing up. We bless deeply, *Shehecheyanu*, thanking God for bringing us to this special day.

Our Daniel, at thirteen, is becoming a bar mitzvah. He leads the service, chants from Torah, and expounds on the lessons of his Torah portion. With shoulders broad enough to carry on the responsibility for our tradition and values, he receives Torah passed *l'dor vador* (from generation to generation). Some now call him a "man," but we know better. This thirteen-year-old is taking the first steps on the road toward adulthood, but he is still so young. With his grandparents surrounding us, our smiles mingle with tears as we bless, *Shehecheyanu*, thanking God for bringing us to this precious day.

Sooner than we are ready, our Noah begins his college search. He spends time writing essays to capture the essence of his life and dreams. He compares college majors, extracurricular opportunities, Jewish life, and dorms. As he contemplates his future, we pause once again, holding back tears, to say *Shehecheyanu*, gratefully acknowledging our appreciation that another child has arrived at this powerful juncture.

These are *Shehecheyanu* moments. So too is writing this book. Garnering wisdom from our life together for a quarter century, it is with humility that we share with you the best of what we have learned on our journey to bring holiness and spirituality into our family life.

As we reflect on these transitional highlights in our lives, we once again intone the blessing we Jews say whenever we arrive at one of these firsts:

Baruch atah Adonai Eloheinu Melech ha'olam,
Shehecheyanu, v'kiy'manu, v'higianu laz'man hazeh.

Holy One of Blessing,
Who has guided us on our journeys through this universe,
We thank You for giving us life, for sustaining us,
And for bringing us to this incredible moment.
Amen.

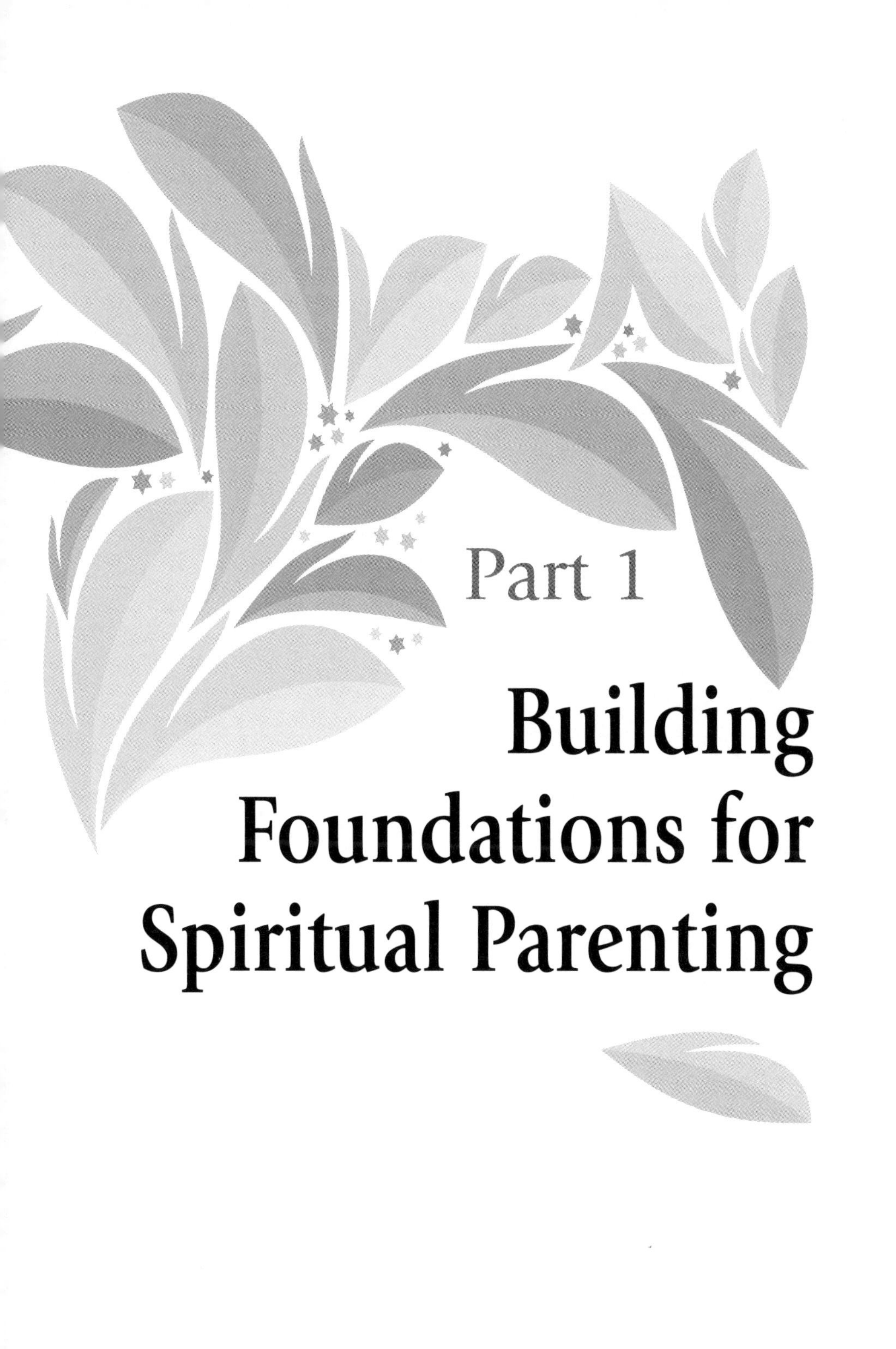

Part 1

Building Foundations for Spiritual Parenting

1 Searching for Spirituality

Fostering *Ruchaniyut* in Our Children's Minds and Hearts

> My religion consists of a humble admiration of the illimitable superior spirit who reveals himself in the slight details we are able to perceive with our frail and feeble mind.
>
> —ALBERT EINSTEIN

Paul: "I Don't Believe in God—Is That Okay?"

David approached me with a look of discomfort on his face. Clearly something was bothering him. "How do I tell my children that I do not believe in God?" he asked. He was concerned about how his children would react to this admission and that it might put a damper on their own spiritual growth.

I have known David for a long time. He has a *gutta neshama,* a good soul. So I asked him, "What kind of God don't you believe in?" He paused for a moment and then explained that he did not believe in a God who was all-knowing, all-powerful, and perfect. In essence, he did not believe in God as God is portrayed in the Torah and prayer book.

"I do believe there is a powerful spiritual presence in the world," he confessed. "But that is not Judaism's idea of God, right?"

My conversation with David clarified for me a nagging feeling I had about how we teach spirituality and belief in Judaism. I was increasingly aware that we Jews have a dangerous problem of definitions. For many Jews (and many people of other backgrounds), the word "God" and the term "religious" are so laden with baggage from self-righteous preachers, cynical politicians, and murderous religious warriors that most of us have difficulty figuring out what we mean when we speak about God.

David felt deeply spiritual, and his description of that spirituality led me to believe that he might even believe in a Holy Presence. Yet in the course of his Jewish upbringing, which seemed to him to be filled with rote ritualism, he never developed the nuanced language to talk about Jewish God-concepts. His spirituality fit in well with some Jewish God-ideas, yet he was sure that what he believed had little or nothing to do with God.

So I admitted to David what I openly admit to many: I am not sure I always believe in the God he described—all-knowing, all-powerful, totally perfect. Human existence and the world I experience all too often seem to call those theological assumptions into question. Still, I believe deeply in God and I live a profoundly Jewish spiritual life.

As we explore *ruchaniyut*, the Jewish notion of spirituality, we begin by thinking deeply about our own beliefs as well as our spiritual and religious experiences. This spiritual self-reflection serves as a first step toward engaging our children in related conversations. We then contemplate what it means to be spiritual and how that might differ from and overlap with being religious. Later, we wrestle with the question of when and how it is appropriate to tell our children about our own faith or struggles with faith while at the same time nurturing their nascent spiritual journeys.

Are Jews Required to Believe in God?

For generations, Judaism resisted outlining a catechism, a set of beliefs to which one must subscribe to be a good Jew. Even after the great rationalist Rabbi Moses Maimonides authored his Thirteen

Articles of Faith back in the twelfth century—later preserved in the daily Jewish hymn *Yigdal*—these articles of faith were not considered compulsory beliefs by any significant portion of the Jewish world.[1] We Jews are a people whose religion is part of our inherited culture and civilization, but belief in God is not a required part of being Jewish. You can be a good Jew, a good human being, a deeply spiritual person, and a sensitive parent—without believing in God.

Even knowing this, many Jews struggle with the idea of God. Some who ceased learning about Judaism after they became a bar or bat mitzvah or who were not blessed with Jewish education cannot begin to imagine that Jewish ideas about God are as diverse as they are fascinating. Others are so influenced by the Western notion of a white-bearded guy in the sky that they fail to recognize that Judaism embraces a whole spectrum of God-concepts.

Jewish tradition teaches that there are at least seventy names for God. Torah calls God *Adonai* (either "my Lord" or "the Eternal") to signify that God benevolently rules over everything. Torah also calls God *Elohim* (God) from the root meaning "strength" or "power." Jews know God by a host of other names, including *Ein Sof* (Without End), *El Shaddai* (either "God Almighty" or "God the Nurturer"), *HaMakom* (The Place), *Makor HaChayim* (Source of Life), *Rachamim* (Compassionate One), *Rofei HaCholim* (Healer of the Sick), and *Oseh HaShalom* (Maker of Peace). God's personal name in Torah is the four-letter name—*Yud-Hei-Vav-Hei*. Spoken aloud euphemistically as "Adonai" but considered unpronounceable, *Yud-Hei-Vav-Hei* is understood as the merging of three verbs—was, is, and will be—rendering God's name as "Existence," "Being," or "the Eternal." Rabbi Karyn Kedar concludes:

> Apparently, our ancestors understood that the vastness of God can be understood only if we use words that include as much of human experience as possible. God is like a judge, like a birthing woman, like a compassionate mother, like a warrior, like a ruler, like a friend.[2]

All these names of God remind us that as Jews we have an abundance of ways to relate with *Adonai Echad*, our God who is one. But with all of those options, Rabbi Arthur Green, one of our generation's great revolutionary God thinkers, explains that because Judaism grew out of the ancient Near Eastern culture that worshipped sky gods, we tend to default to the idea that God lives up in heaven and rules over us.

> "Where does God live?" the child is asked.
>
> "Up there" is the first answer expected, with a finger pointed toward the heavens.
>
> True, we also hope the child will sweep a hand around and say, "Everywhere!" and eventually (though probably quite a few years later) point inward to the heart as well.
>
> But the first answer reconfirms for yet another generation the myth of verticality [that God is up there and we are ruled over down here], the root metaphor of our Western understanding of the relationship between God and world.[3]

We can only hope, as Rabbi Green does, that people who keep searching might stumble into the diversity of Jewish God-concepts. Most of these concepts are not tethered to the traditional definition of a God who rewards good and punishes evil, who knows everything and uses unlimited power to better the world, who lives "up there" and rules over us. We pray that spiritual seekers might encounter the extensive variety of Jewish God-concepts. Why? Because understanding our relationship with God changes the way we view everything else.

Paul: Finding God in Every Place

In Torah, God said, "Build me a sanctuary so that I may dwell among you" (Exodus 25:8). Although we usually expect to connect with God in the synagogue, I believe God is found everywhere in every moment, especially in nature. That's why the ancient Rabbis knew God as *HaMakom*, "The Place," meaning God is in every place, everywhere: skyward, earthward, all around us, and inside you and me. Whenever we can stop focusing on ourselves and our own material needs and open our eyes to the reality and beauty surrounding us, we might find God. The Kabbalists, Jewish mystics, knew God as *Ein Sof* (Without End) because God is everywhere, the Essence that is without end. Moses found God on a mountaintop. Miriam encountered

God at the shores of the sea. The Levites—originally ritual singers and musicians—heard God in the sweet melodies they played. The prophet Elijah experienced God as a still small voice within.

One summer, I too encountered God as *HaMakom*, and it moved me deeply. While our daughter was at URJ Camp Newman, Michelle, the boys, and I minivanned across America. We visited two other Jewish summer camps and nine baseball parks, boated through six waterways, danced at many melodious outdoor concerts, and roamed through countless American history museums. During our summer odyssey, we drove six thousand miles through twenty states in thirty-one days. (But who's counting?)

Most memorable were the incredible national parks. America's natural beauty penetrated deep into our hearts. Wherever we drove, from the mountains in Colorado to the prairies in South Dakota to Oregon's oceans white with foam, I kept encountering *HaMakom*.

Of the seventy names for God referred to in Torah, *HaMakom* stayed with me during that summer. A place is more than just a geographical location. A place is a space that is capable of containing something else. When we call God *HaMakom*, we mean that everything is contained within God, while God is not contained in anything. As our sages say, "God does not have a place; rather God is The Place ... of the Universe" (*Genesis Rabbah* 68:9).

My heart first opened to *HaMakom*, "God as Everywhere," when we meandered up the gorgeous Oregon coast. Each scenic overlook brought us to a view more breathtaking than the last. We lost ourselves in the exquisiteness of our surroundings. It is God's country. It is God. *HaMakom*.

I felt a little like I imagine the first human (*adam*) might have felt soon after creation. After the work of naming the animals and the fun of dallying with Eve, what did Adam do? *Midrash Tanchuma*, a fifth-century collection of Rabbinic stories, tells us that, stirred to the core, Adam stood silent on the shores of the sea, contemplating the majesty around him. Then he lifted up his voice to extol God, saying, "*Mah rabu ma'asecha Adonai*—How great are Your works, O Eternal Creator!" (Psalm 104:24). In both the simple splendor of the ocean and in the world's complexity, Adam saw evidence of the Holy One.[4]

Like Adam, I too perceived signs of *HaMakom* in the ocean, the mountains, and the sky. My ears heard the praise-songs of nature. My heart, inspired beyond its usual capacity, felt as if it might burst.

When our minivan rolled into Grand Teton National Park in Wyoming, my eyes opened as if I were seeing clearly for the first time. I was awed into silence by the grandeur of creation. We were driving by Jackson Lake, planning to scout out Yellowstone in the north. I had to pull off to the side of the road, because I could not catch my breath. My family thought I wanted to take pictures. My son wondered if I was praying. Like Adam, I was just overwhelmed by the beauty. I took out my smartphone and tapped out words of praise about my experience of wonder.

In Torah, we read that when the biblical scouts returned from scouting out the Holy Land, they called it "a land flowing with milk and honey" (Exodus 3:8). I imagine they must have welled up with emotion as they discovered Israel's beauty.

In the Grand Tetons, in the Louisiana bayous, and all across this beautiful country, I too welled up with intense emotion. The eighth-century-BCE prophet Isaiah said it best: "The whole world is filled with the Creator's magnificence" (Isaiah 6:3).

Later, in Utah's Zion National Park, Michelle, Daniel, Noah, and I set out to hike in the Virgin River, a tremendous tributary that bisects the park. After two hours of hiking in the flowing water, we entered the Narrows, so called because of the narrow space created by the towering canyon walls. Though awesome sights encircled us with majesty, rocky obstacles lurking beneath the water's surface sought to trip us up. We used our walking sticks to probe the path ahead for underwater holes.

Here one must tread carefully. Too much attention focused on the surrounding beauty, and a foot misplaced on the slippery upcropping of underwater rocks sends you splashing into the river. This is a lesson of everyday life. Pay attention or you might get tripped up.

At the same time, the Narrows taught us that when we spend too much attention focused on each individual step—so afraid of stumbling and getting soaked—we might miss the splendor of creation: cascading waterfalls, multicolored rock shelves, turquoise blue skies.

We might walk right past Jacob's ladder, *sha'ar hashamayim* (the gateway to heavenly inspiration, Genesis 28:17).

The boys took turns jumping off the rocks and splashing each other while a canyon river wren scolded on a nearby branch. In the song of a river, amidst the giant cliffs that made us think big and feel small, Michelle and I stood silent, mouths agape, eyes open wide at the astonishing landscape. Gazing deep into the soul of that canyon, our boys nearby and giddy with adventure, we found contentment and peace. And we found God.

"Do You Believe in God?"

Children often hit us out of the blue with questions that make us uncomfortable: Where do babies come from? What happens after we die? Did you ever smoke marijuana? It behooves parents—who do not want to fumble their answers and thus create anxiety and confusion—to consider ahead of time how we would respond to these questions. Similarly, most children eventually ask their parents, "Do you believe in God?" Whether we consider ourselves to be spiritual but not religious, religious but not spiritual, both, or neither, we also will want to be prepared with our response.

Instead of waiting until you are caught off guard, take your own spiritual-religious pulse now and think about your own beliefs.

Before we define "spirituality" and "religion," do a Jewish Spiritual Inventory. Ask yourself the questions below and write down your answers. Writing out answers pushes us toward greater clarification. Let your answers flow unfettered. Try to avoid simple answers, which do not add momentum to the discussion. These questions are designed to elicit nuanced, personal, and experiential responses. If you have one, invite your co-parent—and perhaps your own parent too—to do a Jewish Spiritual Inventory as well.

Belief Questions

1. What do I believe?
2. What do I believe about God?
3. What do I *not* believe about God?
4. When have I felt close to God?

Spirituality Questions

1. How am I spiritual?
2. What does spirituality mean to me?
3. Have I ever felt connected to something greater? Deeper? More?
4. When have I had meaningful spiritual experiences?

Religion Questions

1. What do I like about my religion? About religion in general?
2. What about my religion makes me uncomfortable or upsets me? About religion in general?
3. When have I had meaningful experiences with my religion?
4. Which aspects of my religion (or of religion in general) do I want to pass on to my child?

After you write out your answers, sit quietly and review them. What surprised you? Which answers are you certain about, and which questions make you uncomfortable? In what areas might you need to invest more time and thought?

Sitting with your co-parent and/or your own parent, share your answers with each other. Be curious but not dogmatic. Be interested in the *what* (what does he believe, what doesn't she believe?). Be *more* focused on the *when* (when has he felt close to God, when has she felt spiritual, when have I felt the same?).

Our spiritual and religious experiences are often more powerful and life transforming than intellectual ideas about what we believe. These experiences often inform the pathways of our lives in significant ways. Let the conversation open your eyes to who you each are as spiritual and/or religious beings.

Later, you might consider bringing your answers to a rabbi, cantor, Jewish educator, teacher, or Jewish spiritual director to help you further explore and process them. Issues as complex and influential as these deserve additional time and attention so that when we are ready, we may guide our children with intentionality and caring.

What's the Difference Between Religion and Spirituality?

"Religion" is a collection of beliefs, rituals, and prayers intended to help individuals and communities retain a feeling of connection to an intensive spiritual encounter. "Religion," according to *Merriam-Webster's Collegiate Dictionary*, is defined as "(1) the service and worship of God or the supernatural; (2) commitment or devotion to religious faith or observance." Being religious has everything to do with God. At its root, religion aims to continually connect us with certain spiritual experiences related to God. While not every member of the Jewish people believes, Judaism as a religion upholds the existence of God.

For Jews, Torah teaches that generations ago the children of Israel—the Jewish people—had a number of spiritual encounters with the Holy One that embedded within us a clear sense of who we were and how we should live forevermore. Jewish rituals, prayers, and teachings are intended to lead us back to the central experiences of the creation of the world, the Exodus from Egypt, and the spiritual encounter at Mount Sinai that gave us the Torah.

Jewish holidays often recall experiences embedded in our historical or mythic past, most of which point back to God's role in our people's lives. For example, Chanukah commemorates the miraculous Maccabean rebellion against the Assyrian king Antiochus, an event our people saw as God's hand involved in history. Passover relives our people's journey from slavery in Egypt to freedom, the result of God's intentional actions. Sukkot recalls both our people's wandering in the wilderness following God's freeing us from Egypt and God's central role in our successful agricultural harvests in Israel. Daily Jewish prayers are intended to reconnect us with these spiritual events as well as to our arrival in the Promised Land and our *brit* (covenant or agreement) with God.

A "religious person" then is someone who strives to embrace the rituals, teachings, holidays, and prayers. She uses these to identify with her people and to connect with her God. In the ideal, observing rituals leads to a profound sense of *kedusha* (holiness), inspiration, and connection to God and community. Such holiness can be life changing.

"Spirituality" is notoriously hard to define. The Institute for Jewish Spirituality is a revolutionary Jewish organization devoted to guiding clergy to examine their unique experiences of spirituality. The Institute teaches that spirituality is a highly individualized experience. We often associate many concepts with spirituality, including open-heartedness, interconnectedness, gratefulness, meaning, and discernment.[5]

Rabbi Micah D. Greenstein, senior rabbi at Temple Israel of Memphis, Tennessee, explains:

> The English word "spiritual" has its roots in Greek thought and implies a split between the material world and the realm of the spirit, because the opposite of spiritual is material. By definition, in English, spirituality seems to invite the spiritual seeker to exit this everyday, material world to attain some higher spiritual level.[6]

But for Jews, and therefore for Jewish spirituality, only one world exists. Our world is simultaneously material and spiritual. For Judaism the closest word to "spirituality" is *ruchaniyut*, from the Hebrew word *ruach*, which means "spirit." We first encounter *ruach* in Genesis 1:2, when we are told *ruach Elohim* (the spirit of God) hovered over the waters. *Ruach* connotes a presence or connection that is experienced intimately.

For Rabbi Greenstein:

> Spirituality—whether you are Christian, Muslim, a Jew, or a Hindu—is religion experienced intimately. You might say it's the core, the essence of religion. Spirituality is where you and God meet and what you do about it.... Abraham Joshua Heschel, who is a great mystical theologian, suggested that spirituality is life lived in the continuous presence of the divine.[7]

Spirituality, however, is not always or necessarily tied to God. It might be connected to community, family, nature, culture, and/or gratitude. Rabbi Greenstein teaches that Jewish spirituality is "a matter of seeing the holy in the everyday, and invites us to wake up and open our eyes to the holy things happening all around us every day."[8]

Stuart M. Matlins, founder and editor in chief of Jewish Lights Publishing, helped define Jewish spirituality when he started his book publishing company in 1991. The books and authors he published gave shape and academic backing to a growing movement for Jewish spirituality. This body of work, which has grown to over four hundred titles, recognizes that when we talk about spirituality, we most commonly refer to the sense that we are all part of something greater and that this sense of the spiritual necessarily leads to thought processes and behaviors that connect us with that larger reality.[9]

Try This **Revisit Your Jewish Spirituality Inventory**

Now that you have read these definitions of religion and spirituality, revisit your personal Jewish Spirituality Inventory and, with these new perspectives, change or update any answers.

How do these updated answers affect your thoughts about your child's spiritual future? Most particularly, begin to think about—or delve more deeply into—what kind of Jewish spirituality and/or Jewish religious life you want to guide your child to experience and explore.

How Are Religion and Spirituality Connected?

At its best, religion helps us discover, expand, and retain a deep sense of the spiritual. When rituals are meaningful, teaching is inspiring, and encounters within religious communities are warm and relational, religion can help us infuse our lives with a sense that we are part of something greater than ourselves. Rituals and holidays then point us toward our Jewish people's spiritual moments and give us hope that we can experience the same in deeply meaningful ways. Why then do so many people, like David, say they are "spiritual but not religious"?

When religious rituals become dry and monotonous, religion can hinder the spiritual quest and deflate potentially holy moments. When religious leaders become overly concerned with the minutiae of the rituals, when the formality of the prayers gets in the way of organic, musical, and welcoming worship, and when the rules squelch the inspiration, religion can strangle the spirituality out of our quest.

Parents who strive to instill a healthy sense of spirituality in their children want to push through the minutiae and formality to the essence of holiness in life. We want to rise above rote rituals to embrace spiritual wholeness.

Parents need to think carefully about how to nurture Jewish spirituality in the lives of our children. Simple, dogmatic answers can have the effect of shutting down a spiritual search. We encourage parents to prepare ahead as they approach discussions with their children about belief, spirituality, God, and religion.

Teaching Your Child about Spirituality and God

Rabbi David Wolpe, a respected author and the rabbi of Sinai Temple in Los Angeles, in his book *Teaching Your Children about God: A Modern Jewish Approach*, explains that teaching children about God is a way of giving a firm footing to their spiritual life. He offers valuable guidelines for initiating conversations that can be as intimate as any between parents and children. Rabbi Wolpe identifies five parental behaviors that can be exceedingly helpful:

1. *Ask.* Children grow spiritually when we allow them to explore the full range of their spiritual curiosity. Parents should ask their children what they believe or think, instead of telling them what we do (or do not) believe. Inquire rather than evading the subject. Ask questions rather than pronouncing "the truth." We nurture spiritual journeys when we let our children think, speculate, dream, and imagine.
2. *Tell stories.* Younger children understand the concrete; abstract thinking comes at age ten and older. So for younger children, it is helpful to discuss ideas in the form of stories. Parents can teach about God by telling the stories of the Bible, by reading children's books about God out loud, and through conveying their own compelling spiritual experiences. Stories inspire children to form concepts and embrace values. Rabbi Wolpe encourages parents to use descriptive language. Rather

than saying "God knows everything," he suggests trying "God is the one who helps us grow."

3. *Bring God into everyday life.* Let your children feel loved by God by telling them that God loves them. Let them visualize the holiness by showing that the world is filled with the beautiful majesty of God's presence. Let your children feel blessed by reciting blessings—using either traditional formulations or your own words—to express gratitude and connection.

4. *Do not be defensive at challenges.* By their teenage years, most young people will challenge our spiritual and religious ideas. This is healthy and beneficial. Many believing people admit that there are valid reasons to doubt God's existence or goodness. Parents foster spiritual exploration when we welcome—even invite—their questions or doubts.

5. *Be prepared with thoughtful responses.* Simplistic answers fall flat for older and more sophisticated children. Resist the urge to misrepresent the complexity of issues of God, belief, and spirituality. Rabbi Wolpe suggests, for example, that in response to the challenge "'If God dwells everywhere, is he in my pocket?' the appropriate answer is to explain the difference between physical and nonphysical objects. The wind is invisible, but physical. Love is intangible. Ask a child, 'Where is love?' You cannot point to it, but you can feel it. The same is true with God."[10]

Through the years, each of our children has expressed deep spirituality and belief in God. Each has also wandered through periods of nonbelief. We remember moments on mountaintops and during Shabbat at camp when each spoke glowingly about feeling spiritually connected. We recall car rides when one confessed a struggle with God and later when another admitted not believing in God at all. As with other parenting topics, we have learned to be nonreactive to these admissions, seeing them as signposts along the journey of spirituality. We acknowledge and praise the struggle without becoming attached to the results.

American scholar Robert Fowler, in studying patterns of faith development, noted that over their lifetimes many people migrate from childhood belief to skepticism and atheism to expansive and universal faith. Fowler suggested that throughout our lives most of us ride a roller coaster of faith.[11] How and what we believe continually evolves.

For millennia, parents and children have been facing difficult questions about belief in God. There are so many Jewish answers. While not all of the answers will satisfy, as parents our goal is to cultivate spiritual openness and growth, not necessarily to provide definitive answers. When we allow ourselves to be open to spiritual exploration, we also allow our children to open up to the many possibilities that surround us.

Engage in Jewish Spiritual Life Sharing

Some of us had parents who engaged us regularly in conversations about spirituality and religion, sharing their thoughts and experiences. Many did not. Imagine how your life might have deepened if more spiritual conversations had been part of your upbringing. Strive to be the parent who initiates and welcomes those discussions.

Engage in Jewish spiritual life sharing by weaving conversations about spirituality into your encounters with your kids. Make these Jewish spiritual life-sharing moments as regular and normative as talks about sports, movies, or hobbies. You might return to your revised personal Jewish Spirituality Inventory to identify poignant spiritual and religious experiences that, as long as they are age appropriate, you might share with your child. Or choose one of the spiritual life–sharing prompts from the list below. Make sure you allow equal time for both you and your child to address the prompt. When possible, allow your child to respond first. Listen with curiosity to your child's own ideas without judgment or bias. You might also share some of the responses from your co-parent or your own parents. In this way, the Jewish spiritual life-sharing experience is passed down *l'dor vador* (from generation to generation).

1. Ask your child if he ever feels spiritual. Share with your child a story about when you felt a deeper connection to existence or to spirituality.

2. Ask your child what she thinks about God. Share with your child a story about when you felt close to God.
3. Ask your child what gives him the feeling that he has experienced a miracle. Perhaps tell your child about the beauty of his birth or adoption as an example of the miraculous in the world.
4. Ask your child how she feels at the top of a mountain, at the beach, in the middle of a beautiful forest, or wherever else she feels a sense of wonderment. Share with your child the sense of wonderment you feel whenever you are in these special places.

When Can I Tell My Child I Do Not (or Might Not) Believe in God?

Parents who strive for a rich Jewish spiritual family life will want to assume an expansiveness and openness with regard to ideas about spirituality, including the question of God's existence. Rabbi Sarah Reines reminds us that "Judaism does not have a single rigid understanding of God," yet often people are unable to accept the "old man in the sky" image of a God and therefore "assume that the only alternative is to reject God entirely."[12] Yet Judaism offers vastly diverse ways of how we might experience God's presence in our lives.

Ironically, parents who typically embrace multiple perspectives on many other topics sometimes fail to recognize that, regarding God and Jewish spirituality, there is no single "right answer." If we can accept this truth, then we relieve ourselves of the burden of knowing it all. We can approach our children's questions as a way for them to express their burgeoning spirituality.

Throughout a lifetime of work in the Jewish community, we both have witnessed the deepening faith that blossoms as people age. As people gain more life experiences, many develop a richer spirituality. We have heard older people express regret over having inadvertently robbed their young children of opportunities to experience spirituality and to experiment with religion. "I didn't send them to religious school because I disliked my own experience" or "I chose to send them to sports camp instead of Jewish summer camp so they wouldn't feel I was shoving religion down their throat." Many parents explain now that they wish they had acted differently.

We recommend that parents engage in conversation, leaving plenty of room for children to continue questioning and thinking for themselves. Spirituality requires questioning, imagining, and openness. In this way, we can positively reinforce the authentic curiosity of youth.

Go God-Shopping

If you believe deeply in God, you might expand your faith by exploring the spectrum of Jewish God-concepts. If you doubt the existence of God or do not believe at all, first consider that your current nonbelief may be temporary.

Before you tell your young child that you do not believe in God, take the time to truly explore the plethora of Jewish God-concepts that pervade our postmodern Jewish world. If you previously wrestled with belief, you might reengage with the challenge now that you are older and have different life experiences.

We encourage the parents and children in our *Mishpacha* Family Learning program at Congregation Or Ami to go "shopping" in the mall of Jewish God-concepts. To most spiritual questions, you, like them, will encounter a whole spectrum of fascinating Jewish answers. You might:

1. Seek out a rabbi, cantor, Jewish educator, or Jewish spiritual director to help guide your exploration of the many God-concepts in Judaism so that you might open yourself to other potential ideas.
2. Read about the variety of Jewish God-concepts. You might find one that mirrors or expands your own thinking and thus open yourself to a different Jewish view of God. Here are some suggestions:
   - *The Book of Miracles: A Young Person's Guide to Jewish Spiritual Awareness*, by Lawrence Kushner (Woodstock, VT: Jewish Lights, 1987).
   - *The Female Face of God in Auschwitz: A Jewish Feminist Theology of the Holocaust*, by Melissa Raphael (New York: Routledge 2003).

- *Finding God: Ten Jewish Responses*, by Rifat Soncino and Daniel Syme (New York: URJ Press, 1986).
- *God: Jewish Choices for Struggling with the Ultimate*, by Josh Barkin (Los Angeles: Torah Aura, 2008).
- *God of Becoming and Relationship: The Dynamic Nature of Process Theology*, by Bradley Shavit Artson (Woodstock, VT: Jewish Lights, 2014).
- *In God's Name*; *God's Paintbrush*; and other books by Rabbi Sandy Eisenberg Sasso, a parent, spiritual leader, and storyteller, and award-winning author of inspiring books to nurture children's spiritual imagination.
- *Lights in the Forest: Rabbis Respond to Twelve Essential Jewish Questions*, edited by Paul Citrin (New York: CCAR Press, 2014).
- *Reaching Godward: Voices from Jewish Spiritual Guidance*, by Carol Ochs (New York: URJ Press, 2003).
- *Seek My Face: A Jewish Mystical Theology*, by Arthur Green (Woodstock, VT: Jewish Lights, 2014).
- *The Way into Encountering God in Judaism*, by Neil Gillman (Woodstock, VT: Jewish Lights, 2004).

3. Take a class on Jewish theology at a local synagogue or college. If one is not available, approach a local rabbi for independent learning.
4. Read spiritual writings from blogs that provide continually probing conversation and exploration of spirituality and belief in God. Paul's own blog (http://paulkipnes.com) might illuminate for you the wide spectrum of God-concepts within Judaism. His musings are alternately radical, awe-filled, and at times close to blasphemous.

The spiritual search and faith-based religious life can be a joyful, eye-opening, life-enhancing Jewish journey. We hope you will pause before limiting or broadly denying your child the opportunity for a lifelong exploration of his or her belief system. Allow your children to undertake this hike into holiness.

You might begin the next stage of your own journey, as we did in this chapter, by embracing radical truths: that a person can be spiritual but not religious, and that most of us grapple with God and with spirituality. Recognizing that faith development is a lifelong journey that often includes a period of nonbelief or disbelief, you can breathe easier and allow your child's path to unfold naturally.

By limiting how much adult doubt you share, you avoid dampening your child's own search. Parents who want to foster a healthy spiritual journey within the hearts and minds of their children ought to exercise *tzimtzum* (parental contraction), holding back our own adult-sized doubts so as not to encumber our child's quest.

Rather, we can recommit and point to the possibility that there exists a spirituality that enwraps us all. Then our children will be open to the hope, the possibility, and, yes, the holiness that infuses all existence.

Partnership, Pluralism, and Peace

Shutafut as a Spiritual Parenting Strategy

Alone we can do so little;
together we can do so much.
—Helen Keller

Paul: Baby Rachel Goes to Grad School

While I was a full-time graduate student and Michelle worked full time, we patched together a child-care plan that included me taking our three-month-old daughter with me to rabbinical school. Armed with a stash of frozen breast milk and baby supplies for the day, I relished this daddy-daughter time. We did everything together: Rachel napped through Bible class in her cozy carrier, cooed through my study sessions with classmates, and snuggled in my arms as I moved through the library. I suppose I did things differently than Michelle might have, but I kept Rachel well fed, cared for, and safe. Reflecting back, I recognize two important outcomes:

1. The more Michelle evidenced her trust and respect for my parenting skills—and calmly helped me through my mistakes—the more confidently and eagerly I approached parenting.

2. I developed strong relationships with all three of our children because I was an involved, integrated parent from the very beginning.

In this chapter we explore the *shutafut* (partnership) of parenting, a healthy understanding of which includes a perspective of pluralism, an alertness against passing on our own dysfunctions to our children, and an awareness about the influences—both positive and negative—from our own upbringing. We will suggest strategies and attitudes to deepen parenting partnerships and specific activities to examine our parenting role models.

Partnership and Friendship in House and Home

Rabbi Moses Maimonides differentiated three categories of friendship: a person befriended for a purpose, a person befriended for the sake of satisfaction, and a person befriended for the sake of an ideal. The first includes utilitarian relationships—for example, between a leader and his followers, or an employer and her employees. The second type of relationship produces great pleasure and/or deep trust. The third leads to the pursuit of goodness.[1] Rabbi Joseph Soloveitchik, in a teaching conveyed by his student Rabbi Maurice Lamm in *The Jewish Way in Love and Marriage,* extends these friendship categories to the partnership of marriage. While Maimonides does not suggest that strong friendships include all these categories, Rabbi Soloveitchik suggests that the most successful marriages are those based on a combination of personal benefit, pleasure, trust, and higher purpose.[2] We extend this teaching to illuminate the characteristics of partnerships that support successful *shutafut*.

First, a *friend for a purpose* (*chaver l'davar*) is a practical association, which depends on reciprocal usefulness. When the usefulness disappears, the bond of "love" dissolves (*Pirkei Avot* 5:19). Parenting can be exhausting and overwhelming; having another person around is useful as we strive to complete the many tasks that parenting demands.

Second, someone with whom to share sorrows, concerns, and also delight is called a *friend for worrying* (*chaver l'da'agah*).

Happiness can multiply and sadness subside when it is shared. Being on a team with someone trustworthy can add strength and pleasure to parenting.

Third, a *friend for an ideal* (*chaver l'de'ah*) includes shared dedication to common goals. When parenting partners dream together about the type of people they want their children to become, they are more prepared to sacrifice to attain these shared ideals.

Parenting partners, working together on all these levels, create a true collaboration.[3]

The Practices of a Parenting Partnership

We know from parenting specialists that the involvement of multiple adults has the potential to enhance a child's well-being. Raising a child may take a village, but unless that village coordinates its best efforts, the child may suffer from mixed messages and ever-changing demands. *Shutafut* in parenting can be understood as a mindful approach to organizing multiple perspectives into a steady stream of support for that child.

Even when parenting partners are the best of friends, partnership is not always easy. Strong opinions and emotions, disparate sources of information, and unbalanced influence can undermine the partnership.

Shutafut draws on the kabbalistic notion of *tzimtzum,* taught by Jewish mystical rabbi Isaac Luria, as a guiding principle for a parenting partnership. *Tzimtzum,* discussed more fully in the next chapter, grows out of a concept of Creation in which God withdrew in order to make space for humanity. In a parenting partnership, each individual parent pulls back from the need to be in control and lets go whenever possible. Even if we feel we can do it all—which is usually not the case—the involvement of each partner or co-parent can enhance the care and raising of a child. The insights and influence of the other parenting partner can enrich a child's life beyond what we can do alone.

We acknowledge that our partner or co-parent has valuable contributions to make. A parenting partnership affirms a spectrum of perspectives that incorporates and reflects each partner's style. We may not be fond of every choice that a co-parent proposes, but as long as the health or safety of the child is not jeopardized, the partner's input may contribute to the child's thriving in ways we had not imagined. For the benefit of our child, we make room to embrace our partner's wisdom, personality, and authentic love for the child.

In the Torah, Adam and Eve reside in the Garden of Eden as archetypes of lovers and companions. They establish a pattern for subsequent couples to view each other as "one flesh." The partners are *ezer k'negdo*, coequal helpmates for each other. The thirteenth-century biblical commentator Nachmanides emphasizes that the ideal bond of *ezer k'negdo* greatly differentiates human relationships from the arbitrary mating of animals.[4] We are to be partners who augment one another, providing each other with assistance and operating in complementary ways to create a warm home environment and a balanced family life.[5] Whether you are a man and a woman, a gay or lesbian couple, a single parent who finds helpmates in friends and other family members, or a grandparent raising a grandchild, you can build an effective *shutafut*.

Michelle: Partnership Lessons from "Mommy and Me"

As a Mommy and Me program teacher, I interacted with many parents. Some were first-time moms; others were returning to class with their second or third child. Some moms appeared relaxed and confident; others described themselves as exhausted and overwhelmed. Most were married.

Between opening circle, playtime, singing, and snacks, we talked about the blessings and challenges of motherhood and about the developmental stages of childhood. As the moms of six-month-old babies spoke, I observed a recurring theme. Many of the women claimed that their husbands lacked the ability to accomplish a variety of child-raising tasks. They frequently opined, for example, that their husbands were not able to adequately pack a diaper bag or dress their child appropriately. At first this struck me as comical. Many of the husbands had advanced degrees and were CEOs and other professionals with immense responsibility in their jobs. I wondered, how complicated could it be for them to pack a diaper bag? Besides, I knew that neglecting to have sufficient diapers and bottles available is a mistake one makes only once! There *is* a sharp learning curve.

Perhaps wanting to safeguard their role as primary caregiver, some moms might have felt genuine concern about releasing oversight of their children, even to the dads. As their children grew older, most moms relented, learning that packing a diaper bag and dressing a baby were actually simple tasks relative to the meatier challenges they would later face on the parenting journey. Many grew to accept that it does not matter, for example, if the snaps on the toddler's overalls are misaligned or the colors in the top and bottom of an outfit do not coordinate. I wondered, how could moms more generously share parenting responsibilities and child supervision with the goal of strengthening the co-parenting relationship?

When our own children were infants and toddlers, it was fun for me to dress them up in adorable apparel. Paul, however, was not captivated by this exercise and dressed them in more utilitarian ways. Since we believed that our children would thrive with the full involvement of both parents, I understood that if I wanted Paul to feel fully welcomed into all aspects of the parenting equation, I needed to embrace his choices, even when sometimes they differed from mine.

Additionally, Paul and I took time together to address the question of division of labor. Early on, we each assumed responsibility for certain aspects of parenting. Frequently, we would return to the conversation, redistributing responsibilities and shifting as necessary to best benefit our growing family.

Learning from the Failures of Our Ancestors

Wouldn't it be wonderful if we could turn to Torah to find role models of healthy parenting partnerships that result in positive parent-child relationships? Unfortunately, the Torah is fraught with failed familial relationships. It lays out with uncomfortable honesty the potential for familial instability and mirrors the unpleasant realities we see today in some parenting partnerships and many parent-child relationships. But if we read Torah purposefully, we can mine its descriptions of these failures for lessons to apply to our own parenting partnerships.

Right in the beginning, we discover how low the bar has been set. The first children, Cain and Abel, are jealous of each other because of unequal parental attention (Genesis 4). With God in the role of the "eternal parent," the Torah highlights the challenges of managing intense emotions within a family. Cain kills his brother Abel, ostensibly out of jealous rage that their "parent"—in this case, God—seems to prefer Abel's offering to Cain's. From Cain and Abel's story we learn the dangers of appearing to favor one child over another as well as the depth to which sibling rivalry can upend relationships. How might this have turned out differently if God had talked to Adam and Eve about the challenges of raising these two boys?

Ten generations later, Noah and his sons build an ark to replenish a new world cleansed of violence (Genesis 6–9). After forty days on the ark filled with every kind of animal, they stand firmly on dry land. With all human existence depending on his actions, Noah decides to plant a vineyard. He gets drunk, curses his sons and brings hatred back into the world (Genesis 9:24–27). From Noah's story, we learn that our own pressures and vulnerability can lead us to jeopardize the safety of our children. How might this outcome have been different had Noah and his wife, Na'amah, partnered to share and openly discuss the pressures of raising children during a period of overwhelming responsibility?

Ten generations later, the propensity for painful encounters continues as an unwanted gift bequeathed *l'dor vador*. We read about the near-sacrifice of Isaac (Genesis 22). When our biblical patriarch Abraham hears what he believes is God's voice telling him to sacrifice his son, Abraham's passion for his faith blinds him to the possibility that he might have misheard God's request.[6] Thankfully, an angel of God halts the action before Abraham can lay a hand on Isaac, yet nothing can alleviate the psychological damage Isaac suffers from being tied up and prepared for sacrifice by his father. Trust broken is not easily repaired. In the Torah, Abraham and Isaac, father and son, never speak again. They are next together only at Abraham's funeral, as the son buries the father (Genesis 25:8–9). We parents sometimes sacrifice our relationships on the altar of our passions.

Our matriarch Sarah's resentment over Ishmael—her stepson from her husband Abraham's relationship with their maidservant Hagar—gives rise to intense jealousy. In response, when Sarah finally gives birth to her own child, Isaac, she exiles Ishmael and his mother, Hagar, from the home (Genesis 16, 21).

Yet, earlier in the Torah, Abraham and Sarah demonstrate healthy partnership; the *Zohar*, our Jewish mystical text, explains that Abraham needed to gain his wife Sarah's agreement before they could go on the journey toward Canaan. Imagine how Abraham's relationship with both sons Isaac and Ishmael might have fared differently had Abraham and Sarah more regularly engaged in parenting partnership.[7]

Isaac's twin sons, Jacob and Esau, each desperate for their father's approval and jealous of their father's relationship with the other, take sibling rivalry in new directions. Second-born Jacob steals firstborn Esau's birthright and, later, both the firstborn's blessing and claim to the inheritance (Genesis 25–27). Isaac himself is blind to the maneuverings within his family until it is too late. Jacob flees, disappearing for forty years, never fully reconciling with his brother or his own guilt (Genesis 33). The family splits, leaving the parents unable to watch their children grow up. Probing deeper, we discover that Isaac and his wife Rebecca are working at cross-purposes. Isaac favors his hunter son Esau. Rebecca, however, had heard and accepted God's prophecy that Jacob would be a leader over even his brother Esau. So she ensures that Isaac would bestow the gifts of leadership on Jacob. Like Isaac and Rebecca, we parents can sometimes be blind to destructive sibling rivalry. We wonder, had Isaac and Rebecca taken an alternative approach and addressed this behavior while still fulfilling the Holy One's prophecy, might their family have remained whole?

The dysfunction continues as Jacob becomes a father and unwittingly (or naively) plays favorites among his many sons. Jacob presents his beloved son Joseph with a technicolor dream coat. Joseph boasts consistently that his siblings and parents will ultimately serve him. The jealousy burns so fervently among Joseph's brothers that they consider killing their brother Joseph, yet ultimately compromise by selling Joseph into slavery instead. Like his father and grandfather before him, Jacob fails to see the bitter pain and hatred that rage within his family (Genesis 37).

Similarly, after his daughter, Dinah, is raped, Jacob remains silent and offers nothing to help her through her trauma or to guide her siblings through the family's potent rage. Some argue that Jacob's silence enabled the pain to fester, leading his sons to step into the void and respond on their own. The brothers eventually trick and murder the whole tribe of Dinah's rapist (Genesis 34). Might the outcome have been different had Jacob and the stepmothers (he had three other wives) strategized as to how to lower the competitive temperature among and address the pain of their children?

From the parent-child stories of our patriarchs and matriarchs, we learn that we parents can be the last to see the hurt that exists in our families and with our children. Too often we ignore the warning signs or fail to listen to the pleas of loved ones to address our family's problems. Sometimes by our actions or inactions, we become co-conspirators in unhealthy dynamics. The failures of our biblical ancestors need not be our inheritance. Nor do our parents' mistakes need to be ours. As parenting partners, we can share in the task of keeping watch so that we do not fall into the same parenting traps.

Do We Want to Parent Like Our Parents?

We bring our childhood into our parenting, both the positive experiences and the negative ones. One of Paul's childhood rabbis, Rabbi Gary Glickstein of Temple Beth Sholom of Miami, Florida, teaches that we spend our lives drawing closer to and rebelling from our parents, even after they have passed on. For many of us, our parents are the most pervasive role models we have. Their parenting styles are indelibly imprinted into our long-term memory.

Michelle & Paul: Negotiating Expectations from Our Own Upbringing

We grew up in loving families with dissimilar communication styles. Paul's family is uninhibited when stating what is on their minds. Michelle's family exercises a selfless diplomacy. In his introduction to Michelle's family home, Paul was amazed at how challenging it was for him to discern what family members wanted to do or to eat. To Paul, the way Michelle's family deferred to each other in an ongoing effort to accommodate everyone's needs was dizzying. Early on, during Michelle's initial visits with Paul's family, she was astonished by the hard truths that family members customarily shared with one another with a directness that sometimes was startling.

When we began raising our own kids, we negotiated many compromises. Sometimes we brought innovative yet distinct approaches; other times we recognized that our individual upbringing influenced our choices. While acknowledging that compromise did not necessarily mean agreement, we worked conscientiously through each issue. For example, we initially disagreed about the volume of noise in the house while the babies napped. Supposing that they required an uninterrupted sleep environment, Michelle spoke quietly. While we embraced Michelle's ideal, Paul speculated that too much quiet might inadvertently set our kids up to be able to sleep only in soundless conditions. He wondered if they would be able to fall asleep later in noisy places, on sleepovers at friends' houses or at summer camp. Inevitably, with each new baby, our house advanced further away from Michelle's intended "quiet sleep zone." Our children adapted to the evolving increased volume at home such that later, during their adolescence, Michelle smiled when witnessing that even pots and pans clanging, telephones ringing, or commercials blaring on TV would not cause a stir in our teens' deep slumber.

We deliberated about when the kids could use specific technology. Our conversations focused on when a child had the maturity for the responsibilities inherent in owning a cell phone or laptop. A technophile himself, Paul lobbied for earlier access. Michelle, apprehensive about unmediated access to social media, inappropriate content, and cyber-bullying, wanted to protect the children longer. We chose to be stricter here, for our children's emotional safety, although the youngest, Noah—not surprisingly—gained earlier access than his older siblings.

Before the children turned thirteen, we also grappled with boundaries related to watching PG-13 movies. How stringently should we enforce our wait-until-thirteen rules when our child was at a valued friend's house for movie night? Again, we were more successful consistently shielding our oldest; as tagalong younger siblings, Daniel and Noah were exposed to more mature content earlier.

Through it all, we learned that partnership in parenting meant presenting a united front to our children and in turn providing them with a sense of family stability and confidence in us. When we had not fully sorted out how we felt about a topic, we discovered that responding to our children's requests with "Let me think about it and talk to your mom/dad" gave us breathing room to grapple with the topic privately as parenting partners. This response also reinforced to our kids that we were a team.

We made it a priority to let each other know promptly when an issue was pending with one of our kids. Our communication was made much easier as texting allowed us to bring each other up to speed quickly and efficiently. We actively strived to avoid triangulation, guarding against a child seeking answers from one parent and then the other, effectively playing us against each other.

Both before and after the children were born, we engaged in conversation about how we wanted to parent. We agreed that our goal was to raise physically healthy, emotionally balanced, and spiritually connected children. As we explored how we might meet these goals, it was imperative for us to acknowledge that different pathways and child-rearing strategies could yield positive results. We reminded ourselves of this notion frequently, although not always with equanimity. Acknowledging that the other parent was proposing a comparably viable strategy often required us to check our ego at the door.

Do a Parenting Inventory

Honest exchanges of expectations between partners create environments in which children can flourish. Our parenting perspectives are the result of multiple influences, yet our parents often are the primary influence on our attitudes toward parenting. Completing a personal parenting inventory focusing on our upbringing can be a helpful strategy. Ask each parenting partner these questions:

1. How would you describe your parents' parenting styles? In what areas did they work together? In what areas did they seem to be at cross-purposes?
2. What enduring parenting memories do you have from childhood? What did you learn from them?
3. Which characteristics of your parents' parenting styles do you want to emulate? Which parts do you want to ensure are not included in your own parenting?
4. Who are other people—relatives, co-workers, friends—who might serve as positive parenting role models? What makes them particularly skillful and effective?
5. What spiritual practices were part of your upbringing? Which traditions do you want to retain? Which experiences do you want to change?

Discuss the answers together with your parenting partner(s), and identify similarities and differences in your history. In which ways do your attitudes and expectations diverge? Where is there room for conversation and compromise?

Single parents and divorced parents parenting on their own will want to complete a parenting inventory as well. Consider asking a relative or friend to assist. This intentional exploration of your attitudes and values can inform your decisions as you move forward.

Remember that compromise is not easy. School counselors, therapists, and rabbis are helpful resources; parents can turn to them for parenting assistance.

Paul: Benefits of Parenting Partnership

Teaching babies how to sleep through the night is challenging and exhausting. After losing many consecutive nights of sleep as we attempted to soothe our crying infant, we decided to make a change. We chose to follow the then much-touted Ferber plan. This strategy called for allowing babies to establish a pattern of self-nurturing by letting them cry themselves into (and back into) slumber.[8] When we attempted to "Ferberize" our child, we needed each other's emotional strength and physical presence to keep us from "rescuing" our wailing baby. (Our baby girl had staying power!) Locked in a bear hug, reminding each other that we were working toward a valuable goal, we drew strength from one another.

Through this experience and so many others, we discovered that parenting with a partner, and parenting as equal partners, had other significant benefits as well. We bolstered one another's energy level and stamina to power through taxing periods. We pushed each other toward greater self-reflection. We enlightened each other with our unique perspectives.

Before our kids reached elementary school age, Michelle let the kids always be winners in games played at home. In handball, board games, and card games, she accepted what was at times creative rule making. Michelle did not care who won the game as long as everyone had fun. When our son Daniel became particularly invested in who won and who lost, and was headed toward school sports teams, I became concerned that he needed practice mastering the experience of both winning and losing. Over time, we discovered that the more Daniel was shielded from losing, the more difficult losses became.

We sought guidance from coaches and teachers. One wise teacher advised: If you allow your children to bowl only with bumpers, they will never develop the skills to earn their own strikes and spares. Later, we gained reassurance and additional wisdom from parenting expert Dr. Wendy Mogel, who argued in *The Blessing of a Skinned Knee* and *The Blessing of a B Minus* that children thrive through the experience of failure. They learn to pick themselves up, dust themselves off, and face challenges anew.[9]

Over many athletic seasons, we watched each of our children celebrate the exultation of team championships and experience the devastation of play-off defeats. We came to understand that, for children, a true test of strength was not winning the game but managing emotions when facing a loss. Parents can help children discover how to manage feelings of frustration and disappointment. We can guide them to realize that losing a game is an opportunity to work hard again, perhaps to prepare differently, and to hold on to hope for a better outcome. It is in the experience of losing that the spirit of sportsmanship can grow. There is inherent value in children developing resilience, leading to their ability to bounce back and try again. By seeking guidance as partners, we turned our dissonance on this topic into parenting growth.

Try This **Compose a Parenting Vision Statement**

Through conversation and compromise, *tzimtzum*, hope, humility, and a commitment to working together, we parents can create a vision of how we want to nurture our children. Businesses write vision statements to define their goals and to guide their daily work. Similarly, Paul asks parents when preparing for baby-naming ceremonies to write a covenant of family (*brit mishpacha*) as a vision statement that describes the home they intend to create for their new baby.

Try writing a vision statement about your parenting. Bring together co-parent(s) and articulate in five to six sentences your vision of how you want to parent your children. Which values will you prioritize? What kind of home will you create? Make sure to include a sentence about the kind of spiritual life you envision.

Refer back to this parenting vision statement when parenting challenges arise. Use this long-term vision to reframe problem areas and better discern the way forward.

Clarifying Spiritual Parenting Priorities

Cultivating our own spiritual lives requires mindfulness. So too is it with spiritual parenting demands. Raising spiritually comfortable children necessarily requires mindfulness, intentionality, and hard work as well. Partnership is important here too.

"Our Rabbis taught: There are three partners in creating every human being—the Holy One, a father, and a mother. When a person honors his father and mother, the Holy One says, 'I view them as though I had dwelt among them and they had honored Me'" (Talmud, *Kiddushin* 30b–3la). In other words, as we honor our parents, God is with us. Parents are seen as partners with the Source of Life in the creation of each human being. (As always, we extend this teaching to the parenting partnership between two men or two women, in blended families, and to the single parent, who is also a partner with God in the holy task of child rearing.) When we toil in the work of parenting, we can draw spiritual strength and inspiration from the Holy One.[10]

Like other aspects of parenting partnerships, the spiritual dimension of our family's life deserves ongoing consideration. In this arena, many parents find it valuable to engage in conversations with youth education professionals, early childhood teachers, parenting specialists, Jewish educators, and rabbis and cantors. The input of seasoned professionals can help parenting partners navigate the difficult and sometimes intimidating conversations.

Try This: Set Your Jewish Spiritual Parenting Goals

When Paul counsels engaged couples, he asks them to think about many aspects of their future lives together, including the spiritual and religious dimensions. Just as we encouraged you to create a parenting vision statement, we also suggest you set goals for your Jewish spiritual parenting. Each co-parent should spend time thinking about the following questions before recording answers.

1. Describe your childhood religious and spiritual life. What remains meaningful? What would you like to do differently?
2. Based on your own definition of spirituality, what are your goals for your family's spiritual life?
3. How do you feel about your child developing a sense of closeness to God?
4. What Jewish values do you want to infuse into your home and family and to be prevalent in your parenting?
5. How open are you to connecting with a Jewish community—synagogue, youth group, Jewish camp, Jewish day school, Israel experience—to help raise your children spiritually? What draws you to any of these communities?

Once all co-parents have completed the exercise, sit together and share your answers. Note similarities and divergences. Highlight the areas in which you find agreement and those where you can benefit from deeper consideration and more conversation. Identify also what kinds of ritual life and beliefs you want to integrate into your family's life.

Parenting Is One Part Inheritance, One Part Partnership

Parenting children is a lifelong task—the more we experience, the more opportunity for self-reflection. With heightened insight, wisdom develops and we are better equipped to become the parents we long to be.

Although Torah might not present a wealth of positive role models for Jewish spiritual parenting, it does awaken us to a universal truth: parenting tops the list of the most challenging experiences we adults ever face. Our families bequeath us a whole set of attitudes and parenting practices that influence who we are and how we act (or will act) as parents. Recognizing this inheritance, we strive to partner with co-parents to identify the ideas that populate our conscious and subconscious selves. As we unpack the parenting baggage we carry with us from our youth, we are better able to be up front and intentional about our ideals and interests so that we can develop consistency and bring out the best in our parenting partnerships.

3 Holding Them Close, Letting Them Grow

The *Tzimtzum* of Spiritual Parenting

> Parents can only give good advice or put them on the right paths, but the final forming of a person's character lies in their own hands.
>
> —Anne Frank

Michelle: Teaching Baby Noah to Hug

When Noah was six months old, Paul actively taught him how to hug. "You put one arm here around my neck," Paul explained, holding Noah close and curling one of his plump baby arms gently to demonstrate. "And the other arm goes here," he coached playfully, attempting to clasp Noah's two hands together. "And now ... squeeeeze!" Paul instructed while smiling into his scrumptious green eyes. Like his older siblings, he quickly got the hang of it and has been giving great hugs ever since.

When children are young, we teach them by drawing them close and demonstrating how to behave. We describe and model valued actions and attitudes. Like Noah and the hugging lessons, young children are often receptive to the instruction. As they individuate and grow older, we still have lessons to teach, but we do so as they are busy discovering who they are on their own.

A child's process of growing up and maturing necessitates testing boundaries and experimenting with different personas. This requires parents both to step back (easier said than done!) and, because our children are still in need of parental guidance, to lean in. We endeavor to find that tenuous balance between ensuring our child's safety and letting her blossom naturally. On our best days, we trust that our parenting influence will serve as a sturdy sail as she ventures out on her own. We hope it will guide her back to us when she is ready to return.

Parents can intentionally cultivate closeness even as their child is wriggling out of our hugs. As children grow, we can continue to engage and teach them even as we take a step back and let them expand into fuller personhood. From this slight distance, we can watch, listen, monitor, and continue to teach. From a step away, children have space to develop and mature.

Tzimtzum (contraction) parenting is a way of providing our children with physical, emotional, and psychological space in which to expand. A Jewish mystical Creation myth can help us practice contracting and, by doing so, discover how to deepen our bonds with our children.

Pulling Back So They Can Burst Forth

In the sixteenth century, a rabbi named Isaac Luria lived in Safed, a city in northern Israel, where he became the father of contemporary Kabbalah (Jewish mysticism).[1]

According to Lurianic Kabbalah, before the creation of the universe nothing existed but God. Kabbalists called God *Ein Sof*, meaning "without end," to express that God was and is everything and everywhere. When God wanted to create the universe, God needed to create space in which it could come into being. So God began by contracting Godself—God's own essence—to provide an area in which creation could begin. Rabbi Luria called this *tzimtzum*, a process of withdrawing from being everywhere. God pulled back so that the universe could burst forth.

In that space, the Holy One created the universe as vessels, which at that moment were devoid of anything, including Godself.

We might think about the vessels as glass jars or clay containers, though they were without actual form.

So there would be no separation between the Holy One and the holy creation, God poured God's divine light into those vessels. But this light was too pure and too potent for the vessels, and they shattered, sending shards of creation and sparks of God's light everywhere. Rabbi Luria called this shattering *shvirat hakeilim* (shattering of the vessels). The resulting brokenness gave rise to the world of brokenness in which we live. According to Lurianic Kabbalah, every example of imperfection we encounter—pain and suffering, hatred and hunger, violence and evil—is the result of the unintended consequences of God trying to pour pure light into imperfect vessels.

Another consequence of this shattering is the development of a sacred role for humanity to partner with God in repairing the brokenness of the universe. Our purpose in life centers on engaging in *tikkun olam* (repairing the world). Each human action is potentially holy as we lift up the sparks of God's light from the brokenness of the world. *Tikkun olam* is understood in many circles as primarily social justice work, yet at its root *tikkun olam* also embraces spiritual activities, Jewish rituals, and especially the repair of human relationships. *Tikkun olam* brings wholeness to the universe—and to the Holy One.

Imitating God's *Tzimtzum*

We are created in God's image, intended to live by imitating God. We can learn important spiritual parenting practices from Rabbi Luria's notions of *tzimtzum, shvirat hakeilim,* and *tikkun olam*.

Rabbi Lawrence Kushner, a Reform Jewish scholar and mystic, suggests that *tzimtzum*, God's "voluntary self-contraction," is "not unlike what any good parent or teacher must routinely do: get out of the way so that the child or student can have room in which to learn and grow."[2]

Dr. Eugene Borowitz, often referred to as the dean of American liberal Jewish philosophy, explores *tzimtzum* as a mystic model for leadership. He also likens God's self-contraction to that of a parent:

> Take the case of a parent who has the power to insist upon a given decision and a good deal of experience upon which to base his judgment. In such an instance, the urge to compel is almost irresistible. Yet if it is a matter the parent feels the child can handle—better, if making this decision and taking responsibility for it will help the child grow as a person—then the mature parent withdraws and makes it possible for the child to choose and thus come more fully into being.[3]

By gradually contracting our parenting instruction, we provide more space in which our children can develop themselves. We strive to nurture independence. Learning from God's example, or at least Rabbi Luria's vision of how God created the world, we parents can work to avoid *shvirat hakeilim*. We can pull back on our tendency to pour too much of ourselves into our children. We do so gradually; we do so intentionally. By being judicious in how much of our own needs and ideas we project onto them, we bolster parent-child relationships that ultimately will *not* shatter.

Of course, this self-contraction is not easy. Dr. Isa Aron, scholar of Jewish education at Hebrew Union College–Jewish Institute of Religion, recognizes the challenge of *tzimtzum* for us all:

> Anyone who has ever been in a similar situation with a child ... knows how difficult it is to practice [*tzimtzum*], but also how, ultimately, this act of self-restraint allows the other person to develop more fully.[4]

Opening the Channels for Face-to-Face Communication in an Online World

Some of us are blessed to enjoy a lifetime of ease of conversation with our parents. Many of us, though, recall awkward moments—perhaps awkward years—when our parents seemed to be intensely probing into our lives and with equal intensity we tried to block them out. These were especially true when we were preteens and teens.

A new world is being fashioned through social media that further complicates our ability to connect with our children. Their lives are increasingly moving online and are communicated through text-, photo-, and video-messaging and other social media. What appears in social media is instantaneous; what is shared in texts proceeds at a rapid pace. Most children—including teens—lack the ability to process all the messages, to understand them in context, and to slow down enough to address the emotions they evoke. They do not, and often cannot, pause long enough to filter the information and edit their natural, impulsive response. Parents can serve as a sounding board and a secure anchor in the tsunami of instantaneous images and conversations. Children benefit from consistent reminders that what appears online is only a slice of an ever-changing experience.

How parents successfully connect with children is an ongoing experiment. We found success by engaging in *tzimtzum*. Over the years we noticed that certain activities provided opportunities for conversation and enough flexibility for our child to preserve personal space. Four qualities characterize these activities:

1. They take place outside of the home.
2. They are activities you can do together with your child.
3. They are experiences your child enjoys.
4. They preferably include some kind of physical movement.

Michelle: Walking Rituals—"Frapp and Chat"

When a new Peet's coffee shop opened one mile from our house, I was thrilled. I had fallen in love with a great cup of coffee long before I had fallen in love with Paul.

I began walking to Peet's for exercise and to take a break. Soon I began inviting one of the kids to join me for a (decaf) frappuccino. Those "frapp and chats" on Sunday mornings and on warm spring evenings provided much cherished one-on-one time. During the walk to Peet's, we would lose ourselves in conversation about everything and anything: friendships, upcoming sports games, and school pressures. We could brainstorm about a pending science project, debrief ways to study for a test, talk about movies, and reflect on an interaction with another family member.

On those walks I spent much of my time listening, every so often prodding with an open-ended question and then pulling back to ensure our child kept talking. Because we were headed for a frappuccino, to our child the discussion felt like an afterthought. Thus dialogue flowed like casual banter rather than as a litany of parental questions or the dreaded "third degree."

Activity as an Aid to Dialogue

Physical activity paired with conversation seems to aid our boys in particular, opening them to emotional and personal dialogue. Although not an athlete, Paul treasures memories of days spent at a nearby park hitting hundreds of grounders and fly balls to Noah and Daniel. Video games also seem to minimize the feeling of parental probing. In the early years, Paul and Daniel would play Donkey Kong together on their Nintendo 64 as a means of creating a partnership in solving the game's challenge. In between fly balls or video game levels, Paul would toss in a question to invite conversation.

Friends of ours find that taking a walk with their children, dribbling a basketball, or riding bikes provides the perfect entree into conversations about life. Others nurture open heart-to-hearts during daddy-child dinners out and mother-child shopping excursions, and in the midst of coaching opportunities on the ball field. Whether playing or watching sports together, playing Scrabble, or working on a craft project, those shared hours in an activity provide an excuse around which conversations can unfold. Whenever the discussion becomes too intense, we can pour ourselves back into the activity, averting that explosive *shvirat hakeilim*.

Paul: Walking Rituals—Frisbee "Toss and Talk"

When our boys were growing up, we often took them for walks along the beach in Santa Monica, California, and we always brought a Frisbee. Noah, Daniel, and I would throw the Frisbee back and forth as we made our way forward.

As they grew, I would throw the disc farther and farther down the wide-open strip of sand. Returning with the Frisbee, drawing close, we would have time for little bits of conversation. This "toss and talk" activity provided the excuse for recurring dialogue.

Sometimes we talked about simple subjects like television shows or sports statistics; other times we would delve deeper into their schoolwork, social challenges, or emotional well-being. I would toss in a question here or there and see how the conversation progressed. Whenever they seemed to become uncomfortable with the direction, I would throw the Frisbee far and allow all of us a moment to breathe before continuing the conversation. I pulled back and they ventured forth, tension alleviated before anyone or anything shattered.

Establish Your Own Innovative Communication Rituals

The earlier you establish your communication rituals, the more normative the experience becomes in your family life. Each week invite your child to engage with you in a chosen activity. Use this as an opportunity to do something together and to talk. In between moments of activity, share a funny story, ask his or her opinion about something, or dream about an upcoming meal or trip. Practice *tzimtzum*—contracting and pulling back, either physically or with moments of quiet—to keep intensity from overwhelming the encounters. This parental contraction will foster trust and comfort in your communication.

As your child grows up, especially during the intense, hormonal teenage years, it can become difficult to find common ground for conversation. Having this comfortable ritual to return to can serve as a pressure-release valve.

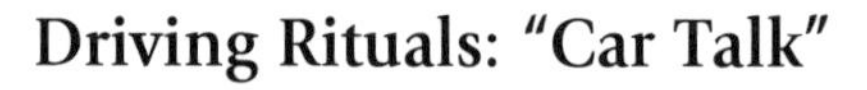

Driving Rituals: "Car Talk"

We parents spend so much time schlepping our children to various places. Car time is pregnant with opportunity for parents to gain glimpses into their child's emotional state and personal well-being.

"Car talk," as we referred to conversations shared or overheard while driving, is a fascinating phenomenon. As parents, we were continually surprised at how much we learned about our kids' lives while driving them from place to place. Captive in the car and benefiting from our parental *tzimtzum*, our children more easily opened up, talked without holding back, and even listened to the advice we subtly dispensed. We came to appreciate these daily opportunities for meaningful connection.

The relative position of the passengers in the car seems to contribute to opening the flow of conversation. When both parent and child are facing forward instead of facing each other, the child experiences an enhanced sense of safety in sharing personal thoughts. We parents, engaged in *tzimtzum* as opposed to being "in their faces" with questions, are viewed as safe sounding boards.

Use "Car Talk" Communication Tactics

We identified certain useful tactics for parent-child car talk:

1. Hold your tongue. Next to keeping your eyes on the road and your hands on the steering wheel, the most important skill for car talk is learning to listen more and talk less.
2. Toss in purposeful questions only sporadically. This makes you a nonintrusive presence. Similarly, being sparing with advice keeps you from seeming overbearing, which could curtail conversation.
3. Identify a useful amount of silence to allow a better chance of getting a conversation going. We found we needed to wait a while before talking on early morning drives. We used certain landmarks as our internal prompts before speaking to our sleepy preteens.
4. Ask questions about what you hear on the radio. Talk radio provides plenty of hooks with which to begin a conversation. Ask "Do you agree with that guy?" or "What do you think about that?" to propel the car talk forward.
5. Ask specific, nonjudgmental questions. At the end of the school day, asking questions like "Did Ms. Teacher explain the math problems you were working on?" or "What was your favorite part of the day?" yields more conversation than asking the more generic "How was school today?"

Similarly, when we drive carpools of our children and their friends, we are given a unique opportunity to learn about their lives, the highlights and the challenges. If we can successfully engage in *tzimtzum* during this time, our children's conversations with their friends will happen naturally. By being quiet, we allow our children the liberty to engage with others without our intervention or judgment. We move from being initiators of conversation to being silent observers of their inner lives.

Carpool Listening Without Interfering

When our children are engaging with others in our presence, we have an opportunity to observe without interfering. In doing so, we enable our children to develop their personalities and relationships as we silently monitor and remain aware. This encourages our children to own their own voice. This listening technique, particularly useful while driving carpools, has its own set of guidelines:

1. Try not to enter into your child's conversation. If you remain quiet, your presence tends to vanish and children share more freely, revealing pieces of their inner world. By not jumping in, we learn about friendships, pressures, crushes, which subjects are challenging, and which assignments are exciting. We unobtrusively gain access to their inner circle.
2. Think before you comment or intervene. When you hear something that significantly concerns you, you first want to evaluate the importance and urgency of the issue. Sometimes what feels important may not be urgent, and what feels urgent may not really be important. At times, it is best to hold off addressing the issue in order to gather additional information during another carpool interaction. Perhaps we misheard the child's intention, perhaps the kids solved the problem on their own, or perhaps they were just blowing off steam and the details originally stated were exaggerated. Taking the larger view, we learn that inaction can sometimes yield the best result. Of

course, we intentionally act when we need to ensure physical or significant emotional safety.

Tikkun Olam: Nurturing Wholeness in Our Children

Back when Rabbi Isaac Luria envisioned the *tzimtzum–shvirat hakeilim–tikkun olam* (contracting-shattering-repairing) Creation myth, he was focused on attempting to understand why, if the Holy One created the world, it could be filled with such brokenness and pain. Luria's conception of Creation was that it was unintentionally imperfect.

Rabbi Luria's insight lends itself to the unintentionally imperfect relationships between parents and children. If the Eternal Parent poured too much of Godself into God's creation, we in contrast can strive to hold ourselves back. While the Holy One's actions led to explosive destruction of the nascent universe, we can learn to act intentionally so as to minimize the volatility that characterizes many parent-child relationships during the child's preteen and teenage years.

Tzimtzum should increase slowly as our children enter middle school and beyond, until it defines more of our parenting in the teen years. Combining activities together with conversations allows for and invites practiced connection. Then we are engaging in *tikkun olam,* healing both our world and inoculating our relationships with our children.

That, after all, is the goal of Jewish spiritual parenting: to bring wholeness and holiness to their lives, our family life, and the world we share.

4

Transmitting Our Heritage Through the Generations

The Spiritual Significance of *Mishpacha* and *L'dor Vador*

Without memory, there is no culture. Without memory, there would be no civilization, no society, no future.

—Elie Wiesel

Paul: Why I Call My Dad Daily

I call my father on my way to work every morning. Why? Because he enjoys the brief update and takes pleasure in knowing what is happening in our daily lives. Because I want my kids and grandkids to follow my lead and call me regularly when I get older. Because he sometimes needs the conversation. And because I love him. My phone call is a small way to show immense gratitude for all that my dad has done for me. (And yes, I call my mother frequently too.)

I also call daily because I take seriously the wisdom of the fifth commandment, to "honor your father and mother" (Exodus 20:12). Honoring parents appears in the Ten Commandments as the link between the first four commandments, mediating our relationship with God and spirituality, and the last five, governing how we treat other people. Accordingly, we learn that treating our parents with respect and honor directly impacts the quality of our spiritual life and the health of our relationships with other people.

The relationships between generations are so consequential that the Holiness Code, another collection of ethical laws in the Torah (Leviticus 19), opens its understanding of holiness with the instruction "You shall revere your mother and father" (Leviticus 19:3). *Kedoshim tiheyu* (being holy) blossoms fully when relationships between generations are filled with mutual respect.

The way we treat our parents also reflects our character. When asked for advice on whether someone might make a good marriage partner, I suggest, "Watch how he cares for his parents. From this, you will learn about the quality of his compassion, patience, and commitment to family." When people wonder how their children will treat them when they get older, I respond, "Just look in the mirror of your life and observe how you treat your parents." After all, we are the role models for our children. If we treat our parents well, our children will learn to do the same. If we do not, how can we expect different treatment?

Accepting the fifth commandment as a guide, we honor our parents by nurturing their relationships with our children. Grandparents can be sources of wisdom and connectors *l'dor vador* (from generation to generation) to our Jewish past and familial lore. Other adults in our family and community can also serve as transmitters of values in addition to, or sometimes in place of, grandparents. (When we write about grandparents, you might also think about these other older adults.)

In this chapter, we share ways to integrate grandparents into our children's lives. We also address the unique challenges of being grandparents of children in interfaith families.

Cultivating the Grandparent-Grandchild Relationship

We need only skim through the Bible to realize that biblical family relationships are complex, impassioned, and filled with drama. In spite of these challenging family dynamics, Judaism places a high value on family relationships. Shabbat and holy days are intended to be celebrated with the *mishpacha* (family); life-cycle transitions become central moments for family gatherings and reconnection.

Family relationships between children and their grandparents are cherished. Proverbs, our biblical book of wisdom, elevates grandchildren as the priceless jewel of grandparenthood, gushing that "children's children [are] the crown of their elders" (Proverbs 17:6). Similarly, grandparents can be enduring positive influences on the Jewish spiritual life of their grandchildren.

Jewish tradition rightly identifies the grandparent-grandchild alliance as essential to the transmission of our most cherished values. In Deuteronomy, we are told to remember significant Jewish spiritual moments and pass them on to the next two generations: our children and our grandchildren.

> Only take heed and watch yourself very carefully, so that you do not forget the things that your eyes saw. Do not let [this memory] leave your hearts, all the days of your lives. Teach your children and children's children about the day you stood before the Eternal your God at Horeb. (Deuteronomy 4:9–10)[1]

Based on this passage, Rabbi Yehoshua ben Levi in the Talmud explains the life-changing, time-defying shift that occurs when grandparents teach grandchildren:

> Anyone who teaches his grandchild Torah is regarded as if he had received the Torah from Mount Sinai, as it is said, "Teach your children and children's children," and then it says, "The day you stood before the Eternal your God at Horeb." (Talmud, *Berachot* 21b and *Kiddushin* 30a)

When grandparents teach their grandchildren, the whole revelation at Mount Sinai is affirmed yet again.

As parents committed to deepening our children's Jewish spirituality, we value the bonds between our children and their grandparents. Thankfully the Torah guides us in this endeavor. At the end of Genesis, while our ancestor Jacob lay on his deathbed, he delivered a heartfelt blessing to his two grandsons, Menashe and Ephraim.

Jacob said, "In you, my grandchildren, shall Israel always bless [future generations], saying: 'May God bless you as Ephraim and Menashe'" (Genesis 48:20). Emulating Jacob's example, Jews regularly bless their sons and grandsons on Shabbat and holy days with those same words: "May God bless you as Ephraim and Menashe" (*Y'simcha Elohim k'Ephraim v'chi'M'nashe*). Daughters too are blessed in the name of our biblical matriarchs: "May God make you like Sarah, Rebecca, Rachel, and Leah" (*Y'simeich Elohim k'Sarah, Rivka, Rachel, v'Leah*).

This singular instance of a grandparent blessing his grandchildren figures much more significantly in the overall perspective of Jewish continuity than do the many biblical instances of parents blessing children. Rabbi Jonathan Sacks, former Orthodox chief rabbi of Great Britain, observes:

> Between parents and children ... there are often tensions. Parents worry about their children. Children sometimes rebel against their parents. The relationship is not always smooth.
>
> Not so with grandchildren. There the relationship is one of love untroubled by tension or anxiety. When a grandparent blesses a grandchild, he or she does so with a full heart. That is why this blessing by Jacob of his grandchildren became the model of blessing across the generations. Anyone who has had the privilege of having grandchildren will immediately understand the truth and depth of this explanation.[2]

This embrace by grandparents encircles our celebration of Shabbat each week. On Shabbat, we begin with the blessing of children, based on the words of a grandparent, the biblical Jacob. When Shabbat ends, some recite words of Psalm 128 as part of the evening service: "May you live to see your children's children—peace be on Israel" (Psalm 128:6). These verses point to the unique connection between grandchildren and peace. Rabbi Sacks explains it this way: "Those who think about grandchildren care about the future, and those who think about the future make peace. It is those who constantly think of the past, of slights and humiliations and revenge, [who] make war."[3]

It behooves parents to cultivate this special grandparent-grandchildren bond. After all, as Jewish educator Kay Pomerantz writes,

> Grandparents have a unique relationship with grandchildren because in most situations they do not deal with day-to-day responsibilities. Grandparents can be selective in what the focus of their time spent together will be. Grandchildren are often particularly receptive to these occasions since they are special and out of the ordinary.[4]

Grandparents need not be overly knowledgeable about Judaism to be able to discuss or model meaningful Jewish spirituality. They need only be loving and joyous. A Jewish grandparent's heartfelt sharing of spiritual experiences or recounting of personal Jewish memories can strengthen grandchildren's understanding of Judaism or spiritual living. When grandparents talk about Judaism comfortably and naturally, they aid in nurturing Jewish identity.[5]

Encourage Grandparents to Bless Their Grandchildren

Emulating Jacob's blessing of his grandchildren, encourage grandparents to bless your children. (If your children do not have grandparents nearby, invite another adult who fills a similar role to bless them.) On Friday nights, Jewish holy days, or whenever they are together with their grandchildren, take a moment to sit together. Choose a quiet moment, perhaps at the beginning of a meal, at bedtime, or just before the grandparents say goodbye. Encourage grandparents to bless their grandchildren with either the traditional or a personal blessing. You might print out these words for the grandparents to read, or read them aloud and have the grandparents repeat each line after you. In some families, like ours, the whole family—parents, children, and grandchildren—repeat the words together. Make sure to link the spiritual with the physical by holding hands while reciting words of blessing.

If you choose the traditional Jewish blessings, here they are in English:

For a boy:

May God make you like Ephraim and Menashe.

For a girl:

May God make you like Sarah, Rebecca, Rachel, and Leah.

For both:

May the Holy One bless you and keep you.
May the Holy One shine light upon you and be gracious to you.
May the Holy One be with you always and grant you peace.

In Hebrew:
For a boy:

Y'simcha Elohim k'Ephraim v'chi'M'nashe.
Y'varech'cha Adonai v'yishm'recha.
Ya'er Adonai panav eilecha vichuneka.
Yisa Adonai panav eilecha v'yasem l'cha shalom.

For a girl:

Y'simeich Elohim k'Sarah, Rivka, Rachel, v'Leah.
Yivareichayich Adonai v'yishm'rayich.
Ya'er Adonai panav elayich vichunayich.
Yisa Adonai panav alayich vayasem lach shalom.[6]

Alternatively, if grandparents choose to create a personal blessing, they might begin, "May God bless you with ..." and conclude with some words of hope for certain attributes and values. If it is more comfortable, their blessing might begin, "I wish for you ..."

For example:

May God bless you with joy and happiness,
with an understanding that you are intelligent and kind,
and with all the love in the world.

or:

I wish for you a nighttime of comfortable sleep,
a day tomorrow filled with optimism and contentment,
and knowledge in your heart that I love you to the moon and back.

Conclude with hugs and kisses, ensuring that meaningful words are sealed with love.

Modeling *L'Dor Vador* for Our Children

Today, extended families live all over the world and gathering together is often expensive and challenging to schedule around busy calendars. We parents need to act intentionally to ensure that our children have meaningful interactions with their grandparents and other extended family.

Parents need to plan ahead to plant the seeds of healthy multigenerational family relationships. Just as Abraham and Isaac passed down their own family dysfunction to Jacob and then to his sons, so too do we see such dysfunction passed down *l'dor vador*. We ought to dream about the healthy family relationships we want our children to have—with each other, with us, and with their grandparents—and to consider how we can model the desired behavior ourselves. When we prioritize time and connection with our parents, our siblings, and our other relatives, our grown-up kids have a better chance of doing the same with us.

Coach Grandparents and Older Family Members to Connect

Create the connection between generations by intentionally drawing the grandchildren and grandparents closer. When visiting is not possible, harness the power of technology.

We foster deeper connections by:

- Teaching grandparents the newest technology.
- Calling grandparents ourselves and then handing the phone to the kids.
- Giving the children questions to ask the grandparents or hints about what to share.
- Providing hints to the grandparents about what the child is interested in.

- Reminding grandparents of their own stories that they might share with their grandchildren. Our children were intrigued by Paul's mother "Lala's" community leadership and social action work, Grandpa's enthusiasm for photography and his long-ago army duty, Papa's businesses and connection to his larger family, and Grandma's positivity, empathy, and interest in their ideas and journeys. Conversation topics like these enable grandchildren to view their grandparents as human beings with compelling dimension and history.
- Contextualizing the "now" of the relationship to older children so they do not regret delaying opportunities to connect while their grandparents are healthy.

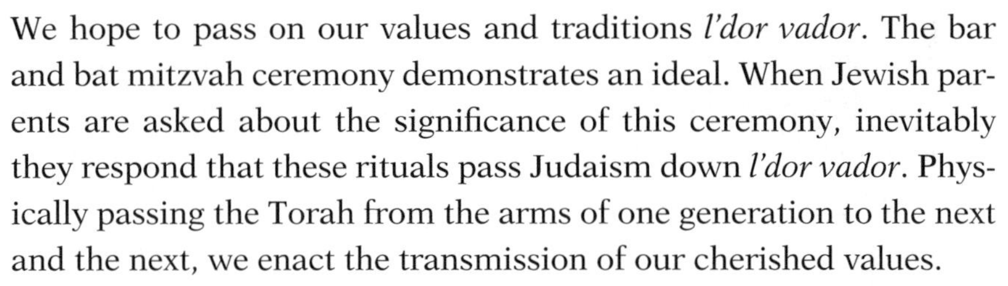

We hope to pass on our values and traditions *l'dor vador*. The bar and bat mitzvah ceremony demonstrates an ideal. When Jewish parents are asked about the significance of this ceremony, inevitably they respond that these rituals pass Judaism down *l'dor vador*. Physically passing the Torah from the arms of one generation to the next and the next, we enact the transmission of our cherished values.

Consider this favorite folktale:

> A mother bird was walking down the road with three baby birds when they came to a large puddle. It was too deep for the baby birds to walk across and too wide for them to go around. So the mother bird said to the first baby bird, "If I pick you up and carry you across the puddle, how will you repay me for it?" The baby bird said, "The next puddle we come to, I'll pick you up and carry you across." The mother replied, "That's a silly answer. You're too small to carry me across." She asked the same question of the second fledgling, and the bird answered, "When I've grown up, I'll carry you across puddles." The mother bird shook her head and said, "Even when you're grown up, I won't need you to get across puddles." Then she asked her third baby, who answered, "Someday I'll be a mother bird and I'll have babies of my own, and I'll do all the things for them that you've done for me."[7]

Among the highest aspirations of Jewish spiritual parenting and grandparenting is ensuring the continuity of all that is good about our people, our families, our traditions, and our spiritual practices. The value of *l'dor vador* succeeds most strongly when we have cultivated a relationship between the generations.

Paul: The Precious Value of Papa's Phone Calls

My parents live on the East Coast, and we live on the West Coast. Since family (*mishpacha*) is so central to all of us, we mindfully nurtured a relationship between our children and "Papa and Lala."

Papa made weekly calls to his grandchildren even when they were just a year old. Michelle and I would put each child on the phone, and Papa would coo, chatter, and earnestly teach them how to say "Papa." Although as a toddler each would only nod and smile in growing recognition, the silence did not discourage Papa. Long-distance calls were expensive back then, but Papa knew that he was laying the foundation for a close-knit bond with his California grandchildren. In time, we saw that this investment in their relationship paid off tremendously.

The phone-calling ritual, I remembered, had begun the generation before. My dad made sure that my siblings and I each spoke regularly on the phone to our great-grandparents and later to our grandparents also. Each Sunday when the cousins were together, we children sometimes kvetched about being pulled away from TV or a game, but we dutifully observed this ritual weekly. The conversations were brief, but they ensured that we prioritized *mishpacha* and maintained an ongoing touch-base relationship.

It was not until I was a parent that I finally understood the import of the phone-calling ritual. My dad was building a bridge between generations. He was embedding *l'dor vador* into our family routine. Michelle and I have since adopted the ritual and made certain that our own kids call each of their four grandparents regularly. We prioritized family visits to grandparents' homes. We kvell that our grown children are now internally motivated to visit, call, text, and Facebook-friend their grandparents. *L'dor vador*, our *mishpacha* thrives.

Build a Sukkah, Refocus Your Life

Jewish holidays offer the opportunity to create lasting memories that can deepen the sense of *mishpacha* and multigenerational bonds, and pass down important spiritual values *l'dor vador*.

The festival of Sukkot especially highlights the poignancy of extending family bonds across the generations. Sukkot is the name of both the holiday and the rickety booths in which we sit during the holiday. Celebrated with joy and an atmosphere of fun, Sukkot can bring anticipation, excitement, and laughter into the family. It also symbolizes in stark terms the fragility of life and the sadness that seems to creep at some point into every home. Sukkot can redirect our attention away from the impermanence of material possessions back to the relationships that make life abidingly meaningful. This holiday reminds us not to wait until it is too late to focus on what—and who—is truly important.

Sometimes our priorities shift and we lose focus. Judaism offers an antidote to that confusion: *"Build a sukkah; refocus your life."* With a little preplanning and a trip to the hardware store or a visit to a pre-fab sukkah website, we can regain our ultimate focus and redirect ourselves to what we value most.

Paul's most abiding Jewish childhood memory took place during Sukkot. He recalls with joy being with his parents as they helped build the sukkah at Congregation Shalom in Chelmsford, Massachusetts. Together they measured and sawed; they hammered and nailed. It took all day, and everyone had fun.

Similarly, many of our own family's fond memories include sukkah building with three generations. Grandparents join us in the backyard. None of us is particularly handy with tools, yet we get the job done, creating and adorning the temporary dwelling. The frame is constructed, the palm fronds affixed on top, and the beautification occurs as each family member digs into the boxed collection of Sukkot decorations and hangs fall-colored fabric leaves, faux fruit, and dried flowers.

Temple Isaiah in Los Angeles beautifully expresses how the sukkah transports us through time and space:

> When we finally sit in this sketch of a home, we are transported to the desert where the Israelites wandered for forty years [Leviticus 23:42-43]. We might remember the rabbinic legend that says the sukkot the Israelites dwelt in were made from clouds God provided for them. We are also transported to Israel, where during the harvests the farmers would live out in their fields in little booths to be able to keep watch over their crops. As we sit in the flimsy sukkah, we might also be transported to Skid Row where people live in flimsy makeshift homes of boxes and scrap wood. We might realize that despite the walls we build up, we are always vulnerable.[8]

Imagine that you are in your house or apartment. In your mind's eye, look around and notice that it might be full of collections: furniture and family heirlooms; artwork and vacation photos; china and tchotchkes. Surrounded by these cherished symbols of your lifetime, now imagine that you are lying in your bed asleep, a warm blanket tucked under your chin. You are sleeping soundly, secure in the knowledge that, come rain or shine, the roof over your head—the place you call home—will protect you.

Those of us from the Los Angeles area recall January 1994. Same blissful sleep, same sense of security. Same *sukkat shalom* (shelter of peacefulness). Until 4:31 a.m., when the Northridge earthquake struck, a 6.7 on the Richter scale. The ground shook and swayed, and in the process turned our lives inside out. One moment our homes were pillars of strength. The next, as we sat among cracked walls, broken glass, and piles of rubble, we were reminded of how fleeting and fragile life can be. After making sure everyone was safe, we felt intense gratitude at being alive. Rabbi Lawrence Kushner, in his book *Invisible Lines of Connection: Sacred Stories of the Ordinary,* raises the challenge of maintaining this sense of gratitude at all times in our lives. He wonders, "Would that there be some way of getting to that heightened gratitude for life without the terror."[9]

Building a sukkah helps parents and children develop perspective and gratitude. The festival of Sukkot forces us out of that ephemeral sense of security by relocating us to a rickety structure. Changing our vantage point can be eye-opening. Gazing through the doorway of a sukkah in our backyard into the windows of our real home, we cannot but marvel at the study in contrasts! The sukkah is shaky, while our home appears sturdy. The cost of a sukkah is minimal; a permanent home costs much more. One reminds us what life could be if tragedy were to strike quickly; the other blinds us with a false sense of what really is. The sukkah experience invites us to gain a better sense of reality, to humbly rearrange our lives—at least for a week—to realign our relationships and our family as central.

Try This **Build a Sukkah and Gain Perspective**

Sukkah building is stress-free, fun-filled Judaism that builds relationships too. Everyone can help: parents, children, grandparents, friends, neighbors, and co-workers. Since modern building codes do not govern sukkah building, you can design creatively. Construction need not be complicated: four walls, three walls, even two full walls with a freestanding half wall will fulfill the tradition. Cover the top with *schach* (formerly living plant material), usually palm fronds on the West Coast, pine branches on the East, and cornstalks in the Midwest. Use just enough *schach* to ensure the amount of shade is greater than sunlight during the day, while allowing the stars to shine through at night.

Decorating the sukkah can be great fun. Use your imagination. Cover the walls with kids' drawings, Rosh Hashanah cards, and other artwork. In cooler areas, you can hang fruit from the sukkah roof. In warmer climates, you might decorate with faux fruit from a craft store.

Eat in the sukkah as often as possible, perhaps inviting friends for a potluck meal. Some families also snooze in sleeping bags in their sukkah under the stars; consider it a Jewish backyard campout.

Sukkah building bonds *mishpacha* together, reinforces your perspective on life, and provides unadulterated fun! Take the challenge: build a sukkah and refocus your life.

While Jewish holidays like Sukkot set specific times for families to come together, we need not limit the bonding opportunities to holidays alone. We have 365 days in every year available to us to strengthen the bonds of *mishpacha* and to honor the value of *l'dor vador*. Scheduling special weekends or multiday vacations when extended families link together establishes the abiding connections that will enrich your children throughout their lifetimes. Our children grow up quickly. Setting aside time for family gatherings facilitates our ability to honor our priorities and live our values.

Michelle: One-Bedroom Palm Springs Vacation Home —Sleeps Thirteen Comfortably

When I was growing up, family vacations often included thirteen of us: my parents and two brothers; my aunt, uncle, and four first cousins; and my maternal grandparents. We traveled to breathtaking destinations like Yosemite, yet my all-time favorite summer vacation memories are those at my grandparents' Palm Springs apartment, where my brothers, cousins, and I spent full days swimming in the pool. The summer heat often exceeded 110 degrees, and we—the youngest by far in this retirement community—were typically the only ones in the pool. Every so often my grandparents called one of us to the side of the pool to say a quick hello to a neighbor, who always knew us by name. My grandparents relished updating them with details about our age, our inches grown, and our recent accomplishments.

At dinnertime, Grandma Ruby wore her brilliantly colored muumuu and Grandpa David his golf garb as they grilled kosher hot dogs on their patio hibachi. After eating, we toasted marshmallows golden while Grandpa sat nearby listening to a baseball game on his transistor radio, grumbling his own play-by-play analysis. When the temperature dropped to 100 degrees, it was time to head over to Thrifty's Drugstore for triple-scoop ice-cream cones. (Inevitably one of us forfeited a scoop to the heat as it slid down our arm and plopped onto the sizzling pavement.) Back at the apartment we played contract gin and Scrabble late into the night. Despite a range of ages, we cousins formed deep bonds in the mutual playground of the pool, ice cream, and a game of cards.

At night, the thirteen of us nestled in my grandparent's one-bedroom apartment, yet we never felt a lack of space.

Through these experiences I learned that what makes family vacations memorable is not fancy hotels or destinations or luxurious travel packages, but rather sharing time away together. We cherished the experience of multiple generations enjoying life's simple pleasures. These uncomplicated vacation routines set the stage for the transcendent value of *mishpacha* and the centrality of family relationships in my adult life.

Time with Grandparents: Vacation or a Family Visit?

Wouldn't it be wonderful if every family gathering, holiday celebration, or vacation was a tension-free, exhilarating adventure? Alas, that is not always possible. There are unique personalities to navigate and competing needs to negotiate. Nonetheless, time with grandparents, relatives, and siblings is crucial to developing healthy bonds.

We discovered that by reframing our time with family, we could define the experience differently and our expectations were more realistic. After one particular visit in which we were unsuccessful in meeting competing needs, Paul's mom, Linda, astutely suggested that we view our time spent together not as a vacation but as "family time." Linda's wisdom permitted us to reassess expectations for our time together, and to set new goals for our interactions with our children's grandparents:

1. *To make time spent with grandparents a priority*. We planned trips to the East Coast during school breaks, and we regularly scheduled weekend time at Michelle's parents' home on the West Coast—a two-hour drive south. We renamed this "family time" instead of vacation time.
2. *To allow the grandparents unfettered access to their grandchildren*. We are fortunate to have four parents who are hands-on grandparents and were capable of caring for young children. We took advantage of their generosity to let us get away and let them bond in our absence. When watching the kids, they kept most of our rules, supplementing them with their own ideas—access to more candy and later bedtimes. At first we

had a hard time accepting that a different menu (french fries and chocolate) and a relaxed bedtime routine were not harmful. Soon we realized that this time with grandparents was full of distinctive memories. Our parents loved having their grandkids to themselves without us hovering, and we deeply appreciated the break.

3. *To spend no more than three consecutive days in each other's homes*. We discovered that after three days in another family member's home, the adults became cranky. So we had loving yet up-front conversations with the grandparents about setting limits for time together. If Paul's parents were in town for a week, they would leave in the middle for a few days to visit other friends. If we were visiting them, we arranged a mini-vacation for ourselves while the grandparents babysat. By talking about our needs and agreeing to a plan, we defused charged emotions and provided each other much needed—and much appreciated—breathing space.
4. *To accept nonjudgmentally the unique contributions each grandparent offered*. Some grandparents express love with presents. Others extend the gift of attention, patience, or silly repartee. Many offer wisdom free of judgment and welcome rule-bending experiences. Some show up at every sporting event, school play, and recital. We learned to embrace each gift and the love it represented.

Try This Clarify Expectations for Grandparent Time

What are your goals for your child's time with his grandparent? Keeping in mind that the time together is finite, one goal might be for your child to have an exceptional experience outside of at-home routines. Safety concerns excepted, the benefit to a child from experiencing a unique set of "grandparent rules" is that it makes the experience indelible. "Papa let us eat hot fudge sundaes for *dinner*!" and "Grandpa let me use his brand-new camera!" become extraordinary recollections from childhood.

Invite your child's grandparents to reflect on their own goals and expectations for time with grandparents. Speak with each other candidly about areas of overlap and divergence, and brainstorm ways to make everyone feel comfortable with the agreed-upon plan.

Develop a kind of *brit* (agreement) to guide you. Some families will write these words down; others will find that a conversation suffices. Differentiate between the ideal versus what works for your family. Let the overarching goal be to embrace opportunities for cross-generational bonding while simultaneously preventing or at least lessening any hurt or frustration. Setting goals and preplanning just might tone down the often intensely charged nature of family gatherings.

Grandparenting Interfaith Grandchildren

In interfaith families, parents do a delicate dance with and around religion. As a rabbi, Paul strongly urges parents of two different faiths to choose one religion, because that gives clarity to the children about their religious identity. But we also know plenty of people who have made different choices. A casual Internet search provides links to like-minded people who have created their own unique strategies.

Parents must also decide what role, if any, grandparents have in supporting the religious or spiritual identity of their grandchild. How can Jewish grandparents of interfaith families be positive role models? Author and maven on grandparenting Sunie Levin, in *Mingled Roots: A Guide for Grandparents of Interfaith Children*, teaches that intentional conversations between parent and grandparent can bring calm to any difficult encounters.[10] Based on her advice and Paul's experience counseling grandparents of interfaith families, we offer two questions to consider:

1. *Who makes the decisions?* Remember that the grandchild's parents, including the non-Jewish spouse or partner, determine the religious identity of the child. Make sure your words and actions support this principle by showing respect for the parents' choices. Their choice may be to raise their children

in one religion (of either the Jewish or non-Jewish parent) or in both religions. Alternatively, they might let the children choose their own religion at a later date. While it may be uncomfortable or painful, let the parents know that you understand that they make the decision.

2. *What Jewish traditions can you share with your grandchild?* First gain permission from the parents and together determine what you may share. Being exceedingly sensitive to the parents' boundaries, check in regularly with the parents and honor their feelings. As you build up trust, they may allow you to share more.[11]

Test These Interfaith Grandparenting Tips

When sharing your Jewish heritage with your grandchildren, think intentionally and act prudently. Plan ahead and gain permission.

1. Write out your ideas for sharing your Jewish identity with your grandchildren, detailing your desires. Be specific. This allows you to think it through clearly before overreaching. Offer to share your ideas with your child and the co-parent and if they agree, give them time to digest and respond to your words. Be open to the give-and-take.
2. Preplan Jewish experiences. Think ahead, even months ahead, about what you want to experience with your grandchild. Begin slowly. You might talk about memories of your parents and grandparents, where they were born and what their lives were like, and how they experienced Jewish holidays. Create a Shabbat experience for your grandchild in your home. Perhaps you will visit a Jewish museum, attend a family concert with a Jewish rock musician, or participate in an interactive family activity at a synagogue, Jewish camp, or Jewish community center. Take your grandchildren to a deli to taste culturally Jewish foods. Plant a tree on the Jewish Arbor Day festival of Tu B'shvat.

3. Give the gift of Jewish books. Share with the parents a list of the books you would like to give your grandchildren. Children's books by Sandy Eisenberg Sasso (*God's Paintbrush* and *In God's Name*) and by Nancy Sohn Swartz (*How Did the Animals Help God?*) are thoughtful, engaging tools for nurturing Jewish spirituality. With the parents' permission, sign your grandchild up with PJ Library ("Pajama Library," http://pjlibrary.org), an organization that sends families Jewish-themed, holiday-related, age-appropriate books each month.
4. Make your home a Jewish space. Affix a mezuzah on the doorpost of each room; these can be purchased in a Judaica shop, in a synagogue, or online. Display Jewish ritual objects year-round. Decorate for Jewish holidays. Buy Jewish children's books for your home library.
5. Teach by example, and practice what you preach. Embrace your own Judaism by joining and attending a synagogue, visiting Israel, and/or taking classes about Judaism.
6. Offer to pay to send your grandchild to a Jewish summer camp. Jewish overnight summer camps have an enduring impact on Jewish identity development. At camp, children build self-esteem in the safety of creative, nonjudgmental, round-the-clock Jewish living. Jewish camps are designed for children with all interests. The Union for Reform Judaism runs summer camps all over the country, including some camps focused on high-level sports, sci-tech, arts, outdoor adventure, and teen leadership.[12]
7. Continually remind the parents that you will adhere to what they feel comfortable with when you are telling your grandchild—their child—about Judaism.

Michelle & Paul: Who Else Can Play the Grandparent Role?

When we think about the role of older adults in the lives of children, we need not be constrained by either proximity or biology. With modern technology, we can guide grandparents who live far away to connect with their young relatives. We can invite into our children's lives people who can play a similar role: adults who live nearby such as neighbors, older members of a local synagogue, or great-aunts and -uncles.

We have discovered in our own family that relationships with older relatives can be meaningful to our children. They love hearing stories from great-aunts and -uncles, and cousins. At a birthday party for Michelle's ninety-five-year-old cousin Hedy, dozens of people stood to voice their gratitude for Hedy and share stories about how they came to view her as a symbolic adoptive mother. Hedy does not have biological children of her own, yet at this gathering men and women ranging in age from twenty-something to sixty-something and speaking in English, Spanish, and Hebrew shared a deep-rooted connection to her.

When our daughter, Rachel, graduated from college, Hedy gave her a beaded necklace that had belonged to her own grandmother. The beads, Hedy told Rachel, were not precious or valuable stones. Yet for Rachel the connection to her ancestor was priceless. Hedy's grandfather, who originally gave her grandmother the necklace, was a "brilliant" interpreter at Ellis Island, who helped open the gateway to America for innumerable immigrants. He reportedly spoke up to fifteen languages. (We smile as his language fluency seems to increase with each retelling of the story.) Rachel was so moved by Hedy's gift that she slipped the beads off the delicate string and used them to make earrings for each of her female cousins so that all of them could hold close their connection to Hedy and this beautiful family legacy.

Try This **Promote Sacred Storytelling**

Create opportunities for grandparents and older adults to share their memories of growing up, going to school, praying in shul (synagogue), serving in the army, falling in love, and navigating the political and economic climate of their youth. Make family time an opportunity to bring the past into the present. Encourage sharing of memories.

While some grandparents are natural storytellers, others need an invitation or a prompt. With your child, create a list of topics that interest them about Grandma or Grandpa. Combine factual questions (Where did you go to school? What did you do for fun?) with value-based and spiritual questions (What life lessons did your parents teach you? What are your Jewish memories from your childhood?). Save that list on a smartphone, stick it on the refrigerator, or keep it in a wallet. When you are with a grandparent, ask the questions—in front of your child—or hand the list to your child to read.

There are plenty of questions that can prompt priceless exchanges. Here are some ideas:

- What made you fall in love with your spouse/partner?
- How did you get engaged?
- Where did you celebrate Jewish holidays, and what were the celebrations like?
- What was your first job, and how did you choose your career?
- What were the major influences in the world at the time?
- Do you remember when ______________________ happened? (Fill in a historical event.)
- Who were your childhood best friends?
- What were your hobbies as children?
- What kind of music did you enjoy?
- What do you miss from your childhood?
- When have you felt close to God?
- When have you felt spiritual?
- What are your proudest accomplishments?
- What do you wish you had done differently?

Whether over the phone, at Thanksgiving dinner, or around a table in the sukkah, be inquisitive. Our parents often share sentimental childhood memories moving us all to tears at family gatherings. When given the opportunity, grandparents and other older adults who are otherwise quiet can surprise us with unpredictable and inspirational tales of courage, grief, strength, and humor.

The Responsibility Is Ours

Over time, we understood that we hit the jackpot with all four of our children's grandparents. Our children are deeply grateful for their grandparents' limitless generosity of heart and for the immeasurable ways they continue to enrich their lives. The Jewish life lessons that our parents have taught their grandchildren—about endurance, resilience, philanthropy, kindness, and humor—are timeless gifts.

We parents hold the keys to the cultivation of those relationships. As we bond one generation to the other *l'dor vador,* we ensure the continuation of important values and we embed a commitment to *mishpacha*. Through it all, we help our children locate their place in time and in the world.

5 Truths We Know

Sharing *Emet* with Our Children

> Learn from your father [and mother] about what is important in life. If you want a life filled with love, you must love.... If you want goodness for your children, hold them close to your heart and tell them of their beauty.
>
> —RABBI KARYN KEDAR, *GOD WHISPERS*

Paul: How Do We Pass On Our Values?

When my friend Becky asked me to officiate at a *minyan* service after her father Aaron's funeral, I stepped forward without question. Friends help friends. It was only as I stood beside Becky and our extended group of friends that I realized the daunting task of trying to find words of wisdom to comfort someone I considered more a family member than a friend. But there we were, so we prayed the prayers. Becky seemed to gain strength from the ritual and comfort from the companionship of the community. I worried still about what to say to bring uplift to her heart and solace to her soul.

I was saved, however, by none other than her father Aaron himself—yes, the deceased. Before heart surgery ten years earlier, being well aware that we can never be sure when the end will come, Aaron had written an ethical will to make sure that his ideals would survive. A short two-page letter to loved ones, his ethical will bequeathed to them the values he held most dear. As I read Aaron's letter aloud, it was Aaron himself who comforted his daughter and family. Aaron led us all with wisdom and humility into a meaningful moment of *kedusha* (holiness).

That is the power of ethical wills; they are poignant precisely because they allow a writer to convey truth as he knows it, long after he is gone.

We each have hopes and dreams for our children and our families. When we begin to raise our children, we envision the values and priorities that we hope will encircle their lives. Sometimes we communicate these by example. At other moments we speak aloud our most cherished values. Too often, too much goes unspoken.

Emet (truth) involves an honest accounting of who we are, what we value, and how we express and share those values with others. We document those values to convey to our families what we hold most dear. We can also use moments of transition—actual and anticipated—to guide our children in the moment and toward the future. The resulting collection of letters bequeaths to future generations our hopes and dreams for their Jewish spiritual lives.

The All-Encompassing Truth

Emet, meaning "truth" or "faithfulness," is the attribute of God that appears most frequently in Torah. The word *emet* comes from the Hebrew root word *aman,* which conveys firmness and certainty. In a powerful moment of self-disclosure, God proclaims God's central attributes: "The Eternal, the Eternal God, merciful and gracious, long-suffering, and abounding in goodness and truth [*emet*]" (Exodus 34:6). The ancient Rabbis note that *emet* is the final characteristic mentioned, suggesting that above all else are God's underlying certainty, dependability, and reliability.[1] The Talmud also states, "The seal of the Holy One is *emet*" (*Shabbat* 55a). When humans who are created in the image of God (*b'tzelem Elohim*) speak words of truth, we act like God. As the prophet Zechariah, ever trying to goad his people to live holy lives, instructed his generation, "These are the things you must do: Speak the truth to one another, render true and perfect justice in your gates" (Zechariah 8:16). Speaking truth and acting faithfully—these are the ways of holiness.

Being truthful, of course, goes beyond the ninth commandment's prohibition that "You shall not bear false witness against your neighbor" (Exodus 20:13). True, we should not lie. *Emet*, however, incorporates much more. Commitment to *emet* includes admitting when we have made mistakes. As parents, we want to be especially careful to teach our children that everyone, including us, makes mistakes. That honesty from parents emboldens children to strive toward truth and to embrace their own fallibility.

Emet involves being true to who we are, both in thought and in deed. Too many people—children and adults—struggle with authenticity. Though we are created in the image of God and so are valued for our uniqueness, we live in a world that seems to reward conformity. We must make ourselves vulnerable in order to embrace the very uniqueness that is our essence. This message is even more significant for preteens and teens as they struggle to embrace their own uniqueness.

Emet encompasses being true to our beliefs—Jewish and spiritual. Maintaining a strong Jewish identity is easier in some places and harder in others. In a world where racism, prejudice, and anti-Semitism give many an excuse to be hateful, we hope our children nonetheless will wrap themselves in our Jewish spiritual tradition and feel pride in being part of a Jewish family.

Similarly, as inheritors of a Jewish tradition born out of enslavement in Egypt and nurtured on resilience in the face of oppression, we Jews have an added responsibility to be aware of and care for the vulnerable—the widow and widower, the orphan, the poor, and the stranger. Doing so requires that we sometimes stand up against the status quo, speaking truth to power. Living *emet* is not always easy, but it does give us a strong sense of integrity.

Rabbi Arthur Green clarifies the essence of Jewish tradition's prioritizing of *emet*. In *These Are the Words: A Vocabulary of Jewish Spiritual Life*, Rabbi Green explains:

> God's seal of truth commands us to be honest and to live with integrity. This has to do with every aspect of our lives, from our business dealings and political system to the way we express

our faith in God. What we do and say should be out in the open, accessible to all who want to see it, and capable of passing common human tests of truth.[2]

V'ahavta: Impress Them upon Your Children

Twice daily, many Jews recite the *V'ahavta* (Deuteronomy 6:4–9), a prayer from Torah that calls upon us to "impress them upon your children and recite them" (*v'shinantam l'vanecha v'dibarta bam*). Just what "them" refers to is unspecified. Does the prayer instruct us to teach spiritual truths—perhaps the words of the *Shema*, which precede the *V'ahavta*? Or are we directed to teach Torah truths, from which the *V'ahavta* is excerpted? Should we convey other kinds of truth: the teachings handed down by generations of rabbis, the 613 *mitzvot* (commandments) enumerated from Torah, the lessons that our parents instilled in us, or those that we have discerned throughout our lives? The task of Jewish spiritual parenting, we believe, is to instill all of this into the minds, hearts, and lives of our children.

The eleventh-century French scholar Rashi (Rabbi Shlomo Yitzhaki) explains that the Torah's instruction "And you shall speak of them" means that speaking timeless truths "should be your principal topic of conversation, not of secondary importance." Quoting a midrashic teaching from *Sifrei*, Rashi reminds parents particularly that teaching our children Jewish spiritual values is more important than anything else we do.[3]

Like Becky's father, Aaron, we want our loved ones to know our priorities and ideals so that they will clearly see their way forward. As parents, we are challenged to find hopeful, nonjudgmental ways to articulate to our children, as Aaron did for his, those truths that we believe are abiding.

Paul: My Ethical Will

A few weeks after the shiva *minyan* for Aaron, emboldened by his example, I sat down to write my own ethical will. I accepted for myself Aaron's implicit invitation to impart words of comfort and wisdom to those who would survive me. Should I live to watch my three children mature, make their way in the world, and create their own families, I hope to have impressed on them these values both in words and by example. But if not, I want them to know what is in my heart.

To My Beloved Children:

We live in a world in which celebrity often seems more important than the goodness you accomplish. A world where America's leading businesses and business watchdogs lied to thousands of investors who counted on their honesty to plan for their future.... Where anti-Semitism—unadulterated hate—has raised its head yet again, endangering our people....Where the conflict in the Mideast flares and persists.

I find myself contemplating the awesome responsibility Mommy and I have to guide you. As you navigate the uncharted waters of life, I wonder, have we filled your life raft with a strong enough set of ethics and ideals to keep your heads above raging waters?

The key, it seems, is to remember that you have all you need to bring goodness to yourself and into the world. Do not allow yourself to be limited by others, whether because of your gender or your religion, race, orientation, or age. These provide you with unique tools with which to navigate our world and focus your mind toward anything you truly wish to accomplish. By the way, that is the central lesson of the modern bar and bat mitzvah. Having completed an arduous, complex task, you will have learned that while some tasks may be difficult, challenges are worth the reach.

My children, you are part of *am bachor* (a chosen people) that is not better than others but is chosen for a special responsibility. You are chosen to receive Torah and its values and to effectuate them in our world. As you grow, immerse yourselves in our Jewish values and become our ideal, an *or lagoyim* (a light unto the nations). To help you understand this, we have prioritized our lives around enabling you to gain a strong Jewish education and to learn the teachings of Torah. Torah encompasses that which is good and worthy. "*Hafach ba v'hafach ba d'chula va*—turn it and turn it, everything is in Torah" (*Pirkei Avot* 5:22): our stories and traditions, keys to our spirituality, our connection to the Source of All, our rituals, ethics, and values. Taken together, Torah goads us into making our special contribution to this world.

Of course, the pursuit of wisdom begins with Torah, but should not conclude with Jewish learning alone. As *am hasefer*, the People of the Book, we value secular scholarship too, for its own sake and as the key to our survival. Complete your studies with vigor; pursue college and continue to educate yourself throughout your life. Combine Jewish knowledge and secular studies to better prepare yourself to pursue your dreams. It is a marriage made in heaven.

Speaking of marriage, back in ancient days, I would have had the privilege of choosing your spouse or partner. Today, thankfully, you choose your own. Allow me to share with you what I have learned about love and marriage. Look not to movies or advertisements for guidance in your search for a soul mate. Look, rather, for a partner who loves you and whom you love, who helps you realize your fullest potential, and with whom you feel enabled to expand your horizons.

Marry a Jew (or at least find someone who has a commitment to Jewish life). With that person you will share a heritage and an ethical and spiritual encoding that was programmed into you at the moment of conception, nourished within you from the time you nursed at your mother's breast. With such a partner, your life will be easier and, I believe, fuller. Yet whomever you choose, Jew or non-Jew, a male or a female, know that we will love you and will aim to support the life you build together.

I have learned that marriage takes as much work as whatever you get paid to do, but the rewards of these efforts far exceed the paycheck you bring home. Continue to date your partner throughout your life. Make your time with him or her a priority, even when you have children, and share the responsibilities of parenting. Know that it is Mom's love that keeps me sane during the unpredictable, seemingly unjust parts of life.

Mishpacha (family) should be a high priority. Mom and I made decisions about where we wanted to live based on our desire to raise you in proximity to your grandparents. Yes, family can push your buttons like no other, but they also accept you and love you unconditionally. Love your family and they will sustain you through the most challenging of times. Let yourself be separated from them when you are adults and the pain of separation will be passed on as a model for your own children. Call your adult siblings regularly and your parents even more. Throughout your life, make *shalom bayit* (peace in the home) one of your goals and you will find unparalleled strength as you venture out into the world.

About work, I have learned this: Find a career path that will allow you to bring goodness into our world. Making money for money's sake, or even just to support your family, will slowly consume your soul. At the end of the day, you will not sustain yourself without seeking a greater good because the sole pursuit of money and material things is unending.

Be ethical in all that you do—especially at work—not because otherwise you will ultimately get caught; rather, be ethical because it is the right thing to do. Pay attention to that old Hebrew National hot dog commercial that cautions that we are "responsible to a Higher Authority."

As you prioritize your time, seek out a synagogue that speaks to your heart. Help it fulfill its mission to educate Jews and to respond *hineinu* (we are here) to support each other. Shabbat services can heal and uplift your soul in ways that you will recognize only after you have expended the energy to show up. *Al tifrosh min hatzibur* (do not separate yourself from the community) since within community we can best feel God's loving Presence (*Pirkei Avot* 2:5).

Pray for the peace of Jerusalem (*sha'alu shalom Lirushalayim*) (Psalm 122:6). Nowhere is the need for *shalom* more clear and yet often more difficult than in relationship with the State of Israel. As you know, Mom and I are drawn to Israel. As a family and as individuals we have made it a priority to spend significant time there. We can discern in our hearts a special love for Israel as we learn about her past and her present. Let this love and connection grow—even when you might not embrace certain policies or politics—and support Israel with your travel, attention, and *tzedakah*.

Within each of us are many diverse tools—physical, emotional, spiritual—to help us navigate the currents of life. We have taught you the power of seeking out others for help and the wisdom of listening closely to their advice and counsel. I hope we have taught you that turning to others for support—friends and school counselors, rabbis and therapists—is the mark of courage and strength, not of weakness or shame. So seek out help when you need it.

Life, you may be learning, is filled with mysteries; to me the most important is why God placed us upon this earth. Recently I have discovered a hint of that ultimate purpose. Embedded in Torah, in a portion we read every Yom Kippur, are the words: *Kedoshim tiheyu ki kadosh ani Adonai Eloheichem* (you are holy because I, the Eternal your God, am holy) (Leviticus 19:2). Life, I believe, is about *kedusha* (holiness), about those significant yet indescribable moments of inspirational uplift that result from right-minded actions and intentions. Holiness, like spirituality, is not just a state of being; it is acting with compassion, pursuing justice, and seeking truth. When we do this right, our actions reflect *shutafut* (partnership) with God.

These are the values I cherish. I hope they carry you through bright days and dark days. I wrote what I cherish most as a way to guide and comfort you in the years ahead. Perhaps one day too, you will follow this example and write down your ethical will. It truly is a holy task.

For now, *mine kinderlach*—my children—honor my memory, and your family's memory, and our Jewish values passed down *l'dor vador* (from generation to generation) since the time of Moses, by being holy, by being *kadosh*. I know you are ... May you know you are too.

I love you.
Daddy

Write Your Own Ethical Will

Imagine the unimaginable: that one day, unexpectedly, you may die and live no more. Now think about your child. What words of wisdom would you want to share with him or her at the moment before your death? Reread my ethical will, read those of others in the book *Ethical Wills and How to*

Prepare Them: A Guide to Sharing Your Values from Generation to Generation, and ask yourself if these values are priorities for you and your family.[4] Consider what other values or ideals you want to include.

Some guidelines:

1. Be concise and personal.
2. Since you will not be around to interpret your intent, be as clear and forthright as possible.
3. Let love flow through your words. Let your child know that he or she is cherished, worthy, and loved.
4. Choose your words carefully. Leave out words of critique so you do not transmit pain to the next generation.
5. Save copies (in sealed, labeled envelopes) in safe places: a safe deposit box, wherever you keep your legal will, and/or with a dear friend who can deliver it after you have died.

Crafting Words of Wisdom for Times of Transition

When a Jewish family announces a child's Hebrew name during a *brit milah* (circumcision ceremony) or a *brit bat* (covenant ceremony for a daughter), parents often share heartfelt words about the child's Hebrew name and articulate a *brit mishpacha* (covenant of family) describing the kind of home and family they want to create for the newborn. When children become bar or bat mitzvah, parents in progressive Jewish communities typically share publicly with their child words expressing their admiration and pride in the child's accomplishments and the abiding significance of this Jewish moment in their lives. Crafting these parental blessings requires time and emotional energy. Sharing these words with your children can create lasting memories and be incredibly rewarding.

We encourage parents to also use other moments of transition as opportunities to document and articulate words of pride, hope, ideals, and values. These transitions might include:

- The beginning of a new school year
- Starting a new sport

- The first day of a new job
- Leaving for summer camp
- A first boyfriend or girlfriend
- Attending a new school (kindergarten, middle or high school, or transferring to a new school)
- Leaving home for freshman year in college
- Embracing a new physical, mental, or emotional challenge
- Experiencing a change of family structure (divorce, remarriage, or arrival of a new sibling)
- Moving to a new house and neighborhood

Paul: A Letter to Our Sons—On Being a Man

When Daniel prepared to go to college, I composed words to help guide both boys, speaking the truth in my heart, to guide him (and later Noah) into an adulthood of love, integrity, and compassion.

To My Sons:

You are about to leave for college, spread your wings, and move forward in your adult life. It feels that you have grown up so quickly, yet I am excited for the experiences yet to come. I cannot believe how fast the time has flown since you were my little boys who would jump off my shoulders in the pool and with whom I could wrestle without worrying that someone (me) might get hurt. Sooner than I will be ready, you will be on your own—living, learning, working, and loving.

I remember the day that Mom and I named each of you. You were so tiny, so vulnerable, so delicious. We chose names that connected you to our family and to our Jewish tradition. We picked names that reflected compassion, confidence, and strength. We aimed to teach each of you to be a mensch (a kindhearted, caring man). Yet ultimately we knew that you alone would determine the name by which you are known in the world.[5]

Being a man is about character. Men—real men—know that manhood is not about size but about quality. The quality of your character ultimately means more than the size of your muscles or the strength of your portfolio. We admire people who risk life and liberty for a cause, like Dr. Martin Luther King Jr., Oskar Schindler, and the 9/11 firefighters. But character is also born in a thousand bit parts that never get written up: like what you choose to do when the clerk gives you the incorrect change, whether you give up your seat on the bus for an older person, and how calmly you react to someone who is being rude. The best index to a person's character is (a) how you treat people who cannot do you any good, and (b) how you treat people who cannot fight back.

Be a gentleman: Judaism teaches that we are all born with a *yetzer hatov*, an inclination to do good.[6] Insulate your soul for good by following your conscience. Being a male is a matter of birth, and being a man is a matter of age, but being a gentleman—a mensch—is a matter of choice. Strive always to be a gentleman.

My sons, be honest, be thoughtful, and be monogamous. Treat women and other men as equals, and never discriminate against people of a different background, religion, race, or orientation than your own.

On being a father: One day I hope you will bless Mom and me with grandchildren. Kids are wonderful and demanding, inspiring and exhausting. From the moment they are conceived, children become your blessing. Both parents, whether married or not, have the lifelong responsibility of raising them. Be an involved dad and not an absent one. If you do not have children, volunteer in the mentoring of others. We all bear responsibility for the next generation.

Your children will carry on your influence long after you are gone. Fathers can model for their kids how to be mensches, so be a positive Jewish role model. Let your children see you at your best—with your family, with your friends, in the Jewish community, and within your career. Help them with homework, play with them in the park, and listen nonjudgmentally to their problems. As a parent, you will—necessarily—develop new skills. I got to learn how to hit 250 baseballs in a row and how to throw a Frisbee forehand, because these activities made you happy and gave us time together. Do the same for your own kids.

Be honest in your work: Being a man is also about working. Many men get a lot of their self-esteem from their work. Seek out a career that you find meaningful. Take seriously your behavior in your work. According to one Jewish teaching, when we die and arrive at the gates of heaven, the very first question we will be asked is "*Nasata v'natata b'emunah*? Did you deal honestly in your business?" (Talmud, *Shabbat* 31a). This question is not just about buying and selling. It is about integrity.

Did you act with honesty in your business relationships? Did you treat your co-workers and subordinates with respect? The question presupposes that we all harbor within us the ability to cheat, lie, and steal and that our business ethics will be tested every day. Resist the temptation to take advantage of people. Be someone in whom others can put their trust.

Own up to your mistakes. Seek help when you are confused. When in pain, if you delve deeply beneath your anger to find the sadness hidden beneath, you begin to heal more quickly.

About money: Remember that money is just a tool, not an end in itself. Money opens opportunities, but working around the clock will not quell the longings of your heart. Do spend time with your loved ones—including your siblings and especially your parents. Devote ample time to elevate your community and set aside plenty of money to give as *tzedakah* (charitable donations).

It's "guy love" that sustains you: You know that my friendships have nourished me throughout my life. On one of your favorite TV shows, *Scrubs*, J. D. and Turk had a name for such cherished friendships. They call it "guy love." Follow the wisdom of fourteenth-century Spanish Talmudic scholar Isaac Aboab, in *Menorat ha-Maor*, who counseled, "Invite [your friend] to your joyous occasions; ... never give away his secrets; help him when he is in trouble; ... overlook his shortcomings and forgive him promptly; criticize him when he has done wrong; do not deceive him; ... and attend to his [family] if he dies."

Be involved in your Jewish community: Being a man involves a relationship with your Jewish community. Next time you are in Shabbat services, notice all the men (and women) who sit down, close their lips, and patiently wait for the service to end. Perhaps they do not know the prayers, do not see their value, or do not understand how to reconcile religion with science. I encourage you to sing the melodies out loud. Ask your rabbi to help you uncover deeper meaning and a personal connection to the prayers. Spirituality and religiosity are a lifelong journey that can nourish your soul when your heart is burdened, broken, or uplifted. Being a Jew means taking the risk that significant meaning may be hidden within our ancient rituals and modern teaching.

On sex and love: Although television and movies suggest otherwise, in reality sex is about so much more than the mechanics of where you put what. (We already had that talk.) Sex can be great, but it should be within a mature, loving relationship. Sex is also about intimacy and love, commitment and responsibility. Trust me, making love is so much better. Regarding sex, try being countercultural and focus first on finding love.

I may not know everything about love, but I do know this: that the love I share with your mother is the most fulfilling, complex, nuanced, and wonderful thing I have ever experienced in my life. Love is not always easy, but it has always been worth it. I hope you are so blessed, because mature love will bring you strength, contentment, and wholeness. Yes, there will be heartbreak; we all experience it along the way. Know that time will help heal most wounds and that exercise, therapy, and prayer can assist the restoration process.

What is mature love? In our youth, we often fall for people who live up to a certain definition of outward beauty. As adults, we jump over the inevitable hurdles of life and see that over the long term the partnerships that remain strong are characterized by trust and a mutuality of values. We recognize that marriage takes significant effort and time. So enter into love relationships with your eyes wide open. First get to know and love yourself. Then consider seriously the person's character and values, concern for others, family, friends, education, and short- and long-term goals.

In today's world, the odds are just barely in your favor that any marriage will last beyond eight years. Put into your marriage as much effort as you do your work and your sports teams. How?

Date your beloved well after you are married. Get dressed up; go out. Romancing each other will be a lifetime gift you give to your partner and yourself, and because it will help keep your relationship fresh and healthy, it will be a gift to your children as well.

My sons, I am here to guide you, to support you, to nurture you, and to celebrate you. I am your #1 fan and I am grateful for you each and every day!

I love you.
Dad

Try This Enlighten Your Child's Life Passages

Compile a list of topics you want to discuss with your child before or during transition moments. Dig deep to uncover your fears, hopes, and dreams for your child. Once you have articulated your values to yourself, write them down and weave them into messages you share with your child. Like the mezuzot that we are instructed to affix to the doorposts of our homes, these messages will guide our children as they face the transitions in their lives.

Paul: A Letter to Our College-Bound Daughter

Michelle and I saw the movie *Toy Story 3* with our children on the day it opened. There we sat, watching a bunch of talking toys, when I noticed the tears streaming down Michelle's face. I squeezed her hand tightly; I too was crying. Like the character Andy, our oldest child, Rachel, was about to leave for college. We long dreamt about and planned for this day, yet when the move-in date was on the calendar and Rachel actually had the gall to go, we found ourselves on a roller coaster of emotions. As she was about to take the lead on her young adult life outside of our home, we wondered if we had openly shared with Rachel what we valued most.

So I sat down and wrote her a letter to share our *emet*, the truth in our hearts about her journey ahead. We wanted Rachel to be true to herself, to embrace our tradition, and to strive to be her highest self.

Dearest Rachel:

You are about to embark on the next leg of the journey called "your life." For all of us, this is bittersweet: sweet, because as you go off to college, exciting new worlds will open up to you, worlds that you did not even imagine existed. They will inspire you and challenge you; you will grow in incredible ways.

This is also a moment for us to pause. Your departure to college makes it undeniably clear that you are no longer a little girl, my little redhead, who lived in a protective bubble of family and community, as safe as possible under the watchful eyes of Mom and Dad.

Although Mom and I fantasized about it, they do not seem to allow parents to be your college roommates. You are off on your own. Although we will undoubtedly connect regularly—texting, Facebook, FaceTime, and maybe even that old standby, the telephone—Mom and I will no longer have front-row seats on your journey; from this day forward, we learn about you from you.

As you leave, there is so much I want to remind you about—values to reaffirm, lessons to repeat. Now I know college is filled with really smart professors. However, I want to share with you eighteen bits of my *chochma*, one piece of wisdom for each of your eighteen years of life.

1. First, last, and in between, remember always that you are compassionate, intelligent, and beautiful. Every time we talk to you, you take our breath away with your insightfulness, the depth of your kindness, your "you." This essence animates you. Our Creator, the Holy One, endowed you with these gifts. Embrace them, honor them, and hone them. Especially because ...
2. The world is about to open up for you. Embrace the excitement and the challenge. Reb Nachman of Breslov wrote, *Kol ha'olam kulo, gesher tzar me'od, v'ha'ikkar lo l'fached klal*—that "the whole world is a very narrow bridge, and the most important thing is not to be too afraid." So step up, step out—be it with people, experiences, or opportunities. Do not be afraid to fall or fail. Where we can, Mom and I will be there to support you,

but we trust your strength and resilience to pick yourself up and redirect. (Of course, be thoughtful. Just because a bridge presents itself does not mean you have to cross it.)

3. Every new experience allows you to reflect upon ideas you take for granted and ideas you have never before encountered. Absorb the knowledge; be challenged by the ideas of others. Listen carefully to their perspectives on the world, their philosophies, and even their theologies. As the Talmudic sage Ben Zoma taught, "*V'eizeh hu chacham?* Who is wise? *Halomed mikol adam*—the one who learns from every person" (*Pirkei Avot* 4:1).
4. Remember that we were all created *b'tzelem Elohim* (in God's image) (Genesis 1:26–28). So seek out the diverse people who populate your college. As the Passover seder reminds us, *ger hayiti b'eretz mitzrayim*, that we Jews were once strangers in the land of Egypt, shunned, pushed to the edges of society by people with narrow minds. Move out of the *mitzrayim* of narrow-mindedness and into the promised land of pluralism.
5. Remember that you are beautiful. Make sure you fall in love with someone who treats you beautifully. And try to fall in love with someone who shares your love and appreciation of Judaism and wants to create a Jewish home. Not because Judaism is the only truth, nor because you cannot find happiness with someone who is not Jewish (you can). Do it because it is who you are.
6. Mom and I pride ourselves on getting you to this point in your life, healthy, whole, and in one piece. Now your safety and future is up to you. Remember the four questions that Dr. Bruce Powell asked you and your high school classmates to consider before making choices during each summer vacation:
   1. Is it safe?
   2. Is it legal?
   3. Is it moral?

   And, because what you do today in your dorm room or at a party is apt to show up that night on someone's social media:

4. Would you want your mother, father, grandparents, teacher, or rabbi to know about it?[7]

   If you cannot say "yes" to all four, perhaps you should not walk down that path.

7. The world will present you with a plethora of opportunities to indulge your wildest urges—intellectually, physically, spiritually, with artificial stimulants, with artificial people. College is a time of experimentation. But heed the wisdom of the wise Ben Zoma, who also said, "*V'eizeh hu gibor?* Who is mighty? *Hakovesh et yitzro*—the one who controls her passions" (*Pirkei Avot* 4:1). Remember: ultimately you are responsible for who you will become and what you make of your life.
8 You are now the guide of your own learning. Make wise choices. Sign up each semester for classes that are thought-provoking and inspiring. Ask questions, and respectfully challenge pat answers so that you can advance from collecting knowledge to developing wisdom.
9. Remember that Judaism is a multifaceted, multivocal, intellectually compelling religion. There is so much you—and I—still do not know about it. Choose a Jewish studies class to learn more about Judaism as an adult.
10. Your college will provide you with a golden opportunity to broaden your horizons. Naturally, Jewish life on campus is not the same as at Congregation Or Ami. Just as you are growing intellectually, socially, and independently, so too allow yourself to grow Jewishly. Do not feel self-conscious about what you do not know. Seek out the Hillel director to explore together what your college Jewish life could be. You might be surprised at the opportunities that appeal to you.
11. Make sure to get to Israel. Take a Birthright trip. Consider doing a semester abroad in Jerusalem or Tel Aviv.
12. And speaking of Israel, you may soon discover that the university world is not always supportive of her. Many people use the open intellectual environment as a cover to bash Israel. You know that I love Israel, her people, and her land. You also know that I believe there is much to criticize about Israeli government

policies. As an *ohev Yisrael* (a lover of Israel), we must separate the critique of policies from our support of the fundamental right of the Jewish people to a Jewish pluralistic, democratic state. Align yourself with a pro-Israel group. Wherever you stand, be sure to differentiate your response from those who seek to harm Israel or the Jewish people.

13. Your religious and spiritual foundations are about to be shaken in exciting and potentially startling ways. As you learn about the plethora of perspectives in the world, you might find yourself considering ideas and beliefs beyond the Jewish ideas with which you have been raised.
14. Do not be afraid to discover that some of our most cherished beliefs have parallels or antecedents in other cultures or religions. I believe that God shares wisdom in many ways with many peoples and that there are many paths to that Truth (*emet*). Buddhism has informed the Jewish spirituality I have embraced; Christianity and Judaism share compelling notions about justice and compassion.
15. I encourage you and all Congregation Or Ami college students to call or email their rabbi—me—or Cantor Doug Cotler, when you are feeling shaken to your core. A lot of life happens in four years. We want to help you to remain grounded and to process complex issues.
16. About grades. Work hard and do your very best. You do not need to be an A+ student. But as you learned at New Community Jewish High School, always strive to be an A+ human being. Living a life of kindness and compassion, integrity and honesty, of *tzedakah* and justice—this is nonnegotiable.
17. Rachel, you amaze and inspire me. Your journey energizes me as I get to watch you in the process of becoming. Know that Mom and I believe in you.
18. May the Holy One bless you on your journey. *B'tzeitecha u'vo'echa*—in your going away and in your coming home too. *Mei'atah v'ad olam*—from this day forth and forever.

We love you.

Daddy

Write Letters at Times of Transition

Write a note or a letter to your child that you will share with him or her at the beginning of a new experience. You might include the following:

1. Observations about this transition time.
2. Your set of beliefs surrounding the transition, such as the value of education, Jewish community, perseverance, or tolerance.
3. Your words of guidance for the transition (without being preachy).
4. Your hopes for your child during this phase.
5. Where appropriate, your pride that your child is taking this step.

After you have shared the note with your child, consider how you will intentionally weave these messages into further conversations with this child (and, if appropriate, with your other children). Look for opportunities to reinforce your priorities so that your child knows what you stand for, what you value, what you expect, and what you cherish.

Whether authoring a bat mitzvah parent blessing, a birthday card, a reflection as your son goes off to camp, or a missive as your daughter begins the first day of middle school, parenting by handwritten (or typed) letter allows our words to sink in well beyond the first moment they are read. In this way, we guide them from childhood to adulthood with meaningful words. We pass on our values and ideals—our *emet*—in a way that we can impress our hopes into their hearts and minds.

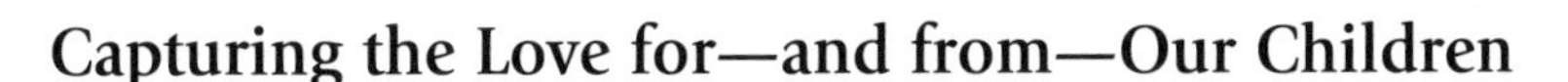

Capturing the Love for—and from—Our Children

When our children were young, during the week before their birthdays, Michelle wrote letters to each child as a way of documenting highlights of the year, emphasizing their uniqueness and reinforcing our *emet*. The letters provided a slice of life of that year. Although the kids might have highlighted different milestones in their own recollections, Michelle's letters included physical and emotional change and growth, challenges they overcame, and activities they enjoyed. She also included a few quotable gems to remember the phrases they used. Sometimes Michelle added comments from relatives, friends, and teachers.

While we are an erratic gift-giving family, we are consistent about giving handwritten cards. We taught the kids from early on the value of expressing themselves on paper by making and writing birthday cards for their grandparents, siblings, and for us. The birthday ritual continues today. To ensure it happens, we buy cards for each non–birthday child and one for ourselves. The kids choose the card that they like best, and they write their message inside. Today, Rachel sometimes handcrafts her own cards. When the children were young, they wrote only a few words. Today, they write paragraphs of sentiments, often infused with a healthy dose of humor. An annual card gives each of us the opportunity to express gratitude and appreciation for what the birthday celebrant has endured or provided for us during the year. We cherish these treasures of honesty, acknowledgment, and good wishes.

Michelle: Happy Seventh Birthday, Noah

Dear Noah,

I am certain that you will be donning a baseball cap backwards as we read this birthday letter together. I love thinking about the warm, affectionate child you are. You continue to capture the hearts of your family members. We adore you!

You have blossomed in school this year. Your teachers are excited by your curiosity and constantly praise your participation in learning. You are an eager reader and your evolving penmanship is the envy of all of your classmates' parents!

You have a heart of gold and you are kind to others. In our family, we describe this kindness as *menschy*. You continue to crack us up with your funny sense of humor. You are sharp-witted and you are learning to pipe up alongside your siblings at the dinner table.

This year, you thrived in Little League baseball. Coach Pete nicknamed you "Silk." He says you are smooth as silk, consistently keeping your head in the game, anticipating and reacting efficiently to each play. You are becoming quite a ball player!

You are a vegetarian by choice and this sometimes means learning to navigate meals in friends' homes when you are on playdates. When their parents are stumped and do not know what to feed you, you take charge, informing them that you are a pastaterian and you eat any pasta with a little butter and Parmesan cheese!

You are an inquisitive, pensive soul who loves to cuddle. At night you sleep peacefully with both arms outstretched overhead; I marvel at the openness of your being.

Happy birthday!

I love you so, so much.
Mommy

As our children grow up, we pray that they will be safe and make wise choices. We hope that they will live by their own seal of truth, reflecting the highest values of our family and our Jewish tradition. Our babies are precious; we need not give them up when they begin new experiences. By embracing the change, we parents evolve also and guide them differently, more subtly, but with the same love and inspiration year after year.

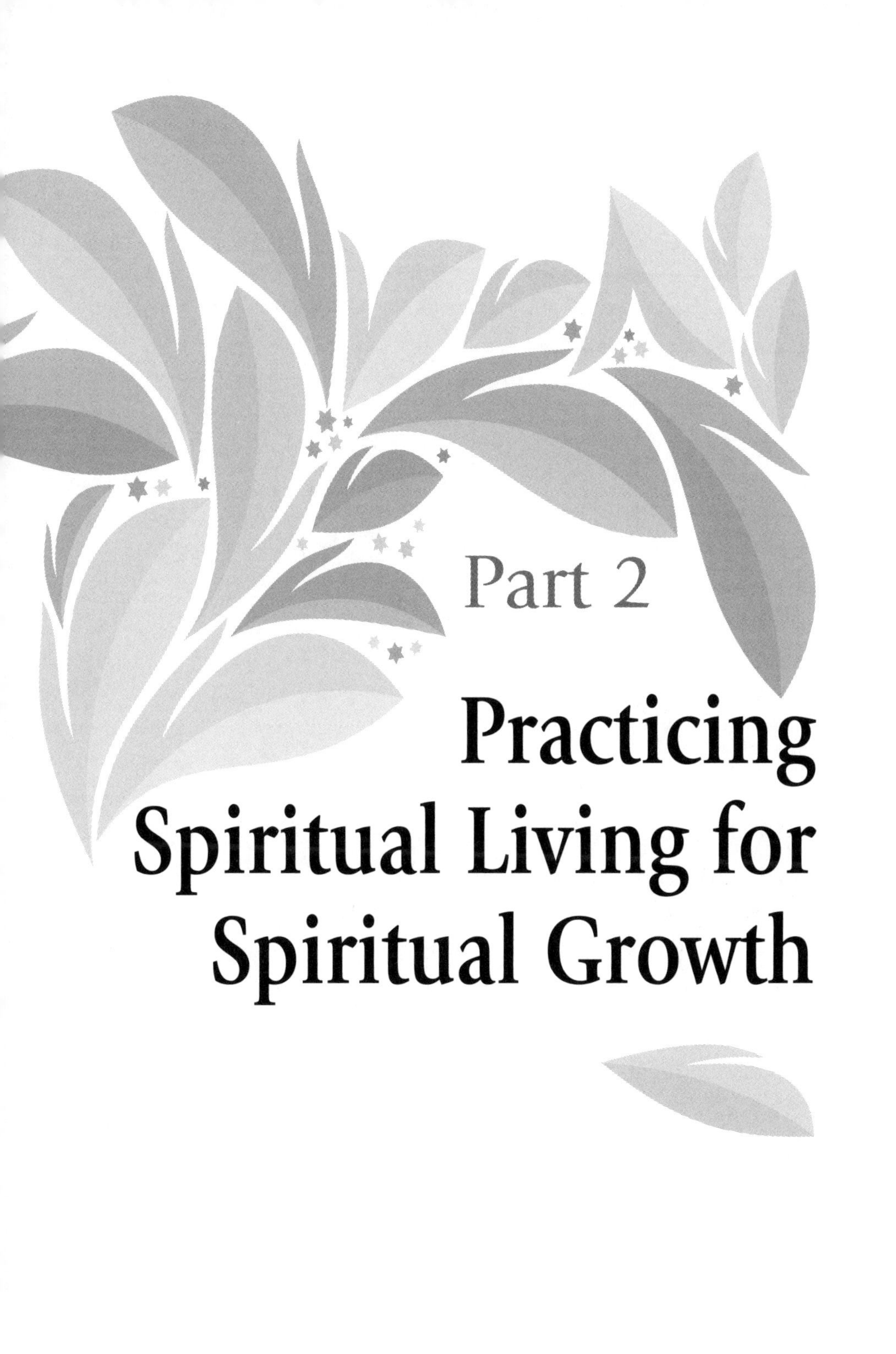

Part 2

Practicing Spiritual Living for Spiritual Growth

6 Living Holy Lives

Kedoshim Tiheyu at Bedtime, at Wake-Up, and Throughout the Day

> To be a Jew means to wake up and to keep your eyes open to the many beautiful, mysterious, and holy things that happen all around us every day.
>
> —Rabbi Lawrence Kushner

Paul: Daddy-Child Day

When our daughter, Rachel, was six, she and I went out for a very early breakfast of chocolate chip pancakes at IHOP, bowled a couple of games at the bowling alley, and then painted ceramics at the local art studio. Once the art projects were completed, a wave of exhaustion came over me. I glanced at my watch and decided it was time to head home.

As we moved toward the car holding hands, Rachel looked up at me and asked, "Can we go bowling *again*? Why do we have to go home *already*? We just got here!" Soon she began pleading in earnest. I thought to myself, "We spent a wonderful morning together doing fun things at three different places. Shouldn't my child be exclaiming, 'Thank you for this special morning, Daddy'?" I was feeling disappointed and surprised that my first-grade child did not express gratitude for our special morning of adventures together.

Through this experience Michelle and I came to realize that feeling and expressing gratitude—while important to us—may not be natural for children. We decided to intentionally intervene to nurture a sense of gratitude. We recognized that instilling this value in our children was critical to their seeing the holiness that surrounds them. So we set a *kavannah* (intention) that gratitude would be essential to our family life.

Seeing the Holiness Around Us

Judaism is rich in opportunities to express gratitude. Our tradition encourages us to wake with words of thanks, to spend our days seeking out blessings, and to power down at the end of the day by taking stock of the blessings in our lives. All of this is possible because we intentionally adopt an attitude that we can be holy because we are, at our essence, holy creations.

Our tradition calls us *kedoshim tiheyu* (to be holy)—recalling the Holy One's words, "You shall be holy, for I, the Eternal your God, am holy" (Leviticus 19:2). As children of God, whose essence is holiness, we strive to uplift each moment of our lives and to transform each interaction with others into a moment of blessing.

Holiness, or *kedusha*, connotes that which is higher, deeper, or more "real." Being holy is living a life of meaning, living in a way that is connected to the universe beyond us and with our own essential worthiness within. Rabbi Bernard Bamberger, a twentieth-century spiritual leader and biblical commentator, taught, "The idea of holiness implies that what we do and what we make of our lives matters not only to us as individuals, not only to society, but to the entire cosmos."[1] People who live lives of holiness are essentially living in ways that center them. They feel gratitude for what they have and regularly express that gratitude.

This isn't easy. Our world seems to conspire to keep us from focusing on what is essential. All around us are messages that tell us that we are not good enough, not pretty enough, not wealthy enough, or not talented enough. We are told that what we have and who we are is essentially lacking. When we listen to these messages, when we try to keep up with the Joneses (or the Steins), we lose sight of what is essential. We begin to pursue the unimportant and the nonessential. We forget Rabbi Ben Zoma's instruction, "Who is rich? The one who appreciates what he or she has" (*Pirkei Avot* 4:1).

As parents, we want our children to value the little things in life, to appreciate the beauty of our world, to practice *chesed* (loving-kindness), and to pursue justice and peace. We want them to count their blessings at each moment, because as Rabbi Abraham Joshua Heschel points out, "It is gratefulness which makes the soul great."[2]

In the daily *V'ahavta* prayer, we are instructed to teach our children our essential values at the pivotal moments of the day: especially "when you lie down and when you rise up" (Deuteronomy 6:7). Teaching our children how to be grateful at the beginning and end of the day guides them to become spiritually grounded, ethically focused, holy living citizens of the world.

The Blessing of Firsts: *Shehecheyanu*

Our all-time favorite prayer is *Shehecheyanu*, the Jewish prayer for first-time events.

> *Baruch atah Adonai, Eloheinu Melech ha'olam,*
> *shehecheheyanu, v'kiy'manu, v'higianu laz'man hazeh.*
>
> Holy One of Blessing,
> who has guided us on our journeys through this universe,
> we thank You for giving us life, for sustaining us,
> and for bringing us to this special occasion.

We say *Shehecheyanu* whenever something new happens, like the birth of a baby or beginning to learn a new skill. Given the Jewish penchant for finding blessings in each moment of life, this prayer is also recited for those occurrences that happen for the first time in a given year, like the first night of Chanukah or the first time we sit in a sukkah. And on birthdays.

We have sweet memories of singing this prayer with our kids when Noah's first tooth fell out, when Daniel and Paul jumped in the pool for the first time each summer, and when we dropped each child off on the first day of the new school year.

We recited *Shehecheyanu* when Rachel was elected to student council in high school, and when Daniel and Noah were each elected to the North American Federation of Temple Youth (NFTY)–Southern California Regional Board. We attempted to notice and kvell at all the firsts with *Shehecheyanu*: the first time each baby rolled over, the first time Noah or Daniel went up to bat each season and Rachel served the volleyball, her first period, and their first time driving off in the car alone. Even today, when something new happens, our children will recite the whole prayer or sometimes just shorthand it by whispering, "*Shehecheyanu*." Saying *Shehecheyanu* with our children empowered their Jewish spiritual growth as we raised up the ordinary and expressed gratitude for it.

How do we understand the special meaning of *Shehecheyanu*? Rabbi Samuel Stahl, emeritus rabbi of Temple Beth-El in San Antonio, suggested that *Shehecheyanu*'s power comes from its articulation of three reasons to thank God. He taught:

> In the first instance, we thank God for keeping us alive, for maintaining our physical existence. Here we have limited control. Ultimately, the length of time that we spend on earth is in God's province.
>
> In the second instance, we thank ... God, as Sustainer, [who] gives us the boundless power to achieve. [We] find happiness with our immediate circumstances, regardless of what they are. If we can truly be "in the moment" and not focus on we haven't amassed, what we haven't done, what we need to do or where we should be going, then we can know happiness as deep spiritual satisfaction.[3]

This means letting go of the to-do list of steps to propel us forward, allowing us to plant our feet solidly on the ground and contentedly take note of where we stand today.

The third reason we praise God, explains Rabbi Stahl, is for bringing us to this occasion. "To arrive at the celebration of a joyous event is beyond our human power. It is no longer a matter of choice, as before. Rather it is a matter of chance. Here we recall the Yiddish proverb that 'Man proposes, but God disposes.'"[4] Yet the willingness to honor the special occasion, to raise it up with our words as a holy moment—that is assuredly within our power.

There are no limits to when we can recite the *Shehecheyanu* prayer. Nor are there limits on how much holiness we can experience. Reb Nachman of Breslov wrote:

> When we start to pray, it is as if we were picking beautiful blossoms and flowers and blooms. Just as when someone walks in a field and gathers beautiful blooms and flowers one by one, bringing them together in a bunch, and then continues to pick others one by one, making another bunch, and continues on further making more and more beautiful bouquets of bunches of flowers—so, too, when we pray.[5]

Our task as parents—as historians of childhood—is to collect precious *Shehecheyanu* moments like wildflowers, gathering them into radiant bouquets. Reciting *Shehecheyanu*, we allow these moments to blossom into the blessings they are.

Say *Shehecheyanu* Together

Teach your child the words to *Shehecheyanu*, and learn to sing the blessing together.

Whenever something new happens—for the first time or the first time that year; for a specifically Jewish moment or a totally secular one—wrap him in your arms, look her in the eyes, and quietly or loudly say your prayer. With words and through ritual, you raise up the moment, encircle it in Jewish spirituality, and call it what it is: a moment of holiness.

Waking Up with Words of Thanks

How do we cultivate a sense of thankfulness in our children? "Practice makes perfect." We parents nurture gratitude by rehearsing it with our children until the experience becomes ingrained and the expression of gratitude becomes routine.

Our Rabbis instruct us that upon waking in the morning, we should recite the *Modeh Ani* prayer, which cultivates a heart of thankfulness:

*Modeh ani [*females say *Modah ani] l'fanecha,*
Melech chai v'kayam,
shehechezarta bi nishmati b'chemlah;
rabah emunatecha.

I give thanks to You, O God,
eternal and living Ruler,
who in mercy has returned my soul to me;
great is Your faithfulness.

A more child-friendly interpretation might be:

Thank You, God.
You take care of every living thing
and You take care of me as I wake up this morning.
You are awesome!

Modeh Ani, rooted in the ancient belief that our souls leave us when we sleep, addresses the fear that our soul might not return to us in the morning. On a literal level, the prayer thanks God for directing our soul back into our bodies. Although the idea of a departing and traveling soul may seem irrational to some, the core message of *Modeh Ani* endures: that each morning we ought to be thankful for our lives.

As Tamar Frankiel, president of the Academy of Jewish Religion in Los Angeles, and Cantor Judy Greenfeld, founder of the Nachshon Minyan in Los Angeles, point out in *Minding the Temple of the Soul, Modeh Ani* also spurs us to holy action:

> This is what it means to say a prayer first thing in the morning. As the Torah teaches, we are to bring the "first and best" to God.... This service begins immediately when we wake, so that we consecrate the moment of our first awareness to God.[6]

At some Jewish summer camps, the whole community gathers in the morning to sing *Modeh Ani*. Similarly, some Jewish families begin their days with *Modeh Ani,* letting it become their morning ritual for cultivating gratitude.

Sing *Modeh Ani* as a Morning Ritual

When children are young, you might wake them by sitting on their beds, showering them with hugs and kisses, and together singing *Modeh Ani*. Or because we may adapt rituals to our family's reality, you might find that late-morning moments better lend themselves to morning rituals. (That might mean any time after mom's first cup of coffee!) As your children grow older—and getting them out of bed is more of a challenge—you might consider singing the prayer at the breakfast table. One friend sings *Modah Ani* with her children as they walk to school; another recites it in their car ride to preschool.

You might deepen the gratitude experience by encouraging family members to first share their own feelings of thanksgiving. Parents model the behavior, perhaps saying, "I am thankful that you are part of my life." "I am thankful that we get to spend today together." "I am thankful that I have a whole day to make others smile." "I am thankful that going to work gives me the opportunity to bring goodness into the world." Then invite your children to share their words of gratitude.

You might also choose other songs of gratitude. Some friends sing the children's songs "Good Morning Sunshine" and Craig Taubman's "Boker Tov" to create the right mood.[7] However you develop your morning ritual, use it to begin your day with thankfulness.

Counting Our Blessings

Our Rabbinic teachers of the Talmud sought guidance for cultivating gratitude and spiritual living (*Menachot* 43b). They studied a verse in Torah: "Now, Israel, what does the Eternal, your God, ask of you?... To walk in God's ways ... and to serve God" (Deuteronomy 10:12). The Hebrew word for "what," *mah*, sounds similar to the word *me'ah*, which means "one hundred." The Torah verse seemed to be saying, "Now, Israel, *a hundred* does the Eternal, your God, ask of you." Recognizing that we often fret about the future or pine for the past instead of finding joy in the present, the sages instructed their students to count one hundred blessings daily. These Rabbis wisely understood that if we do not slow down and draw attention to the holy moments in life, we will miss them entirely. The Talmudic sage Rabbi Yossi explained, "Alas for people who see but do not know what they see and for people who stand but do not know on what they stand" (*Hagigah* 12b).

For these Rabbis, blessings were statements that began with a standardized formula: "*Baruch atah Adonai Eloheinu, Melech ha'olam* (Blessed are You, Eternal God, Guide of the universe, who ...). They were a means of acknowledging God's role in the creation of that moment. The Rabbinic formula also includes the phrase *asher kid'shanu b'mitzvotav* (who makes us holy through doing *mitzvot*), attesting to the interconnection between words, actions, and holiness. They recognize that by adding articulated intention to our actions, we can experience *ruchaniyut* (spirituality). Whether we consider these actions to be sacred commandments decreed by God, traditional Jewish acts passed down *l'dor vador,* or unique opportunities for spirituality, they fill the moments of our lives with the blessing of holiness.

Begin a Blessing Practice

The ancient Rabbis suggest we count one hundred blessings each day. You might easily count to one hundred because your outlook quickly lends itself to this spiritual practice. Or you might find the scale of this activity onerous or overwhelming. To make the goal more attainable, we suggest that you and your children each practice finding three moments for which you are especially thankful.

Alternatively, you might sit with your children at a meal, talk with them on the ride to school, or pause some other time you are together. Choosing one prompt below, invite everyone (including yourself) to respond:

- Think about your family. What experience of joy did they bring you recently?
- Consider your friends. In what ways have they provided you strength, hope, love, caring, and companionship?

- What about your community? How has your temple, club, school, or organization provided you with a sense of belonging and meaning?
- For adults, think about your job or your daily responsibilities. How have they sustained you and inspired in you purpose and meaning? For children, think about how you spent your day. What part made you feel special?
- Or, simply, what are you thankful for today?

The Central Conference of American Rabbis' smartphone app Daily Blessings (http://ccarnet.org/ccar-press/blessings-app) provides access to many kinds of blessings for when you see the beauty of nature, when you interact with a special person, when you eat different kinds of food, when you do acts of justice, and when you learn new things. Alternatively, you can say personal spontaneous blessings like "Wow, that is awesome/special/inspiring. That is a blessing." You can also express blessings with words like "I thank God for this blessing of ..." Or "We thank Holiness (or the Holy One or Life Itself) for ..."

Imagine starting every morning or concluding every night by counting your blessings. Such a spiritual practice would promote thankfulness within your heart and within your family.

An Attitude of Gratitude

As parents, we can point out those moments for which we feel blessed. Over time, we create a narrative of blessing that our children can adopt as their outlook on life. From the birth of our children to the beauty of a sunset to precious time spent with grandparents, blessings are found when we pause and recognize the uplifted moment as holy. "This is one of the goals of the Jewish way of living: to experience commonplace deeds as spiritual adventures, to feel the hidden love and wisdom in all things," writes Rabbi Abraham Joshua Heschel.[8] Daily thankfulness can be a powerful antidote for a world otherwise filled with unabashed coveting and lacking in appreciation.

Create a Gratitude List

Each day, before he goes to sleep, Paul records his three blessings of the day. Revisiting this list regularly reminds him of the holiness in his life.

Set aside a regular moment each day—perhaps at bedtime or before getting out of bed—to write down three things for which you were thankful that day. You are likely to embed gratitude in your life if you take the time to record your thankfulness. You might record notes in a document on a computer, begin a list on your smartphone, or tack up a piece of paper on a bulletin board.

When adults count our blessings, we are more inclined help our children do the same. So take this on as your own spiritual practice and then guide your children to make their own gratitude lists.

Setting a *Kavannah* (Intention) to Start the Day

Older readers and those who are fans of vintage television might remember the morning police roll call on an old favorite television show, *Hill Street Blues*. Sergeant Phil Esterhaus routinely cautioned his officers, "Let's be careful out there!" Week in and week out, without fail, the sergeant's *kavannah* ensured that everyone knew the primary goal of the day: to be as vigilant as possible as they all went through their dangerous days on the beat.

"Intention" means thinking ahead about what we want to accomplish so that, instead of haphazardly reacting to events, we have a clearer picture of where we want to go and what we want to accomplish. By talking about what is planned and what we hope will happen, we remind our children that we each have the power to transform a regular day into a holy day, an experience of blessing and joy. That is living with intentionality.

Many parents have routine send-offs for their children before school.[9] Along with a kiss on the *keppie* (head), they say:

"Remember to ask good questions."

"Make sacred choices."

"Do a mitzvah."

"Make today special."

Michelle's preferred parental prompt is "Make good decisions."

Other friends hang a *middot* chart to choose the kind of intention their family wants to set for the day. *Middot* are divine qualities that we try to emulate, like compassion, patience, and courage. Another friend encourages her children to set their own intentions by simply asking them over breakfast, "What do you hope to accomplish today?"

Set Your Daily *Kavannah* (Intention)

We parents can help our children set a *kavannah* for the day. As you send your children off for the day, look in their eyes and deliver a few choice words—"make good decisions," "ask good questions"—to set a hopeful tone for the day. While your children might roll their eyes at your repetitive mantra, rest assured that the message will become part of their subconscious, reminding them at meaningful junctures throughout their lives what is most important.

Bedtime Rituals to Wrap Up the Day

Bedtime rituals can often be one of the most poignant Jewish spiritual parenting practices. They help guide children through the process of winding down at the end of the day. Deborah Echt-Moxness, a marriage and family therapist who writes about creating new family rituals, observes in *Keeper of Traditions: Family Activities to Strengthen Connections and Celebrate Life Every Day*:

> When they are little, the familiarity of the same routine each night helps children feel safe and secure. When they get older, bedtime is often the time they unwind and share their thoughts and feelings with you.... This is definitely a sacred opportunity to reconnect and pour your love and devotion into them; so they are

ready to face the next day with confidence and strength, knowing they are loved and cherished.[10]

Michelle: Sweetening the Bedtime Struggle

Getting young children in bed can require the endurance of a marathon runner and a backbone of steel. Second only to waking them and getting them off to school, few times of the day in our home were fraught with more predictable challenge. Eventually we discovered that habitual bedtime rituals could sweeten the task.

During our experiences in Jewish summer camps and youth retreats, Paul and I each cherished *siyum* (nighttime closing ritual) during which we stood outside in the moonlight in a circle of youth and counselors, arms over each other's shoulders. As the song leader strummed his guitar, we swayed under the stars and sang the bedtime prayers. We reflected on the day gone by. Later, at Camp Newman, we ended the day singing, "*Hashkiveinu Adonai Eloheinu l'shalom*—Shelter us beneath Thy wings, O Adonai. Guard us from all harmful things, O Adonai. Keep us safe throughout the night, 'til we wake with morning's light...." *Siyum* with its prayers and reflections allowed us to power down from a high-energy, intensely social day and move toward lights out.

As parents, we decided to adopt the ritual of *siyum* at home. We began when the children were little and were happily surprised that the ritual continued into their midteens. When they crawled under the covers, we would lie down beside them and snuggle. Cuddling, we read books together, shared stories of our day, and sang nighttime prayers and songs, some with silly improvised family lyrics and accompanying hand movements. These bedtime rituals brought closure to a long day and enabled our children to relax into the quiet of the night. Quickly we saw that these sweet moments provided poignant opportunities for closeness with our children and cherished Jewish spiritual memories.

Setting Goals for Bedtime Rituals

Bedtime serves as a major moment of connection in three realms: between parent and child, between children and the realities of the day now ending, and between our children and the Holy One. Bedtime rituals allow reflection, a return to core values, and a nurturing of Jewish spirituality.

We crafted our family's bedtime rituals to accomplish four goals:

1. To provide regularity in the "powering down" phase of nighttime
2. To review the day gone by and preview the day ahead
3. To reinforce to our children that they are surrounded by people who love and support them
4. To take a spiritual journey together and make real our belief that we are part of (and connected to) the Holy One

Whether your bedtime goals mirror these or include others, creating and facilitating a ritual each night is a priceless gift you give your children.

Done with forethought and love, our bedtime rituals can calm our children, centering them as they lie down to sleep. They can build self-esteem as children take comfort in the knowledge that they have succeeded in many ways during that day. Beyond the physical act of tucking them in, bedtime rituals provide a sense of safety and protection as the quietude and darkness of night descend.

Develop "Powering Down" Rituals

After the tumult of changing into pajamas, brushing teeth, and packing up items for the next day, moving onto the bed creates separation between the frenetic and the calm. Once your children climb into bed, turn down the lights, and lie down with them. (With video chat, parents away on business or vacation can still share in nighttime rituals.) Soft, soothing voices set a peaceful tone.

Review the day. Encourage your children to notice both the positive and the negative. Sometimes prompts are needed: "What went well today?" or "Were there disappointments?" At other times, a smile and your warm presence will elicit an avalanche of comments and revelations. Push aside judgment and critique; surely your children have experienced plenty of this during their day. Rather let these moments bring peacefulness.

"Is there something you are excited about for tomorrow?" you might ask. Undoubtedly, they are thinking about this themselves. "Is there anything that concerns you?" By sharing the concern, they can better fall asleep, knowing they are not facing it alone. "What are you looking forward to tomorrow?" builds excitement and hopefulness. Encourage your children: "Let's prepare for a wonderful day."

We found that this private face-to-face time was cherished by each of our children and served as a constructive way for them to stave off the inevitable lights-out moment. It also gave us a much welcomed glimpse into the hidden corners of their daily lives. In fact, on many nights, our kids would reveal just about anything to extend the moment, thus granting us significant insight into their activities and inner thoughts.

Jewish Bedtime Prayers

Judaism encourages us to say two prayers at bedtime: *Shema* and *Hashkivienu*.

The *Shema*, often called the "watchword of our faith," is simultaneously a statement of monotheism—there is but one God—and the recognition that we are all part of that Oneness.

> *Shema Yisra'el: Adonai Eloheinu, Adonai Echad.*
> *Baruch shem k'vod mal'chuto l'olam va'ed.*

> Hear, O Israel: the Eternal One is our God, the Eternal alone.
> Blessed is God's glorious majesty forever and ever.

Shema, as a central prayer in Jewish life, appears throughout Jewish time and space. Written on parchment in mezuzot placed on the doorposts of our house and in tefillin worn by some on the arm and head during prayer, the *Shema* is a constant reminder of our connection to the One God. We recite *Shema* when we wake up and when we lie down, when we take the Torah out of the ark, and at the end of Yom Kippur. *Shema* is traditionally the last words on the lips of the dying, attesting to our belief in the Oneness that connects everyone and everything.

To understand the *Shema* we need to remember that God's primary name in Torah is *Yud-Hei-Vav-Hei* and that *Yud-Hei-Vav-Hei* points to Existence, as discussed in chapter 1. While some relate to God as Being, others experience God in relationship, and still others understand God as the connectivity between all things. Each has roots in Jewish thought. Some do not feel connected to God at all.

The central idea of the *Shema* appears in its final two words: *Adonai Echad*. Usually translated as "God is one," *Adonai Echad* reminds us that we are all part of the Oneness we call Existence. God—the Being, the Existence, the Connectivity, the Idea—is that which links each of us to everyone and everything. God connects those living now with those long gone with those who are yet to be. God loves us. Or God is love. Either way, we are connected. Singing the *Shema* at night reconnects our children to this central Jewish idea and reinforces the idea that we are not alone.

The *Hashkiveinu* prayer—especially the Hebrew/English mash-up favored in Jewish summer camps and NFTY regions—speaks directly to the fear of nighttime.

Hashkiveinu, Adonai Eloheinu, l'shalom, l'shalom
V'ha'amideinu Malkeinu, l'chaim.
Ufros aleinu sukkat shlomecha (2x). Amen.

Shelter us beneath Thy wings, O Adonai.
Guard us from all harmful things, O Adonai.
Keep us safe throughout the night,
Till we wake with morning's light.
Teach us, God, wrong from right, O Adonai. Amen.[11]

The *Hashkiveinu* prayer—literally, "cause us to lie down"—can assuage our children's fear that bad things might happen to them while they sleep. It reminds them that they are watched over by the Holy One and by their parents. *Hashkiveinu* gives our children the comfort that goodness will come with morning's light. The sweet tune calms and soothes.

Some families add or substitute other prayers or songs into their bedtime routine. We often sang *Shalom Rav*, a prayer for peace, and occasionally other love-filled children's songs. Our goal was to calm, console, and connect.

Sing Bedtime Songs and Prayers

Lie down with your child on the bed or hold her in your arms. Allow your bedtime prayer to express your love. Wrapping your child in a hug, you remind him that he is cherished. Quietly sing bedtime prayers, perhaps accompanied by music or a YouTube video of *Shema* and *Hashkiveinu*.

Surprisingly, bedtime can become a favorite part of the day. All children—toddlers, middle schoolers, and teenagers—desire the reassurance that they are valued and their lives are significant. Thus the reason for our bedtime rituals: to bring an everyday sense of purpose and preciousness into our children's lives.

Finding Holiness in Every Moment

Being holy requires our attention at more than just wake-up and bedtime. As parents seeking to nurture spiritually aware children, we view each moment of every day as an opportunity to point our children toward holiness. We guide them, with love and intentionality. Answering the call—*kedoshim tehiyu*—can become second nature because life itself is filled with holiness. Our task, then, is to name it and embrace it.

7

Each Child Is Unique

Embracing *B'tzelem Elohim*

Beloved is humanity, for humans were created in the image of God. Still greater was God's love in that God gave to humanity the knowledge of having been so created.

—Rabbi Akiva (*Pirkei Avot* 3:14)

Michelle & Paul: Three Children, Each Wonderful and Unique

We are blessed with three children. All share traits we cherish: sensitivity toward others, deep compassion, an ingrained sense of fairness, a comfort as leaders, and a love of family and Judaism. Each child is a sacred gift; each one is a holy creation. Each is unique.

Our youngest child, Noah, is quick-witted and possesses a sense of humor that continually entertains. He is an especially loyal friend who interacts in the world with a warm, gentle heart. Noah is curious and has keen observational skills. He thoughtfully gauges his surroundings, weighs options, and values having sufficient time between activities. His natural proclivity for examining life's details makes him the family historian; he amazes us as he easily recalls minute facts, including the dates, places, and timing of events. Drawn to sports, Noah amasses sports statistics ready to share at any moment.

Our second child, Daniel, lives in perpetual motion. In the primary grades, Daniel stood instead of sat at his desk at school and at the kitchen table during dinner. We discovered that Daniel learned best through physical activities. Complementing Daniel's energy is an abundant creativity. Young Daniel loved constructing objects—mock computers, baseball stadiums, guitars—from boxes, containers, egg cartons, and other recycled materials. (His grandparents kept a bin full of these for his visits.) Daniel is a doer. He loves an opportunity to build things—an idea, a club, a team—from nothing. Daniel dives in with passion and is action and accomplishment oriented.

As a little girl, our first child, Rachel, loved to play house, cooking in her pretend kitchen and inviting relatives—in person or as imaginary guests—to her table. Rachel finds meaning in relationships. She has an innate openness to people. She is curious about communities around the world and is drawn to searching beneath the surface of cultures. The kitchen remains Rachel's happy place; cooking for others brings her immense joy. Rachel is a gatherer of friends, and she rejoices in the broad inclusion of others. During family celebrations, being surrounded by loved ones especially energizes her.

Genesis 1:27 teaches that humans are created *b'tzelem Elohim* (in the image of God). *Tzelem* means "image," like what we see in a mirror. *Elohim* means "God." *B'* means "in." Being created *b'tzelem Elohim* means that when we look at our reflection, we can get a sense of what God is like.

B'tzelem Elohim points to the core belief that every person is born in the image of God. As humans, we accept the inherent worthiness of every person. As parents, we try to nurture an abiding Jewish spirituality in each one of our children. We aim to discover the best way to embrace each personality so that we can nurture each child's uniqueness. Striving to see *tzelem Elohim* in each child, we learn to approach his or her spiritual journey with the same individuality that we do every other part of his or her life.

What Does God Really Look Like?

In the Ten Commandments, the second commandment decrees that we should not create images of God (Exodus 20:4). Our Rabbis took seriously not wanting physicality inserted into the *tzelem Elohim* concept. In the twelfth century Rabbi Moses Maimonides said that anyone who believes that God has corporeal form—that is, a body—is both a heretic and has no share in *olam haba* (the world to come).[1] So, since we lack physical depictions, what can we really say about God's image?

Rabbi Arthur Green, in his book *Radical Judaism*, offers this teaching in the name of Rabbi Abraham Joshua Heschel:

> "Why are graven images forbidden by the Torah?" I once heard Abraham Joshua Heschel ask. Why is the Torah so concerned with idolatry? You might think (with the Maimonideans) that it is because God has no image, and any image of God is therefore a distortion. But Heschel read the commandment differently. "No," he said, "it is precisely because God *has* an image that idols are forbidden. *You* are the image of God. But the only medium in which you can shape that image is that of your entire life. To take anything less than a full, living, breathing human being and try to create God's image out of it—that diminishes the divine and is considered idolatry." You can't *make* God's image; you can only *be* God's image.[2]

We do not create images of God; instead, by living our lives in a godly way, we become God's image. We do not need a physical depiction of God because we are it.

Rabbi Jonathan Slater offers the teaching of the Hasidic rabbi Mordecai Yosef Lainer of Izbica as a surprisingly modern interpretation of *b'tzelem Elohim*:

> The likeness of God is made up of tiny fragments, each fabricated to appear as one part of the totality that constitutes the mosaic image. Every piece of tile used to compose the image in the mosaic is necessary. The absence of one would diminish the image.[3]

Through each individual tile, the splendor of the Holy One is increased as the image is made greater—and whole.

> Not only is the mosaic made up of many diverse tiles, each necessary for its wholeness. Each tile itself is the image of God—or at least one quality, one aspect of the divine.[4]

Every child represents a tile in the mosaic. That tile—the unique combination of various talents and skills, personality characteristics, emotional intelligence, physical abilities, gender orientation, self-awareness, cultural and ethnic background, family structure, and more—makes your child, indispensable and valued.

Modern Orthodox rabbi Yitz Greenberg clarifies the essence of the Jewish value of *b'tzelem Elohim*:

> Human images can be duplicated, but the hallmark of God's creative power, God's distinctive infinite creative capacity, is that each and every image of God is absolutely unique. Even identical twins are not identical. Ideally, one should respond to the uniqueness of each person in every moment of contact.[5]

When Seeing the Image of God Is a Challenge

It is not that difficult for most of us to see *tzelem Elohim*—infinite value, equality, and uniqueness—in the family and the friends we cherish. The love, strength, compassion, wonder, and beauty we feel in their presence are almost divine.

The challenge of *b'tzelem Elohim* is being able to find the divine likeness in those we do not know, in those we dislike, or in those we cannot figure out how to easily embrace. Sometimes those people are unfamiliar, and sometimes they are members of our family. How do we teach our children to see the world through *"b'tzelem Elohim*–colored glasses"?

Try This Play the Messianic Age Game

In Jewish tradition, the messiah is the one who will usher in a time of peace and an end to violence, war, poverty, and famine. For Jews, the messiah has not come. We know this because the world is still fraught with violence, war, poverty, and famine. Some Jews are waiting, and wondering who the messiah will be. Some Jews are not waiting for the messiah but are anticipating a messianic age when all people will do their part to bring forward a period of peacefulness. Either way, we seek human action to transform the world.

Danny Siegel, poet and lecturer on Jewish values about *tzedakah*, shared in *And God Braided Eve's Hair* this poem about how we should treat others:

A Rebbi's Proverb

(From the Yiddish)

If you always assume
the person sitting next to you
is the Messiah
waiting for some simple human kindness—

You will soon come to weigh your words
and watch your hands.

And if the person chooses
not to be revealed
in your time—

It will not matter.[6]

With your child, play the Messianic Age Game. Explain to him that one way we will bring forward a world of peace without war, famine, or pain—a time called "the messianic age"—is by creating the conditions ourselves. Every person has important gifts that can help us move toward this era.

When passing through areas populated with many people, look at each person and imagine why he or she might be the one who tips the balance of the world toward peacefulness. Whisper to each other, "Maybe he is the one!" and "Maybe she is the one!" Identify the special gifts you imagine that this person might bring to the pursuit of peace and goodness. Then remind your child that while we really know little about this person, he too is important because he was created *b'tzelem Elohim*. This means that each person possesses value and blessing and is deserving of our kindness and compassion.

How do we parents embed within the heart and mind of our child the idea that she is created in the image of God? It begins with our own attitude and awareness.

Rabbi Abraham Joshua Heschel actualized his belief about *b'tzelem Elohim*. He believed that each human being, regardless of skin color, must be considered an individual deserving of compassion and understanding. Before the Civil Rights Act was passed, in a time when people were beaten and killed for espousing the rights and the humanity of blacks, the white-skinned Rabbi Heschel marched in Selma, Alabama, arm and arm with dark-skinned Dr. Martin Luther King Jr., in support of equal voting rights. There was no question about which one of them was created in God's image. He knew that they both were.

Like Rabbi Heschel and Dr. King, we should regularly affirm our own child's infinite value, equality, and uniqueness. We can say specifically to her, "Just as each and every other life is valued and holy, so too are you, my child, valued and holy." The Torah does not say that white people, heterosexual people, citizens of a certain country, able-bodied people, or even Jewish people are created in God's image. The Torah says *all* human beings are created in the image of God.

As Rabbi Yitz Greenberg explains:

> Being in the image of God means that each human being is born with three intrinsic dignities—infinite value, equality, and uniqueness. These dignities are mine, and yours, and everybody's. They are independent of any other factor, such as heritage, status, wealth, health....
>
> Since every human being is an image of God, there is *no* preferred image—God is neither white nor black, male nor female, Jew nor non-Jew. Then all people should be treated as if they are equal.[7]

The final words of the *Shema—Adonai Echad* (literally, "God is one")—may be rendered "God is the Oneness" that connects us all. We remind our children that they are connected to the Source of

Life, which means that they have a double responsibility: to respond to others with justice, kindness, and compassion, and to respond that way to themselves.

Try This **Adopt a Spiritual Practice of Blessing Others**

When we recognize that another person has infinite value and distinctiveness, we are called to affirm that she too is deserving of goodness. By adopting the spiritual practice of blessing others, we create within ourselves more capacity for peace, joy, love, and compassion.

Rabbi Sheila Weinberg of the Institute for Jewish Spirituality leads a spiritual practice of *metta* (loving-kindness) meditation designed to help us acknowledge the *tzelem Elohim* in ourselves and in others—especially in those we do not know and those we do not care for. We learn that even they are deserving of kindness and compassion.

Begin your blessing practice this way: Sit comfortably and breathe deeply. Choose four people: yourself, a family member or friend, someone you feel neutral about, and someone for whom you do not really care. Closing your eyes, visualize one person, beginning with yourself, and recite each sentence of blessing below. You may choose to speak the words aloud in English, Hebrew, or both. Repeat each blessing series for each person.

> May you/I be blessed with love (*chesed*).
> May you/I be blessed with compassion (*rachamim*).
> May you/I be blessed with joy (*simcha*).
> May you/I be blessed with peace (*shalom*).[8]

Once finished, sit and be still for a few minutes. Rest in any feelings of loving-kindness that envelop you. Let the feelings of gratitude expand and seep slowly into your whole body. Imagine the gratitude spilling into the room, stretching across the country, and blanketing the whole world.

Once you become comfortable with this spiritual practice, teach it to your child. Together, choose the people you want to bless. Let your blessing practice deepen your appreciation for each person.

Whenever the opening arises—at the beginning of the day, in the car, at bedtime—help your children find the *tzelem Elohim* in all people. Explain that since we are all created *b'tzelem Elohim*, we cannot dismiss people we do not care for or do not know. Though we might be different in looks, religion, or orientation, we are all children of God and part of the same human race. Invite your child to join you in setting a *kavannah* (intention) that the notion of *b'tzelem Elohim* will guide your interactions all day.

Embracing Our Child's Unique Qualities

Sometimes it is hard to move from theory to practice, from the lofty notion that every person is holy and valued to actually accepting that this specific person is holy and valued and that her unique perspectives, aptitudes, and needs must be acknowledged. How much more difficult it is for parents who struggle to understand a child whose unique qualities are so different from their own.

Teachers, who spend abundant time with them in class, can shine a light on the unique gifts and talents of our children. Coaches and camp counselors can enlighten us too.

At parent-teacher conferences, Mrs. Wargon, a favorite teacher of first Rachel and later Daniel, provided us with valuable insights as she enthusiastically shared perceptions about their dissimilar but authentic classroom contributions. A baseball coach of Daniel's taught us parents the art of the insightful compliment. At the end of each game, with the enthralled players seated around him, Coach Mike reviewed each player's contributions to the game. Like a longtime sports announcer, he doled out compliments, relishing the myriad talents of his beloved team. He publicly highlighted each player's moment of growth. We parents also listened intently, learning from this generous man how to perceive the uniqueness of our children and how to make each one feel like a million bucks.

Four Children Who Motivate Us to Individualize Our Parenting

In a child's life—physical development, emotional journey, and spiritual growth—one path does not fit all. Our children are not the same nor are they copies of us, even when we share appearances, abilities, or interests. We parents sometimes wrestle with how to raise different children. Seasoned parents—raising their second, third, or fourth child—sometimes feel like they are starting over because each subsequent child requires us to approach parenting anew. We want to avoid trying to parent all our children in the same way, or even trying to parent our child in the same way that our parents reared us. Each child is deserving of our attentiveness and our appreciation of his or her individuality.

Judaism has long encouraged parents to address each child's unique self. In fact, the Passover seder, Judaism's central educational ritual, insists that parents focus on each child and respond to his or her unique learning style.

For some Jewish families, the seder (literally, "order," meaning an ordered meal) has become a rote recitation of ancient words and a mindless performance of a very old ritual, but it was not meant to be so. When the ancient Rabbis created the seder, it was an engaging pedagogical innovation designed to provide parents with a multisensory, age-appropriate, highly experiential tool with which they could teach their children the central story of the Jewish people. As it turns out, the seder also was the Rabbis' guide for parenting each unique child.

The Passover Haggadah (literally, "the telling," referring to the book that we use to guide the seder) preserves the Rabbis' teaching theory. It discusses four children: *chacham* (the wise one), *rasha* (the rebellious one, although often misinterpreted as "wicked"), *tam* (the simple one), and *she'eino yodei'a lishol* (the one who does not know how to ask). Recognizing that our children learn things differently, this Four Children passage instructs parents to individualize their responses for each child.

The *chacham*, or wise child, is imagined to inquire, "What is the meaning of the laws, traditions, and rituals that God has commanded us?" The Rabbis explain that this child, who already considers herself as part of the Jewish journey, seeks to understand the Exodus from Egypt and the meaning of all the Passover rituals. For her, parents need to create a seder experience that is intellectual and comprehensive so that she can delve deeper into Judaism's abiding lessons.

The *rasha*, often misdefined as the "wicked child," asks, "What does this service mean to you?" He is characterized as one who removes himself completely from this personal experience. To the ancient Rabbis, this child was a danger to the continuity of the Jewish people and had to be dealt with sternly. The Hebrew text—harsh and inappropriate in its prescription—suggests that such a child might be shaken "such that his teeth are set on edge." He needed to be forced to accept our Jewish past.

Today we view the *rasha* as "disconnected." We imagine this child as one whose inclinations do not easily mirror those of his parents or the Rabbis. Many families have a *rasha*, a person who frequently challenges the outlook of his parents or family. In fact, families with multiple children might notice that at some point each child spends time as the *rasha*, when innate inclinations differ from those of the parents. By asking, "What does this service mean to *you*?" the *rasha* distances himself from the seder and from the Jewish experience. This might be the result of uninspiring Jewish experiences, a family bias against religious rituals, the drive to individuate (especially among preteens or teens), or, more simply, a lack of understanding. Parents of a disconnected, cynical, or rebellious child can take time to craft an especially engaging seder experience that weaves drama, visuals, and learning games together to draw the child into the experience before he thinks about disengaging. We can invest our children in the experience by working with them before the seder to devise specific opportunities for their active participation.

The *tam*, or simple child, asks, "What is this all about?" Because this child is unclear about the significance of Passover, her parents strive to create a seder filled with age-appropriate, meaningful explanations. The Rabbis instruct parents to prepare the seder thoughtfully beforehand, so they may teach the story of the Exodus to this child using the symbols and foods to pique her interest.

As for *she'eino yodei'a lishol* (the one who does not know how to ask), parents create a seder experience that begins and ends with a clear message: "It is for the sake of this, that God did for *me* when

I left Egypt." By personalizing the seder—with new readings and personal stories—parents illuminate the Jewish past and begin to inculcate this child into Jewish spiritual life.

All children can benefit from seder leaders who are vibrant storytellers, weaving past, present, and future together into a poignant spiritual journey. Just as we choose bedtime stories that are tailored to each child's preferences and animate them with our enthusiasm, our seders ought to be equally energetic, designed to engage children with different interests, abilities, and learning styles. The underlying lesson of the Four Children is that we parents must strive to connect each child individually to our people, to holiness, and to his or her best self.

Try This **Identify Your Child's Learning Preferences**

When is your child the *chacham*? When is she the *rasha*, the *tam*, and the *she'eino yodei'a lishol*? When does your child want to intellectualize? When does he need games, drama, movement, or other processes to be more engaged in learning? Connecting your child's learning style to the design of spiritual experiences will enhance his spiritual growth.

Examine how your child best engages in learning experiences. You might want to consult with her teachers.

Does your child like to:

- ☐ Sit and ponder
- ☐ Talk about ideas
- ☐ Move around
- ☐ Listen to others talk
- ☐ Make up stories
- ☐ Share opinions
- ☐ Play games
- ☐ Create games
- ☐ Search the Internet
- ☐ Watch videos or YouTube
- ☐ Sing songs
- ☐ Play music
- ☐ Make up songs
- ☐ Wear costumes
- ☐ Act
- ☐ Dance
- ☐ Cook
- ☐ Organize activities
- ☐ Draw
- ☐ Other: ________________

Use this analysis to develop spiritual experiences—including a Passover seder—that reflect your child's learning style.

Similarly, identify your own learning preferences. Note that if your style matches your child's, creating the experience might be easier. When your styles differ, you will need to experiment to discover engaging learning methods that will best suit your child.

Developing a Spiritual Passover Seder for Everyone

A key challenge of parenting is discovering how to tap into our child's individual energy and sources of inspiration. Once we understand each child's unique way of perceiving and pacing, we can work to broaden our holiday gatherings. Over time, our Passover seders, our Shabbat dinners, and other celebrations became energetic, fun-filled events, combining the best of our inherited Jewish tradition with engaging Jewish innovation.

For Daniel, who liked to move around, we learned not to sit the whole time in one place. Over the years we have enjoyed making our seder a moving experience, literally moving multiple times during the evening to different rooms in the house, including our backyard. For Noah, who likes to think and plan, we learned the benefits of reflection time and of preparing ahead. Since some seder participants felt put on the spot when exploring the Haggadah, we now preassign a topic we want each participant to address during the seder. For Rachel, who loves to explore the intersection between ideas and our lives, we recognize the benefits of gathering new people with fresh ideas and insights. For ourselves as adults, we invite a wide variety of guests so that our seder changes annually, as does the prism through which we reexperience the Exodus from Egypt.

Seeing and Celebrating *B'tzelem Elohim*

B'tzelem Elohim reminds us that each child is unique. Parents with more than one child know that while it might hold the promise of efficiency, utilizing the same parenting techniques for each of our children is not necessarily effective. Seasoned parents grow to understand that parenting keeps us on our toes and prevents family life from being boring!

Thus, as we recognize *tzelem Elohim*—the image of God—in our children, we are better able to nurture their finest traits. As we guide our children to recognize *tzelem Elohim* in themselves, we empower them to become their best selves. That, after all, is the goal: for them to identify *tzelem Elohim* in themselves and others, and thus to create a world of kindness and connectedness.

8 Caring for Body, Mind, and Spirit

Strengthening and Preserving God's Gift with *Shmirat HaGuf*

This body is a reflection of
God, exactly as I am.

—Rabbi Rachel Barenblat,
Velveteen Rabbi blog

Paul: What a Tush!

When she was just five years old, Rachel, like many young children, had a fascination with her own reflection. She would gaze at her image in the mirror, make faces, and sometimes even watch herself dissolve into tears.

One morning I looked in on her just as she had finished dressing for the day. Wearing her pink pants and a long-sleeved shirt with tiny flowers, she was, in my mind, the vision of perfection. I smiled as she smoothed down her clothing. Then, as I have seen many women do, she turned around 180 degrees, looked over her shoulder into the mirror, and checked out her backside.

I sighed. I didn't know if I should laugh or cry. Here at five years old, my darling daughter barely had any protuberance behind her, yet she had already picked up the societal expectation that, along with the rest of her, her tush had to be just so.

A resigned sadness enveloped me. Why did my little girl have to become so concerned about her looks at so young an age? How could we, her parents, help redirect her focus from the shape of her body to the more important shaping of her character and soul?

Learning "Ugliness"

We live in a world that bombards little boys and girls with unrealistic definitions of beauty and attractiveness. It happens so pervasively that their self-images can take a hit early in their lives. In the Disney classic *Snow White*, the evil queen asks, "Mirror, mirror on the wall, who is the fairest of them all?" When the answer does not come back as "You, my queen," the queen launches into a rage that almost kills Snow White. Is that what we want our children to emulate? To assume that if they are not deemed the most attractive, they are not worthy at all?

Unless we opt to sequester our children and divert our collective gaze from supermarket magazine covers, movie billboards, social media, and television commercials, it is too easy for us to slip into believing that the image of a slim, sculpted fashion model or celebrity is the ultimate goal. While children and teens—boys and girls alike—are particularly vulnerable, many intelligent, grounded adults also wonder: Perhaps if I wore my hair like hers, or if my muscles were toned, I would be happier, more lovable, have more friends, be invited to more parties.

The pressure to conform can become so intense that it leads many of us to see only imperfection in our otherwise healthy, capable, and beautiful bodies. As parents, we sometimes unwittingly promote this mentality through our own words and actions.

Kasey Edwards, author of *30 Something and Over It*, remembers the moment she discovered that her beautiful mother was "fat, ugly, and horrible." Her words are a poignant reminder about the dangerous influence of parental self-image.

> *Dear Mum,*
>
> I was 7 when I discovered that you were fat, ugly, and horrible. Up until that point I had believed that you were beautiful—in every sense of the word. I remember flicking through old photo albums and staring at pictures of you standing on the deck of a boat. Your white strapless bathing suit looked so glamorous, just like a movie star. Whenever I had the chance I'd pull out that wondrous white bathing suit hidden in your bottom drawer and imagine a time when I'd be big enough to wear it; when I'd be like you.
>
> But all of that changed when, one night, we were dressed up for a party and you said to me, "Look at you, so thin, beautiful, and lovely. And look at me, fat, ugly, and horrible."
>
> At first I didn't understand what you meant.
>
> "You're not fat," I said earnestly and innocently, and you replied, "Yes I am, darling. I've always been fat; even as a child."
>
> In the days that followed I had some painful revelations that have shaped my whole life. I learned that:
>
> 1. You must be fat because mothers don't lie.
> 2. Fat is ugly and horrible.
> 3. When I grow up I'll look like you and therefore I will be fat, ugly and horrible too.[1]

Our children are impressionable and easily influenced by our foibles. They learn what we consider "ugly" when they see us look unfavorably in the mirror or hear our self-critique. Our words influence them to do the same. Our actions can lead our children to quickly embrace stereotypes and to cast aspersions on anyone—including themselves—who appears different.

Shmirat haguf is the Jewish value of caring for our body, mind, and spirit. Our bodies are gifts to be nurtured. Each is worthy of our appreciation and care. *Shmirat haguf* views rest and exercise as holy gifts for our emotional and spiritual well-being. Guiding us toward spiritual practices that bring peace in the face of life's pressures, our focus on *shmirat haguf* provides our children with a very clear, countercultural message: that they are beautiful just the way they are.

Appreciating Our Bodies Through Jewish Tradition

Even in ancient times, Jewish tradition put strong emphasis on physical well-being as a spiritual practice itself. As the Hellenistic Jewish philosopher Philo said, "The body is the soul's house. Shouldn't we therefore take care of our house so that it doesn't fall into ruin?"[2] Throughout the generations, Jewish scholars encouraged their disciples to be healthful. Rabbi Moses Maimonides taught:

> Maintaining a healthy body is among the ways of serving God, since it is impossible for one who is not healthy to understand or know anything of the Creator. Therefore one must distance oneself from things that harm the body, and accustom oneself to the things that strengthen and make one healthy.[3]

Lest anyone think that such healthy behaviors are merely secondary to other kinds of spiritual work, Rabbi Hillel raised them up to the level of mitzvah (religious obligation). He even called bathing a holy act (*Leviticus Rabbah* 34:3)!

Popular "Ask the Rabbi" columnist Rabbi Yirmiyahu Ullman similarly recognizes the need to maintain the body for the sake of the soul. He explains:

> In order for the soul to exist in the material world, it must be clothed in a body through which the soul may achieve its purpose. For this reason we must supply the body with its essential needs like food, water, sleep, and exercise, without which the body could not exist and the soul could not fulfill its potential.[4]

Give Thanks for Our Bodies

In the *Asher Yatzar* ("that You created") prayer, we offer thanks for our bodies, recognizing that they are wonders beyond imagination. Praising the fact that our orifices are functioning properly, this prayer was originally recited after every use of the toilet. Today, many recite it instead during morning prayer or as part of their morning wake-up routine.

Develop a blessing practice with your child to give thanks for the wonders of our bodies. Choose a few times a week—before a bath or shower, or after physical activity to praise your bodies. Begin by saying something positive about your own body. Be creative and do not focus on looks:

"I like that I am growing stronger each day through exercise."

"I am thankful that my ears allow me to listen to my favorite music."

Then ask your child to say something positive about his or her body, like "I am grateful that my body allows me to run (or pitch or climb) so well."

Then open a prayer book to the *Asher Yatzar* blessing and recite it together.[5]

Eating as a Holy Act

Frequently, we hear from families like ours about the challenge of preparing meals that accommodate a variety of diets: vegetarian, gluten-free, vegan, allergy-averse, dairy-free, and paleo. Parents chuckle as they detail the varieties of soup they need to serve at Passover seder to accommodate each guest's eating practices. In "Making Every Forkful Count," Rabbi Carole B. Bailin, a scholar of Jewish history, explains why: "Everything about food—how we acquire it, who prepares it, what we consume, and with whom we eat—matters."[6] Parents who are concerned about Jewish wellness focus attention on what, when, and how they eat, ensuring healthy eating choices.

Our Jewish tradition provides a buffet of entrées and wisdom about food. It guides us to practice Jewish spiritual living by blessing the food we eat as an expression of gratitude or to recite blessings to remain mindful of each bite we put in our mouths. We can express Jewish spiritual values by minimizing any adverse impact of our food choices on the environment.

We can choose to keep kosher, but even if we do not, its lessons about mindful eating are instructive. In *The Sacred Table: Creating a Jewish Food Ethic*, holy eating maven Rabbi Mary L. Zamore, who is also executive director of the Women's Rabbinic Network, enumerates the Jewish dietary system's many lessons. The one that is most noteworthy to us is the recurring reminder to think before eating and to scrutinize our food choices. Whether keeping kosher or eating mindfully in other ways, we acknowledge the sacred nature of food and its connection to God by elevating the mundane activity of consuming it. Rather than engaging in mindless eating, or worse, abusive eating, eating for wellness and spiritual wholeness generates an enjoyment of food and an appreciation of its power to feed and sustain us.[7]

Looking Beyond Our Bodies to Find Balance

The Jewish concept of *shmirat haguf* (guarding the body) encompasses more than the physical body. Strengthening and preserving our total well-being means caring equally for the spirit and the mind.

For Jewish families, Shabbat as both a concept and as a traditional day of rest can be a ready-made opportunity for taking care of our whole self. Shabbat traditionally serves as a regular appointment for self-care and retreat. Shabbat always seems to arrive just in time. A break from constant forward motion, this weekly respite from energy-sapping momentum is an opportunity to soak up an infusion of peace. As the wise sage in Ecclesiastes advised, "Better to work a little in joy than to be obsessed with work at the expense of tranquility" (Ecclesiastes 4:6).[8]

We explore Shabbat more fully in chapter 11 on *simcha* (joy). Yet what would it be like to bring a foretaste of that respite into the middle of the week? Imagine the feeling of being able to empty your mind, making room to appreciate all that is good.

Enjoy Shabbat-like *Menucha* (Rest) During the Week

Parents and children can benefit physically and spiritually from receiving the gift of Shabbat-like *menucha* (rest) during the week. These brief respites benefit us by giving us a break from everyday pressures.

In the midst of your day—whether you work at home or outside—mindfully make some space for your soul. Do the same with your child. For example:

- Have lunch with a friend who lifts your spirits.
- Leave your workspace for a five-minute walk.
- Text words of affection and colorful emojis to your spouse or partner, your child, or parent.

Alone or with your child, you might:

- Read a chapter in a favorite novel.
- Flip through family photo albums.
- Savor a scoop of your favorite ice cream.
- Listen to a soothing piece of music.
- Take a break to toss a Frisbee or a baseball.
- Have a brief at-home dance party.
- Stand up and stretch your body as if you were just waking up.

Michelle: Finding Tranquility in Yoga

I discovered yoga and over time persuaded Paul to begin a practice too. One of my first yoga classes was taught at the temple where I worked. It had been decades since I had spent school recess doing handstands and swinging upside down on the monkey bars. This yoga class challenged me as a more cautious adult—eager to exercise but hoping not to injure myself—to practice headstands and shoulder stands. I grew to understand that yoga poses were like life tasks, more accessible on some days than on others. Craving and cherishing the opportunity to straighten my spine and sharpen my focus, I began to appreciate the value of viewing the world from a different—in this case, upside down—perspective. Through practice, I gained balance and insight in other areas as well.

The Institute for Jewish Spirituality describes yoga—and, by extension, any physical embodiment practice—as a spiritual practice:

> We work with our bodies by intentionally assuming poses that stretch, lengthen, and strengthen the body. We learn to pay attention more fully to sensations in our bodies as they move into

> various shapes and forms, and to the breath that flows in and out.... As we release tensions and blocks in the body, there is often release of tensions and constrictions held in the mind and the emotions as well. As this process unfolds, we can experience more spaciousness and renewed capacities for movement and growth in our lives.[9]

From yoga, I discovered how to find balance within the unpredictability of parenting. The most enduring spiritual embodiment lesson transpired when the yoga instructor brought her two-year-old son with her to class. A last-minute babysitter cancellation left the instructor with no other choice. She introduced her son and began teaching, calmly demonstrating the "down dog" pose while her toddler ran back and forth beneath her as if she were a human bridge. What was remarkable to me was that the instructor maintained her focus even though her child-care logistics had suddenly shifted. We students followed her lead and soon transferred our focus from the little boy to the yoga practice. I learned to "go with the flow."

Time for exercise is rare and precious for many of us. Yet we benefit significantly from integrating life-balancing practices into our daily lives. Whether a gym workout, a pickup basketball game in the park, walking on a home treadmill, or going for a run in the neighborhood, we can each replenish our energy and recenter ourselves. In fact, most exercise promotes well-being: family hikes, swimming, biking, skiing, tennis, dance, and more. Movement directs us toward the spiritual ideals of forgiveness and release.

Selicha: Forgiveness

We humans live on a continuum of strength, flexibility, and intention. In yoga, in exercise, and in parenting, we strive to accept what is. We learn to forgive ourselves. Some days our bodies allow us to hold a certain pose; other days our minds get in the way. Not accomplishing a goal on one day does not mean that the goal will not be accomplished on the next. We are drawn to the forgiving practice of yoga.

Shichrur: Release

Yoga and exercise lead to healthy release of pent-up emotions. The final pose in a yoga class is called *shavasana*, or "corpse pose." *Shavasana* imitates death. We lie on our backs and surrender ourselves to the earth. Sometimes during this pose emotions held at bay quietly seep into our hearts. I recall one such *shavasana* a few months after my Grandma Ruby died. Caught by surprise as tears filled my eyes, I found myself grieving deeply. In this moment of stillness, I ceased to worry about others and, in a much-needed release, let my own sorrow envelop me.

Practice Simple Yoga Poses Together

Unroll your yoga mat against a wall and place one for your child next to yours. Lie on your side, with your tush up against the wall. Slowly turn onto your back so that your legs swing up the wall. Remain in this pose, called *viparita karani*, for about five to ten minutes until you feel a cascade of calm and restoration.

Soul-Uplifting Friendship

Friendship has long been considered soul-uplifting by our Jewish sages. *Pirkei Avot* (1:2) tells us that in addition to finding a teacher, we each should acquire for ourselves a friend. Declaring, "Either friendship or death," our sages mandated that we exert great effort in cultivating friendship (Talmud, *Ta'anit* 23a). Asher ben Yehiel, a thirteenth-century rabbi known as the Rosh, wrote a guide for ethical living in which he advised, "If you have a faithful friend, hold fast to him. Let him not go, for he is a precious possession."[10] We find wisdom in a saying attributed to Hasidic rabbi Mordechai of Lechovitz that, "Friendship is like a stone. A stone has no value, but when you rub two stones together properly, sparks of fire emerge."[11]

Good friends enhance our lives with their unconditional support, warm comfort, and companionship. Friendships—even those punctuated by long periods of absence from each other's daily lives—need not preclude reconnection; long-shared history can be especially rejuvenating.

Michelle: Friendship's Deep Roots

As children grow and require more mental and emotional attention, we parents can benefit greatly from contact with our own friends. We can learn from their parenting styles and, with them, we can replenish depleted energy.

Reuniting with old friends—whether from college, high school, or childhood—can be precious; shared history allows us to leapfrog over the "getting to know you" part to delve deeper. Soon after we each turned fifty, I met a dear friend for a long weekend on Salt Spring Island, Canada. Jill and I had become fast friends as college freshmen and maintained a long-distance friendship from Seattle and Los Angeles. With the responsibilities of six kids between us, our time together was rare and treasured. Over the last two decades, we had typically seen each other at baby namings and bar or bat mitzvah celebrations.

There on Salt Spring Island, Jill and I gleefully caught each other up, talking constantly, as if in one run-on sentence, stopping only to sleep at night. With our morning coffee, we picked up the conversation. We exchanged stories about our families and our careers, about crushing realities, significant achievements, and dreams still on the horizon. We laughed with happiness and gratitude. We found serenity in a friendship with roots that had grown deep.

One afternoon, Jill and I happened upon an "aerial yoga" class where yoga is practiced in deep-purple silk hammocks suspended from the ceiling. New for us, the opportunity was enticing; this antigravity practice seemed perfect for two women marking their half-century birthdays. Afterward, while relishing a facial in an outdoor spa, I lay peacefully on my back, the eye mask blocking out the skylight. Birds nearby chirped and within moments, I imagined an unfamiliar fountain flowing with purple liquid.

After the facial, I shared with the aesthetician the odd sensation of purple. "What cream fragrance did you use?" I inquired, thinking there was a scent I identified with the color purple. "The cream was unscented. The purple was only in your imagination," she answered. "But in yogic tradition, indigo/violet is the color of the *ajna* chakra, the energy of intuition."

Between the purple silk hammock, the spa, and the depths of laughter with this cherished friend, I temporarily let go of my parenting responsibilities. There on Salt Spring Island, suspended in a soothing spiritual realm, I found inner balance.

When parents model "me time," we find renewed balance and spiritual centering, and our children learn from us healthy habits that will be crucial to their own self-restoration. As they go off to college and beyond, we will have gifted them yet another lesson: that they, like us, are capable of reaching within and finding ways to continually rebalance themselves.

Try This **Restore Your Spirit Through Friendship**

In *N'siah*, a women's spiritual journey group Michelle facilitated at Congregation Or Ami, we reflected on the need for caregiving moms to care for themselves. All the women in this group were raising teenagers. Acknowledging that our kids took their cues from us, we knew that our own agitation or, conversely, our tranquility, could be especially contagious. We identified ways to nurture ourselves:

- Spend time with other adults who maintain a sense of humor, and practice laughing out loud at the continual demands of parenting.
- Stay in touch with parent friends you admire and whose judgment you trust. Make it a practice to swap parenting strategies for creating an atmosphere of calm.
- Schedule dinners out with friends or phone dates with those to whom you are closest. (Allow the unpredictability of life to give you a pass, whenever needed, to reschedule or cut short your time together.)

Paul: Reinforcing a Healthy and Complete Jewish Vision of Beauty

We began our exploration of caring for body, mind, and spirit with poignant anecdotes about our inclination to focus on the physical imperfections of our bodies. None of us are immune to the pressures of society to conform to specific, randomly assigned measures of beauty. As more and more young people become disheartened about their physicality, parents need to become more aware of the dangers to their child's self-esteem and self-image.

Today, when I stand before the holy ark to bless our bar and bat mitzvah students, I aim to reinforce a healthy Jewish vision of beauty. While the congregation listens to the cantor sing, I tell the student privately:

> You know what beauty is, right? Every movie, TV show, and magazine depicts what they think is the definitive image of beauty and attractiveness. For them, the best-looking people have this kind of body shape with that kind of hair and skin type. But that's just advertising.
>
> Do you want to know what beauty/handsomeness looks like? Real beauty is this [I draw a circle around the student's face]. Our Torah teaches that we are all created *b'tzelem Elohim*, in the image of God. This means that the face and body you have been given is a reflection of the awesome preciousness inside that is you. *You* are beautiful. Never forget that.
>
> Remember also that anyone in your life who is worthy of this beauty/handsomeness [again I circle the student's face] must also take care of and honor this wonderful mind [pointing to the student's brain] and this precious heart [pointing to the heart]. Love lifts you up and should make you feel wonderful. So love yourself first, and love will come back to you.

Try This **Bless Real Beauty**

As a daily practice, remind your children how precious they are. Stand in front of your children, and draw an imaginary circle around their faces. Tell them that they are beautiful, valued, and loved.

Do the same for yourself. Stand in front of a mirror, draw an imaginary circle around your face, and tell yourself that your features are God-given, created in the image and likeness of God.

When we practice this exercise with our children when they are young and then we adhere to it as they grow into older teens, we bequeath to them an essential reminder of how truly beautiful they are.

We reap what we sow. When we plant seeds of self-love in our children by exhibiting appreciation and care for our own bodies, minds, and souls, our children will be better able to develop their own healthy self-identity. Our bodies are on loan to us; we are in them for just a short period of time. May we nurture the "temple of our souls," so that we—and our children—become stronger physically, deeper spiritually, and more resilient emotionally.

9

Reframing and Decision Making

Empowering Our Children to Explore Alternatives Through *Davar Acher*

> The greatest discovery of all time is that a person can change his future by merely changing his attitude.
>
> —Oprah Winfrey

Michelle: Shut Up!

Five-year-old Daniel (to a sibling): Shut up!

Mom: Daniel, we don't say "shut up" in our house.

Daniel (pausing thoughtfully): Mommy, where *do* we say "shut up"?

I grew up in a home in which my parents instilled kindheartedness. My mother and father, by their words and their deeds, made real the vision of Psalm 89:3, "*Olam chesed yibaneh*—the world will be created out of kindness."

My mom, Teri, lives a life that reflects the words of *Eshet Chayil* (Woman of Valor; Proverbs 31), a biblical poem that is recited in some homes on Shabbat evenings as a blessing of the woman of the house. She is a compassionate woman who "opens her mouth in wisdom, and words of kindness are on her lips" (Proverbs 31:26).

My dad, Murray, also is one who easily doles out compliments and uplifts people around him. He wears his kindheartedness on his face, an expression of warmth you can see from across the room.

When Paul and I married, I imagined that the home we would create would similarly be filled with kindness above all. When hurtful words and accusations were uttered in the heat of the moment, we required family members—both children and adults—to follow up on that same day by owning up to what was said. We expected that they would offer both an apology and an explanation of context. For example, "I was hungry, and I should not have lashed out at you. I am sorry." Or "My feelings were hurt when I did not get to voice my opinion. I am angry but I should not have called you that name. I apologize." Or "I am feeling pressured by deadlines, but I should not have been so abrupt with you. I apologize for not listening, and I do want to hear what you wanted to tell me." We aspired toward *chesed* in word and deed.

When we felt the lesson was useful, Paul and I would ask our children to explore ways to reframe their thoughts and feelings, remaining true to what they felt, yet expressing their experience in kinder or more constructive ways. For example, instead of telling a sibling to "shut up!" they could say, "I'm too tired to talk. Can we please continue later?"

We believe that the words we say frame the way we see the world. Words are more than reflections of what we think. Words can serve as self-fulfilling prophecies; when we repeat the words that we know should be true, we can create a reality to experience and live.

The Value in Many Perspectives

In classic Torah commentary, *davar acher* (another meaning) signals a second opinion, typically composed by the same author who wrote the prior comment. As Rabbi Jan Katzew, director of service learning at Hebrew Union College–Jewish Institute of Religion, suggests,

> [*Davar acher*] offers proof that multiple simultaneous interpretations of a text are possible, and often desirable, even, and perhaps

> especially by the same person. One Jew, two opinions is not only a joke; it is also a virtue. "The test of a first-rate intelligence is the ability to hold two opposed ideas in the mind at the same time and still retain the ability to function" (F. Scott Fitzgerald).[1]

As parents, we often consider multiple perspectives to ensure that we are doing our best to nurture our children. Jewish spiritual parenting partnerships also embrace *davar acher* as a method for two (or more) parents to open themselves up to multiple views of how to raise children.

There is a deep comfort in Jewish tradition with multiple interpretations. Rabbi Lawrence Hoffman, a creative, deep-thinking scholar of liturgy and prayer, notes:

> Without apology, the rabbinic editors of our midrashic texts state one meaning, and then say, "Another meaning is ..." (*davar acher*) to introduce another equally valid interpretation of the term in question.... Experts may hold diverse but equally correct interpretations of what little things mean.[2]

As a parenting technique, *davar acher* invites parents to guide their children in rethinking challenging moments, opening themselves to consider alternate interpretations of the same situation. We strive to help children "get unstuck," to move beyond the simple or convenient interpretation of a conflict. We teach them to reframe their own experiences so they can practice responding to situations with the appropriate amount of attention and level of concern.

When children express distress or that they are feeling overwhelmed in a social, school, or family interaction, we can utilize *davar acher* to assist them in reframing their perspective on the circumstances. Asking questions prompts children to consider new interpretations. We start with, "Is it best to respond now or should we take time to gather more information?" By modeling composed restraint when confronted with a difficult situation, we teach children the value of evaluation. They learn that by maintaining equilibrium and focus, they can gather their thoughts and collect germane facts. They discover that thoughtful reflection can lead to positive outcomes that were initially unimagined. As parents, we want our children to become adept at detecting alternative interpretations and to develop confidence in their ability to address and manage obstacles in life. We aim to fill our children's spiritual toolbox with powerful techniques for approaching challenges.

Rearranging the Building Blocks of Our Stories

Davar acher creates new ways of comprehending the present and the past by reframing our perspective. Drawing on the writings of late eighteenth-century Hasidic rabbi Elimelech Weisbaum of Lizhensk, Poland, Rabbi Fred Guttman, spiritual leader of Temple Emanuel in Greensboro, North Carolina, teaches,

> When it comes to change, reframing is taking a particular belief about a situation or context and trying to let go of that belief in order to have new insights and interpretations. As such, we see the situation in "another frame." From these new insights, we grow and we may change. New possibilities may open up.[3]

Boston Hebrew College's Rabbi Ebn Leader offers a fascinating *davar acher* of the meeting between the biblical twin brothers Esau and Jacob. The two had gone their separate ways after the younger twin, Jacob, stole the birthright from the older brother, Esau, and gained the blessing of leadership from their father, Isaac. Jacob, fearful of his brother's boiling anger, ran off for forty years. They meet up again in the wilderness. Jacob seems afraid for his life, especially given the report that Esau is arriving with four hundred men. Must Jacob become defensive? Must he view the approaching men as a fighting force coming to punish him? Like all of us, Jacob has options of how to view the anxiety-inducing situation and therefore how to respond to it. Sharing another teaching of Noam Elimelech, Rabbi Leader helps us reframe the Torah story:

> What is the "miracle" Jacob performs to transform a potential clash with his brother into an embrace? Initially, Jacob can see the situation only through the prism of an old conflict with his brother.... From this perspective, the fact that his brother is

> coming to meet him with "four hundred men" (Genesis 32:7) can only be interpreted as a threat.
>
> According to Noam [Elimelech's] reading of the story, Jacob spends the whole night attempting to change his perspective, to find within himself the capacity to move beyond fear and to love Esau fully as a brother. Jacob's success is evidenced in the fact that at the moment of the meeting with Esau, Jacob's whole family is present (after first dividing his camp in half as a tactical measure), and with his full household present, he can walk toward his brother and embrace him—miraculously, conflict is averted.[4]

Although life happens to us, we get to determine how we respond to each occurrence. Will an experience be a blessing or will it be a curse? Will we see it as a failure or will it be an impetus for new possibilities? The classic question—is the glass half full or half empty?—reminds us that our perspective explains as much about us as it does about the situation. We hold tremendous power to rethink and reframe any given situation.

There is a well-known Jewish folktale that illustrates the power of perspective:

> A man and his companion lost their way in a forest. The companion despaired but the man said maybe some good would come of it. They came upon a stranger who needed the man's help. After helping the stranger, they discovered that he was a prince, who gave the man a beautiful horse.
>
> His neighbors praised his good luck and said, "How blessed you are to have such a magnificent animal."
>
> The man said, "Who's to say whether this is a blessing or a curse?"
>
> The next day the horse ran away, and the neighbors said, "How horrible that you were cursed with the loss of your horse."
>
> The man replied, "Who's to say whether this is a curse or a blessing? Perhaps some good will come of this."
>
> The next day, the horse returned leading five wild horses. "You were right!" his neighbors exclaimed. "The curse was a blessing in disguise. Now you're blessed with six horses."

The man replied, "Perhaps, but who's to say whether this is a blessing or a curse?"

The next day, his only son tried to ride one of the wild horses. He was thrown to the ground and broke his leg. The neighbors said, "How wise you were. Your blessing really was a curse."

The man replied, "There may be good yet. Who's to say whether this is a curse or a blessing?"

The next day, soldiers came through the village and took every able-bodied boy to fight in a war where it was almost certain all would be killed. Because the man's son was injured, the boy was the only one not taken. "How blessed are you to keep your son!" the neighbors said.

The man replied, "Who's to say? I don't know whether there's a curse in every blessing, but I am sure there's a blessing in every curse."[5]

Each moment is pregnant with possibility. We rarely know how a moment in time will play out over the course of our lives. Much of that depends on how we frame it and how we respond to it.

Detect the Blessing Within the Curse

Challenges can blossom into opportunities. A job ends; the ensuing job search exposes an exciting new career path. A child's failed test leads to intensified study, which yields deeper understanding of the subject matter. Behavioral patterns in school, labeled first as "problems," shed light on learning differences, prompting interventions and tools to better teach the child. What appeared to be a curse holds the keys to greater blessings.

Read with your child the above folktale about blessings and curses. Together identify experiences in your lives that at first appeared to be painful curses, but that later led to new opportunities or blessings. Think about:

- Friendships
- Sports activities
- Teachers or school subjects

- Relationships with siblings and other family members
- Play rehearsals or dance practices
- Art projects
- Learning differences

Explore what actions or changes in attitudes helped you to detect the blessing hidden within the curse.

"Need," "Want," and Other Words That Matter

Parents can become practiced at responding to children with questions designed to help them think through a situation. By not immediately answering or reacting to the struggles, objections, or concerns, we give our children the skills and space to reframe their own experiences. We engage in *tzimtzum*, stepping back to help them navigate through their own struggles and disappointments and evaluate their own needs. The following reframing questions can guide children to reflect on the urgency, importance, or quality of an issue.[6] You might make them part of your conversations.

Helpful or Harmful?

Like many children, ours went through periods when they seemed to take pleasure in aggravating each other. When we would confront the apparent instigator after a snide comment or a sly poke of a sibling, the accused would inevitably throw up his hands and say, "What did *I* do? I didn't do anything." Although we tried, it was impossible to determine who did what to whom. Feeling frustrated, we pivoted and employed a new tactic. Instead of saying, "Why did you do that?" we probed deeper and asked, "Do you consider your behavior to be helpful or harmful?" Harmful behavior, we explained, provoked an escalation of conflict or pain. With this question, we returned the responsibility to our child; we allowed him to steer himself through the effects of his actions and words. Over time, we observed that simply by being asked "helpful or harmful?" our children could move from denial to responsibility, and from active provocation to growth and reflection.

Big Thing or Small Thing?

Ascribing an appropriate amount of consideration to dilemmas can reduce pressure. Not all predicaments are equal in scale. It is useful to ask our children to first determine whether their problem is a "big thing or a small thing." Our own kids learned this concept from Dr. Bruce Powell, who asks the same of his students each year at de Toledo High School. The teenagers there learn, for example, that a car accident is a big thing. Not passing a driver's test on the first try is really a small thing. Younger children can grow to comprehend that, while hearing that your best friend is moving out of town is a big thing, not being invited to an acquaintance's birthday party, though it hurts, is really a small thing. Scaling issues to size helps children—and especially teens—approach problems with a suitable amount of gravity and learn how not to overreact.

Need or Want?

How many times has your child come forward insisting on a need? She *needed* to buy something. He *had* to eat something. They *must* do something. In response to these insistent entreaties, we started asking our children, "Do you *need* it or *want* it?"

We teach children that we *need* food, shelter, clothing, education, and love, but we merely *want* a new toy, a new pair of shoes, or a ticket to a concert. While the former are necessary to a person's life, the latter are luxuries. Although children still might want something very much, when they realize that it is a "want" and not a "need" they can reframe their request. They might develop a sense of humor about the way they ask for things. Over time, they might even learn to moderate their cravings.

Move from "Need" to "Want"

When your child has repeatedly requested a material object or permission to do something you are not eager to sanction, talk about the difference between needing something and wanting it. Together make a list of things that your child needs and those that your child wants. Ask: What are the differences? What are some things that feel like "needs," but are really "wants"? Teach your child how to more accurately phrase her wish. For example, "Mom, I would really like to go to my friend's house so we can hang out" instead of "I have to go to my friend's house right now!" Or "I really want that new video game" instead of "I need to have that new game; I'm the only one who doesn't have it!" Helping our children reflect on their desires leads them to be more self-aware.

Now or Later?

Parents' questions can also encourage children to accurately evaluate urgency. When one mother we know is confronted with a child who requests an immediate response, she pauses, takes a deep breath, and asks the child, "Now or later? Do you really need to know right this minute, or can you wait a little while?" This question helps children recognize that their request might be an impulsive ask and encourages recognition that Mom might be handling other tasks at the time.

Beg or Persuade?

Parents can guide children to transform a pleading request into a thoughtful moment of articulate persuasion. A friend of ours offers this creative approach: when a child pushes him to do something or to buy something, he encourages the child to offer persuasive logic instead of pleading. This dad invites the child to research and list three substantial reasons to support the idea. He believes that the child will grow from the experience, even if ultimately the request is denied.

Noah wanted his own Facebook account at an age earlier than we had allowed each of his older siblings to open one. When months of petitioning did not yield results, he changed tactics. At a family brunch, he borrowed his brother's computer and created a video to playfully and strategically build his case. He interviewed each aunt, uncle, grandparent, and cousin, asking why each believed he was responsible enough to use this social media tool. Noah's sense of humor shined brightly as he cleverly moved from person to person.

In the end, it was the persuasive video testimony of his sensible Grandpa Murray that convinced us that this boy was ready for his own Facebook account.

When Noah changed his approach, articulating his desire in a pleasant, non-pleading style, he demonstrated to himself and to us that he had the maturity to be strategic. This same maturity would be helpful as we all faced other challenges of social media.

Persist or Take a Break?

Sometimes frustration can impede our ability to deal adequately with a task. When parents observe a child's growing impatience, we can gently suggest, "What do you think about taking a break and trying again later?" The invitation to step back gives the child room to recompose herself and reevaluate. If she wants to keep trying, parents might ask, "Do you think the answer will come to you more easily now or after you have had lunch and a break?" The child is offered another chance to breathe, appraise the situation, and problem-solve from a calmer, fortified place.

Hurt or Scared?

Some children are nonchalant when they scrape their knee or they are accidentally hit with a ball at recess. They may have no idea when or how they got any schoolyard bruises. They bounce back quickly. Other kids exaggerate their reactions, making it challenging for parents and the children themselves to evaluate if the child is hurt, caught off guard, or perhaps embarrassed. In these situations, parents might ask, "Does it hurt, or are you scared?" This invites children to identify what they are actually experiencing. What they imagine to be pain might instead be fear. Once they grasp the difference, they are empowered to verbalize how they feel. Soon they provide parents and themselves with more clarity and direction about how they should respond.

Breathe and Visualize

When children are unsure about how to respond to circumstances, their discomfort and confusion can contribute to their apprehension.

We advise our children to stop and think before reacting. Asking "What are you feeling right now?" gives the child an opportunity to identify his feelings and name them out loud. "I am sad/angry/frustrated/embarrassed." This question gives children time to reflect before they respond.

When our children struggle to make sense of the issues friends are facing, we might use this same "breathe and visualize" exercise to teach empathy. We prompt our child to imagine, "If that experience were happening to me, how would I respond?" The child can visualize the challenges her peer is working through and begin to reflect on feelings she too might experience. For example, when Rachel was eight, her close friend's great-grandmother was hospitalized, and the child wanted to visit. Her friend's parents' decision that the girl was too young for a hospital visit upset Rachel. We gave Rachel an opportunity to express her dismay by asking her, "How did your friend's parents' decision make you feel?" We then asked her to consider what else, besides visiting, her friend might do to show her love for her great-grandmother. This question provided Rachel an emotional outlet and a chance to propose alternatives.

Alternate Choices: Facing Challenges That Perplex Us

We parents encounter challenging decisions every day about the safety, health, and well-being of our children. Amongst these decisions are:

- When should we start preschool?
- Which school is the best fit?
- How long should I breast-feed?
- Should our child play on a sports team? What about dance lessons?
- At what point are we overprogramming our child?
- Will I be a stay-at-home mom or dad, work part time, or work full time?
- In choosing childcare, should we hire in-home care, or use out-of-home day?
- What length of time is best for a first sleepaway camp experience?

- When is an appropriate bedtime?
- Do we give an allowance? If so, how much?
- Do we assist our child with his homework or let him work it out to the best of his ability?

Safety aside, rarely are child-related decisions clear cut. There is usually an attractive *davar acher*—an alternate choice. Internet searches amplify possibilities, and, in turn, unearth more and more questions. Along with reading about the topic and turning ideas over with friends and professionals, we want to take stock of our core values and identify what is essential to our family. Identifying those core values helps us wade through competing viable options to arrive at the best choice for us.

Reframing Uncovers Unique Options

When there are multiple good options, we sometimes belabor the decision. Long before the 1980s rock group the Clash sang about staying or going, our biblical ancestor Abraham was struggling with that same dilemma. How he framed the situation determined how he saw the decision he faced.

Abraham, then called Abram, lived a comfortable life in Ur, at the intersection of the Tigris and Euphrates rivers, the cradle of civilization (Genesis 11). With his wife, Sarah, then called Sarai, and his extended family, he thrived as a merchant. He stood to inherit the family business from his father, Terach, a prominent entrepreneur. Taking over the business, however, came with a price. Abraham would be selling idols. In his heart of hearts, Abraham knew he would be perpetrating a lie, because idolatry was a practice he did not believe in.[7] But Abraham also knew that if he did not take over the business, his family's financial situation might quickly become precarious. Without the idol shop, it would become difficult to remain in Ur. So Abraham had a choice to make: inherit the business or strike out on his own? "Should I stay or should I go now?"

Genesis 12 reports that God told Abraham, "*Lech lecha*," often translated as "Go for your own good." How, though, did Abraham know what was for his own good? Did he listen to his conscience? Did he just follow his *kishkes* (gut)?

In the *Zohar*, a foundational text of the Jewish mystical tradition, Abraham is depicted as speaking at length with his wife, Sarah, pleading with her and ultimately making decisions with her. Perhaps in this instance he confided in her that by selling idols he felt he would be selling false hopes. We imagine that together they weighed the risks: an uncertain future, financial instability, and an arduous and dangerous journey across the desert. They reached that *davar acher* moment when, facing a difficult situation, they had to decide how to frame it.

Should they leave Ur, the cultural, political, and theological center of the ancient world, to enter unknown territory? Or should Abraham compromise his integrity, stay with the business, and maybe even start a family? Was this about financial security or personal integrity?

Abraham and Sarah, at a crossroads, had to make a decision. Ultimately they heard God's command, *"Lech lecha,"* as a call to strike out and start life anew. They decided that personal integrity trumped financial security. Reframing the situation in this way, they reconstructed their reality.

Moving Forward with Confidence

Once we have made a decision, how do we keep ourselves from revisiting it again and again? Michelle gained practical perspective on decision making when she was at a career crossroads in her twenties. A job offer awaited her on one coast, while acceptance to graduate school invited her to another. Both were good, viable options. As she deliberated, a mentor in her office suggested that she move forward in either direction but that when she did, she embrace wholeheartedly the idea that the choice she made had to be the right choice. The advice was brilliant in its simplicity. This insight removed the pressure to guess which was the absolutely perfect choice. With so many decisions to be made and so many sources of information, second-guessing whether we made the right choice can quickly overwhelm us. When we must choose between multiple viable options, accepting our choice—and walking forward with confidence—allows us to spend more time living with our choices and less time worrying about picking the right one.

Examine Your Own Decision-Making Process

We want to teach our children to make decisions in a way that will build confidence. We strive to raise them with spiritual balance so that they will have the wherewithal to dig deep inside themselves to find answers that make sense. Most importantly, we want our children to grow into young adults who can respond to challenging situations with courage and clarity. Approaching our own decision making with self-awareness and patience, we want to model for our children a calm, thoughtful process.

Think about two or three significant personal decisions you made in recent years. Ask yourself:

1. When did I realize that this situation needed to be addressed?
2. Whom did I speak with for guidance and insight?
3. How did I explore the various options before me?
4. What were the values that influenced my final decision?
5. How did I feel during each decision-making process?
6. What commonalities can I find in the way I make decisions?

Be aware of your own decision-making process. Think about:

1. What kinds of issues make you anxious?
2. When do you think quickly?
3. When do you require more time to examine an issue?
4. Are there times when you overreact?
5. What causes you to freeze up?

Share your answers with a parenting partner. Consider how your decision making compares with that of others, especially your co-parent. What kinds of situations lead the two of you into conflict? Which situations can you address together, and which are you able to handle on your own?

Who Chooses?

Parents are responsible for framing many situations for their children. We determine who in the family gets to make the decision and how we respond to it. Of the plethora of decisions families face, some are appropriately determined by children, others by parents only, and still others by a combination of parents and children.

As our own children were growing up, we increasingly let them choose their hairstyle, wardrobe (within reason), room décor, extracurricular activities, music, and friends. Starting in preschool, they decided what to wear. In elementary school, they chose sports they wanted to play; they were also allowed to give up extracurricular activities in which we had enrolled them when they were younger. One day, Rachel, then in third grade and who had always sported long locks, surprised us by asking the hairdresser to chop off seven inches and give her a bob-style haircut. In another chair, years later, sixth-grade Noah cautioned the barber to make sure his bangs remained over his eyebrows and his hair length reached his collarbone. Haircuts, insignificant to us but vital to them, let our children experiment with their own personal style.

Decide Who Gets to Decide

Parents reduce stress when we are able to be clear about who gets to make the decision. Whenever an important decision is before you, consult with your co-parent (when available) to determine who controls the locus of decision making. Ask yourselves if this a decision that:

- We parents must make?
- Our child may make?
- We make as parents with the input of our child?

When you choose, recognize these variables:

- As children grow up, the locus of decision making changes.
- Different children gain the ability to make decisions at different ages and stages.

- Parents need not give up decision-making responsibility until we believe that the child has the maturity and experience to make that particular kind of decision.

While children may not say it aloud, they are often relieved when they do not need to take responsibility (or full responsibility) for a decision. Long into their later teens, children are comforted by and grateful for the knowledge that their parents are still guiding certain elements of the decision-making process. They are reassured by knowing that we are looking out for their best interests. Although they are better able to express gratitude about this when they are older, we parents should not abdicate this decision-making responsibility prematurely.

Getting to the Heart of the Matter

In time, we understand that determining the heart of the matter—whether a situation is a blessing or a curse—depends in large part on how we choose to view it. Like our ancestors Abraham and Sarah, we can learn to reframe choices for ourselves and with our children. We can ease their anxiety and bolster their skills at making healthy life decisions. Small things stay small, needs do not get confused with wants, and their behaviors move from harmful to helpful. Ultimately, our children become expansive in their thinking, exploring life's *davar acher* opportunities and seeing the world as filled with a host of exciting possibilities.

10 Opening Our Hearts with Kindness

Instilling *Chesed* and *Gemilut Chasadim* into Everyday Life

> As we learn from Abraham, we cannot wait for the seekers to show up at our door; we must go out to meet them where they are and invite them in. Audacious hospitality is a transformational spiritual practice that changes all of us for the better.
>
> —Rabbi Rick Jacobs, President, Union for Reform Judaism[1]

Paul: The Simple Act of Reaching Out

Like other parents, we wanted our children to do their best in school. Yet fundamentally, we focused more on the kind of people they would become. At de Toledo High School, where Michelle works, the faculty inspire their students to strive to become A+ human beings excelling in treating others with kindness.

When Noah reached out to a shy teenager at a youth group event, what seemed a simple act ended up having a significant impact. To draw the boy in, Noah asked what he liked to do and then introduced him to a like-minded teen. In time, this boy developed a large circle of friends and blossomed into a leader in the youth movement. Sometimes people just need an invitation to come in from the sidelines.

By being kind to others, engaged in *tikkun olam* (repairing the world) at its elementary level, Noah learned that the simple act of walking up to a newcomer and starting a conversation could make a difference. It is never fun to be an outsider, but our son discovered that by extending himself, he could convert outsiders into insiders.

This sense of inclusion is rooted in the idea that each individual matters. Judaism has always been a mosaic, a beautiful collection of different colored and shaped pieces. The Jewish people are also "Mosaic" in that we connect back to Moses. Moses was a Hebrew child, raised by Egyptians, who married a non-Jewish woman of color and became the leader of his people. Additionally, according to the midrash *Exodus Rabbah* 1:26, Moses had a speech impediment and even suggested to God that because of this he was not up to the task of standing up to Pharaoh (Exodus 4:10).[2] Yet Moses's special challenge, and multicultural and multiethnic background, did not stop God from insisting that Moses lead the Jewish people. Are we holier than the Holy One that we can choose to be more restrictive about who gets to be included in the communal tent? It is important that we model divine inclusiveness for our children so that they too can act with *chesed*, welcoming everyone into the Jewish and general community.[3]

The Jewish people was and still is a mixed multitude. We rejoice that at least 25 percent of the American Jewish population is racially and ethnically diverse, including African, African American, Latino/Hispanic, Asian, Native American, Sephardi, Mizrahi (Middle Eastern), and mixed-race Jews by heritage and marriage.[4] Cross-cultural and cross-racial adoptions have been part of our history from biblical times. Most Jewish families include extended family members who were not raised Jewish. Additionally, up to 20 percent of the Jewish population is living with some kind of disability at any given time.[5]

Judaism has also been an open *mishkan* (tent). Rabbi Rick Jacobs, president of the Union for Reform Judaism in New York, explains:

> Early in Genesis, Abraham and Sarah set the standard. On a blisteringly hot day, Abraham runs after three desert wanderers, insisting they come inside for nourishment. What makes his act so memorable is that he doesn't wait for the wanderers to knock on his door; instead, he goes out to meet them where they are and invites them in.[6]

He practiced what Rabbi Jacobs calls "audacious hospitality." By welcoming these strangers into the tent, Abraham and Sarah articulated a kindness that should be the fundamental focus of every Jewish family and every Jewish community: that everyone who wants to throw her lot in with the Jewish people is welcome.

Jewish spirituality aims to instill in our children the welcoming value of *chesed*, understood as "kindness," "love," and "loving-kindness." Children can learn to share the love in their hearts through openly embracing others, especially those who once sat at the margins of our community. Our commitment to *chesed* ensures that we convey to families with seemingly atypical situations, who may feel like they live outside the tent of Judaism, that we believe they are truly worthy of inclusion.

Loving-Kindness: A Pure Expression of Judaism

Chesed is the core *middah* (ethical virtue) of Judaism. It is embedded in the DNA of Creation. Our Rabbis understood Torah to be Creation's blueprint and saw within Torah how the Holy One infused Creation with loving-kindness. Rabbi Simlai in the Talmud (*Sotah* 14a) asserts:

> The Torah begins with *chesed* and ends with *chesed*. It begins with *chesed*, as it is written, "And the Eternal, God, made for Adam and his wife Eve garments of skins and clothed them" (Genesis 3:21). It ends with *chesed*, as it is written, "And [God] buried [Moses] in the valley in the land of Moab" (Deuteronomy 34:6).

Just as the Holy One acted with loving-kindness—clothing the naked and burying the dead—so too are we called to loving-kindness.

Rabbi Rami Shapiro, poet, author, and translator of Jewish texts, defines *chesed* as "God's unlimited, unconditional, unconditioned, and all-inclusive love for creation."[7] *Chesed* encompasses a maternal aspect, like the love of a nursing mother and child, as well. In *The Receiving: Reclaiming Jewish Women's Wisdom*, Tirzah Firestone, author of books on mysticism and spiritual leader of Congregation Nevei Kodesh in Boulder, Colorado, likens *chesed* to:

> the surge that a nursing mother feels when her milk lets down. As any lactating mother knows, milk lets down when the baby's hunger hits, regardless of how far away Mama is, how many bottles Grandma has on hand, or how beautiful the chiffon evening dress she is wearing when the call comes.[8]

The *Zohar*, a primary text of the Jewish mystical tradition, expands the *chesed* image. Daniel C. Matt, a leading scholar of Kabbalah and Jewish mysticism, teaches that *chesed* "represents the God of love, calling forth the response of love in the human soul as well."[9]

While Torah and the Talmud make statements that are decidedly not embracing—including, for example, a condemnation of homosexuality (Leviticus 18:22) and a prohibition for those who are blemished (that is, having disfiguring disabilities) from approaching the holy *mishkan* (Leviticus 21:23)—much of the Jewish community rejects these exclusionary verses as products of a less enlightened period. The work of *chesed* involves encouraging those who have not yet repudiated (or reinterpreted) these verses to see the blessing of doing so.

Turning Concept into Action

Rabbi Simon the Just taught, "The world rests upon three things: Torah, *avodah* [service to God], and *gemilut chasadim*" (*Pirkei Avot* 1:2). What are *gemilut chasadim*? *Gemilut* means "that which brings about," and *chasadim*—related to *chesed*—points to loving-kindness. *Gemilut chasadim* are "acts of loving-kindness."

A goal of Jewish spiritual parenting is for children to incorporate *gemilut chasadim* into their daily lives. We nurture young people to feel loyalty toward others—both those they know and those they do not—and to act to help others whenever possible. We teach them to respond to others because kindness is a foundational value of our *mishpacha* (family) and *kehillah* (community).

When our people stood at Mount Sinai, the Holy Presence covered them as a cloud. Exhibiting great *chesed*, Moses drew attention to the breadth of our community:

> You stand this day, all of you, before the Eternal your God—you tribal heads, you elders, and you officials, all of the men of Israel, you children, you women, even the stranger within your camp, from woodchopper to water drawer. (Deuteronomy 29:9–10)

We imagine everyone who was there: young and old, healthy and ill, typically abled and differentially abled, and heterosexuals and LGBTQI individuals. People of all backgrounds, colors, and tribes showed up, both the Israelite and the *ger toshav* (non-Israelites, today called "non-Jews") who dwelt among us.

Paul: The *Chesed* of Saying Yes to Inclusion

I take pride in knowing that the synagogues and organizations I have worked with throughout my rabbinate have educated every person who sought Jewish learning experiences, regardless of his or her unique learning challenges. With Congregation Or Ami, I have celebrated along with countless families as they kvelled when their child with special needs ascended our bimah to fully participate in Jewish rituals. With abiding loving-kindness, the congregation has welcomed and either mainstreamed or created special Jewish learning paths for so many children.

Congregant Michael Kaplan likes to tell the story about one Rosh Hashanah morning when he, his wife, their son, Brandon, and Brandon's guide dog entered the sanctuary as visitors, not yet members. Brandon is profoundly developmentally challenged and cannot speak, care for himself, or move about safely without help. Sitting in the front row, the family prayed and sang. Michael and Dina were overjoyed with Brandon's smiles and carefree clapping. After services, I approached to welcome them and, upon meeting then eight-year-old Brandon, asked, "So when is his bar mitzvah?"

Michael speaks about falling in love with our congregational community at that very moment. He notes that there were no discussions about obstacles that Brandon's challenges would bring to the learning process; no concerns raised about whether Brandon could make it in a classroom or whether he would need special attention or an individualized educational plan (IEP). There was just a firm expectation that Brandon would follow the ritual path that Judaism sets out for all young Jewish men and women. So the Kaplans joined the synagogue, and years later Brandon became bar mitzvah in a very moving ceremony. Many tears of joy were shed as Brandon used sign language to read his *parasha* (Torah portion) and an ingenious computer to articulate his *d'var Torah* (speech).

We teach our children about fully embracing others when our communities rejoice with pride in the full inclusion of children with disabilities. At our synagogue, these children have included:

- A child with developmental delays who read Torah beautifully from a transliteration before a congregation of 1,200.
- A teen *madricha* (teaching assistant) on the autism spectrum describing to the whole congregation how autism affects her, and how people can help her integrate into the youth community.
- A twenty-two-year-old becoming bar mitzvah alongside his thirteen-year-old brother in a ceremony marked by mutual respect and joy.
- Children with challenges honored with special ritual responsibilities, such as opening the ark or asking congregants to rise or to be seated.
- Participants in Chaverim, a local Jewish Family Service–sponsored group for developmentally disabled adults ages eighteen to eighty-eight.

On the most fundamental level, there is nothing remarkable about physically, mentally, or emotionally challenged and exceptional children following a Jewish path. *Chesed*, at its core, demands that we reach out and draw in each person. We can do this on a communal level and on a personal level, modeling this value for our children so that they will imitate our actions.

Encourage Disability Inclusion in Your Jewish Community

If your child has special challenges, and the synagogue you approach cannot imagine how to include him, you can educate the synagogue on the possibilities. As a starting point, offer these suggestions:

1. *Find teachers who have creativity, grit, and patience.* Ask the congregation to consider investing in them and training them to work with people with special needs by sending them to a training program.
2. *Ask the clergy and educators to develop a unique Jewish learning path that is a good fit for your child.* Agree in advance that the road ahead may be bumpy, but that you will all do your best.
3. *Work as a team to map out a Jewish educational path for each child.* The parents, rabbi, educator, and teacher (and perhaps the child's secular school educational therapist) can each add value to the team. Since young people grow and mature month to month and year to year, commit to reevaluation every six months to refine the path.
4. *Encourage the leadership to set a clear inclusion policy* like the one we adopted at Congregation Or Ami: "That any child of a member is entitled to a Jewish educational experience at the temple, and that any child of a member who works to the best of his or her ability has the right and privilege to become a bar or bat mitzvah."[10]
5. *Publicize the temple's commitment to inclusion.* Tell stories frequently about the involvement of families with children with special needs. Weave their comfort and successes into sermons, at board meetings, and posting on blogs and social media.
6. *Participate in community discussions on inclusion,* including:
   - *Hineinu* (www.rac.org/hineinu), a comprehensive interdenominational Jewish guide to creating inclusive communities hosted by the Religious Action Center of Reform Judaism
   - Jewish Leadership Institute on Disabilities and Inclusion (http://nlcdd.org/jli.html)

- "Jewish Special Needs Education: Removing the Stumbling Block" Facebook group
- *The New Normal* blog (www.thejewishweek.com/blogs/the-new-normal) of *New York Jewish Week*
- *Or Am I?* (http://paulkipnes.com), Paul's blog posts on inclusion and disabilities
- *Ruderman Family Foundation* blog (www.rudermanfoundation.org/rudermanblog)[11]

Many Jewish summer camps offer mainstream and/or special sessions for children with disabilities. The camps of the Union for Reform Judaism (htttp://urjyouth.org/camps) and Ramah (http://campramah.org), spread throughout the United States, are particularly engaged in inclusion.

Remember to embrace shortcomings as growth opportunities. No synagogue, camp, or community is perfect. There will always be moments when they fail to live up to your hopes and expectations. We remember our own shortcomings: the time we did not adequately or proactively work with a camp to embrace a certain child with special needs; the time when a unique learning path would have been more beneficial to a child than mainstreaming him. Each learning experience, though peppered with pain, leads to greater understanding, better expertise, and more successful inclusion.

Judaism teaches that all Jews were at Mount Sinai to receive the Torah. Every individual, including your child, can enjoy a meaningful Jewish spiritual journey.

Identifying and Removing Stumbling Blocks with *Chesed*

Reflecting on the Torah's injunction "You shall not curse the deaf nor place a stumbling block before the blind" (Leviticus 19:14), our Rabbis unpack two kinds of intended kindnesses: (1) refraining from acting and (2) acting. Torah instructs us to *not* place obstacles before people with disabilities and also to actively remove obstacles. Sometimes children with special needs and their families feel isolated. We might lessen that isolation as we instill the value of *chesed* in our children through intentional outreach.

By increasing our children's awareness of the marginalized, the isolated, the lonely, and the seemingly different among us, we are teaching our children to say *Hineini*! ("here I am") in the most powerful ways. Bible and midrash scholar Rabbi Norman J. Cohen writes:

> Our responsiveness to others, which is embodied in the utterance of *hineini*, enhances the entire human condition. We can heal our broken world—promoting *tikkun olam* (repair of the world)—when we are willing to see the world through the eyes of other people and respond to them with an open heart. Thus we can shape the future of our own descendants, transcending the confines of our own lives.[12]

Teach Your Child to Be Welcoming

Identify where there are children with special needs in your child's classroom, in your synagogue, or in your neighborhood.

- Introduce yourself to the children's parents and introduce the children to each other.
- Make it a family priority to be warm and welcoming, to invite the child to sit or play with you. Include the family in celebrations and on playdates.
- With your child, seek out opportunities to volunteer. Many sports leagues sponsor a "VIP" team to involve children with disabilities. Other communities host Special Olympics. Our local universally accessible playground, Brandon's Village, hosts a monthly group called Brandon's Buddies, which creates afternoons of fun for typically abled and specially abled children. Each experience invites volunteers to partner with children who have unique challenges.

After they spend time together, ask your child: How are you two alike? Where did you discover the *tzelem Elohim* within him?

Loving Others as They Are

Members of the LGBTQI community can also experience profound feelings of isolation. These emotions can particularly affect young people who are especially susceptible to the pressure to conform. Over recent years, too many young people in the LGBTQI community have felt bullied, with some even driven to suicide.

The story of Abraham, Sarah, and the three strangers reminds us to reach out proactively to prevent estrangement and loneliness. Welcoming others is a key part of demonstrating *chesed*. The Talmud states, "*Hachnasat orchim* [welcoming strangers] is a greater mitzvah than welcoming the *Shechinah* [God's presence]" (*Shabbat* 127a). Rabbi Elyse Frishman, of the Barnert Temple in Franklin Lakes, New Jersey, and editor of the Central Conference of American Rabbis' *Mishkan T'filah* prayer book, points out that we experience God's presence when we reach out to others:

> [The *Shechinah* is] the way we experience God in the details of daily life and the physical world.... But, the *Shechinah* isn't just my life, or yours alone; it is all of our lives, all Jews, all people, all the world. To hear the call of the *Shechinah* is not just to hear one's own heart; it is to hear the heart of the stranger, to look into her eyes, to touch his soul.[13]

Combat Bullying by Telling Your Children They Matter

Bullying is a serious concern in today's world, both in person and in social media. A child who is bullied can easily forget how deeply loved, valued, and blessed he is.

We have been deeply saddened by the anguish and deaths of young people who were subjected to bullying because of their sexual orientation. Fully accepting of LGBTQI individuals and couples as created *b'tzelem Elohim*, we reached out to congregant teens, sending a personalized letter and asking their parents to read it together with them. Our message is universal: that each child is created *b'tzelem Elohim* and therefore is intrinsically valued, equal, and blessedly unique.[14]

Read this letter with your pre-teen and teenage children. Tell them it is written by rabbis and a cantor to other young people their age. Afterward, ask them what they have heard about bullying in their schools or online. Their response to the letter may provide you with some valuable insights into their experiences and give you ideas for future conversations.

Dear ___________ (insert your child's name),

Sometimes issues are so heavy, so serious, that words seem insufficient. We are writing to you following the suicide of another young person whose tragic death has saddened us deeply. Whether you are gay, straight, bisexual, transgender, questioning, intersex, or just plain confused, Judaism teaches that you are created *b'tzelem Elohim* (in the image of God). You are beloved and unique.

It does not matter what other people think about you as you are discovering who you are. What does matter is that you feel comfortable being you—at temple, at school, in your community, and in your home—and you learn how to manage those individuals who do not accept you. No matter how badly you feel about your life, you will always have someone to talk to and a community that will accept you, support you, and love you for who you are.

Please turn to a caring adult—a parent, teacher, rabbi, cantor, counselor, youth advisor—if you are in pain or thinking of hurting yourself. (Suicide is a permanent solution to what is a temporary problem.) Reach out if you ever need help.

We live in an imperfect world where some people hurt others because they are different. They may fear what they do not understand and harm people because of whom they love. Alternatively, you may be hurting due to acts of anti-Semitism, cyber-bullying, social exclusion, breaking up with a first love, using drugs or alcohol, or countless other pressures. The effects of such harm will not always be physical, but words, name-calling, and lack of acceptance can leave scars just as deep as the wound from a knife. The good news is that most people in the world support your right to be who you are. Torah teaches *kedoshim tiheyu*—that you are holy—and valued (Leviticus 19:2). We accept you and want you to feel welcome, respected, and loved.

We have each been blessed with beloved friends and relatives, colleagues and congregants who are gay or lesbian, bi, transgender, questioning, or intersex. Some come out easily; others struggle with their identity; still others remain "in the closet." As long as prejudice and bigotry exist, we cannot be silent. Jewish tradition teaches that we are all responsible for one another.

Your Jewish community—rabbis, cantors, educators—cares for you. If you are ever feeling sad, angry, scared, or any of a myriad of confusing emotions and you need someone to talk to, please be in touch with one of us. Always remember that you are part of a community that cares deeply about you and accepts you for who you are. *No matter what.*

Let Your Children Know You Love Them Always

In *Promises for My Gay Children: Reflections of an Orthodox Rabbi for Yom Kippur*, Rabbi Avi Katz Orlow made a series of promises to his children, leading the way for parents to be prepared with a response should their child realize and reveal that he or she is LGBTQI.

From when they are little, let your children know that you value love and relationships in their many forms. Let the depth of *chesed*—your unlimited, unconditional, unconditioned, and all-inclusive love—lead you to make some promises to yourself. We have made the promises below and invite you to consider those you might adopt.

"If I have gay, lesbian, bisexual, transgender, questioning, or intersex children, I will ..."

- *Love them unconditionally.* My children are my children, whoever they are.
- *Stand up for them.* Bigotry and hatred do not belong in a *kehillah kedoshah* (sacred community). I will hold fast to the ideal that the Jewish community fully welcomes all children.
- *Celebrate their partnership.* I will embrace my child's partner in the same way that I would embrace a partner in a heterosexual relationship.

- *Teach others.* I will be a role model by enlightening those organizations that exclude or impose limitations on LGBTQI children.
- *Support Jewish LGBTQI groups.* This is a good promise to make even if you do not have LGBTQI children. Keshet (http://keshet.org) advocates for LGBTQI Jews. Nehirim (www.nehirim.org) is a national community of LGBTQI Jews, their families, and supporters.[15]

Embracing Non-Jewish Spouses and Partners

We value families in all configurations, including those with one or two parents, both Jewish or not, with biologically conceived or adopted children. We each grew up in a family with an adopted or foster sibling, the result of our parents' overflowing *chesed*. We extend that warm welcome to the non-Jewish spouses, partners, and relatives who are part of our community.

At critical moments in the story of our Jewish people, *gemilut chasadim* by non-Jews ensured our very survival. Pharaoh's daughter saved Moses from the river Nile (Exodus 2:5–10). Moses's father-in-law, Yitro, a Midianite priest, taught him how to construct a system of courts and judges to extend Jewish law throughout the Israelite people (Exodus 18:1–27). Hundreds of righteous gentiles hid and saved thousands of Jews during the Holocaust; they are honored at Yad Vashem, the Holocaust Martyrs' and Heroes' Remembrance Authority in Jerusalem.

In many communities, non-Jewish spouses and partners are fully integrated. They stand on the bimah as their children become bar or bat mitzvah, and they also share *simcha*s (joyous moments) and sorrows with the congregation. How can we convey in a clear, unambiguous way our deep appreciation and embrace of the non-Jewish members in our community? We offer the following blessing to our non-Jewish readers, who are raising a Jewish child.[16]

A Blessing for Non-Jewish Spouses, Partners, Relatives, and Friends

We want to thank you for your willingness to cast your lot with the Jewish people. We want to offer our deepest appreciation to you for helping to raise your son and/or daughter as a Jew.

You are part of a very important, diverse group of people. You might be living a Jewish life virtually in all respects. You might be devoutly committed to another faith. You might not define yourself as religious at all.

In a world that not so long ago saw one-third of its Jewish population destroyed, every Jewish child is precious. We are a very small people, and history has made us even smaller. Our children represent hope and they represent life. Every Jewish boy and girl is a gift to the Jewish future. With all of our heart, we want to thank you for your strength of spirit and generosity in giving the ultimate gift to the Jewish people.

Through your actions, you explain to your child why it is important to learn to be a Jew. You take classes or read Jewish books to deepen your own understanding. You create a Jewish home. You learn to make kugel and latkes; you try to like gefilte fish; you learn to put on a seder; and you build a sukkah in your backyard. You drive the carpool for religious school, and you join your spouse, partner, family, or friends around a beautiful Shabbat table.

You hum along to Hebrew songs and help guide your child to become bar or bat mitzvah. You tell them how proud you are of them and how glad you are to see them grow into young Jewish men and women.

We know that some of you have made personal sacrifices with the decision you made to raise a Jewish child. You may have given up the pleasure of sharing your own spiritual beliefs or passing down to your children your own religious traditions. It was Pharaoh's daughter, a non-Jew, who with *chesed* (kindness) nurtured the baby who became Moses our leader. Moses saved our people from Egyptian slavery, received Torah for us, and brought us to the gateway of the Promised Land. Similarly, you nurture your children, ensuring they grow up connected to the Jewish people. You are ensuring that Jewish values, Jewish tradition, and our community continue to shine brightly.

We want to express our deeply felt *chesed* for you by offering you this ancient blessing from the Torah:

> *Yivarech'cha Adonai v'yishm'recha.*
> May God bless you and watch over you.
>
> *Ya'er Adonai panav eilecha vichuneka.*
> May the light of the Holy One shine upon you and be gracious unto you.
>
> *Yisa Adonai panav eilecha v'yasem l'cha shalom.*
> May God be with you always and grant you the precious gift of peace.

Todah rabbah. Thank you very much.

Interact with Other Intermarried Families

If yours is an intermarried family and you feel disconnected, seek out a rabbi at a synagogue or a professional at the Jewish federation or community center to help you integrate. Such community leaders can help you find your way in.

Visit Big Tent Judaism / Jewish Outreach Institute (www.bigtentjudaism.org), an independent, national, transdenominational online organization reaching out to unaffiliated and intermarried families. Whether you are a parent of another religious background raising Jewish kids, a Jewish grandparent with interfaith grandchildren, or a Jew-by-choice, there is a point of entry.

Multicultural and Multiracial Jews Bring Beauty to the Mosaic

The Mishnah, a compilation of Jewish discussions from the second century CE, perceived the vast diversity of humanity as a miracle of God. Using the metaphor of imprinting coins, the Mishnah illustrates the miracle of our creation:

> When people create coins, they stamp each coin with the same image of the king. When the Holy One, blessed be God, minted all human beings with the divine seal with which the first person was made, not one of them is like anyone else. (*Mishnah Sanhedrin* 4:5)

According to Jewish tradition, in loving-kindness the Holy One breathes the *nishmat chaya* (living soul) into every human. We parents celebrate the diversity of creation when we draw our loved ones close and embrace their differences. We help our children see that they are gifts from God and vessels of deep spiritual import. We teach them *chesed* by ensuring that they see themselves and others as worthy of *chesed*.

Connect with Other Multicultural and Multiracial Families

Visit Be'chol Lashon—In Every Tongue (http://bechollashon.org), an online community that strengthens the Jewish people through ethnic, cultural, and racial inclusiveness and advocates for the diversity that has long characterized the Jewish people. Be'chol Lashon fosters an expanding Jewish community that embraces its diversity. However you define yourself, you will discover many in the Jewish community who celebrate this mosaic.

Guiding Our Children to Widen the Tent

We teach our children that they are intrinsically valued. Our desire to live with *chesed* leads us to shower them with unlimited, unconditional, unconditioned, and all-inclusive love. We hope that they too will shower others with this same God-inspired loving-kindness. At each moment, everywhere, we guide our children to widen the tent to embrace all of creation by modeling *chesed* in our everyday lives. Doing this, we too become beacons of spirituality, living that timeless truth: no one is more welcome than you!

11 Living Joyfully

Finding *Simcha* at the Center of Life

It is an enormous mitzvah to be happy always.

—Rabbi Nachman of Breslov, *Likkutei Moharan* 2:24

Michelle: Family Mystery Days—Finding Joy in the Unexpected

Building on the idea that the ordinary has the potential to become extraordinary, we planned "Family Mystery Days" filled with surprises for our young children. On these predetermined days, Paul and I woke early to pack the minivan with swimsuits, sleeping bags, and anything else required for the secret destination. When we woke the kids, asking, "Who is ready for a Family Mystery Day?" all three jumped out of bed, readily welcoming the day of surprises. As we backed out of the driveway, they excitedly plied us with questions and we slowly revealed clues.

Our first surprise destination was to the Mystery Spot, a house in the redwoods of Santa Cruz, California, where a gravitational anomaly grabs visitors' attention, challenging their perceptions of the laws of physics. We determined it was a perfect choice for a mystery day for Rachel, who loved all surprises; for Daniel, who could run and climb; and for Noah, whose mind would be drawn to the site's peculiarities.

At the Mystery Spot, we walked through a house where the floors, doors, and ceilings were at such impossible angles that they seemed to defy gravity. We looked at each other quizzically and, like all visitors, wondered how this could be. As we each stood at an unlikely angle, Paul and I observed that our kids were especially captivated by this activity. We realized that it did not take much to create a sense of adventure: a little preplanning, an openness to trying something new, and a desire to have fun.

Family Mystery Days soon became part of our family life. The mystery destination might be an overnight at a hotel with a big pool and a buffet breakfast (Daniel's favorite), a day at the beach or an aquarium (Noah's favorite), or a trip to Disneyland (Rachel's favorite).

On longer drives, Paul and I would point out shapes in the clouds that were "clues" to our destination: "Hmmm ... this one looks like an ice-cream cone; that one reminds me of a whale." The kids giggled, trying to decipher our clues. Their investigative minds raced to detect whether we were being straightforward or attempting to throw them off course. After much practice gazing into the sky, they began noticing and pointing out fascinating cloud shapes and beautiful sunsets. "Wow, look at all that red sky," Noah observed. "It looks like God," Daniel said. In those comments, we felt our goal was met; we wanted our children to build for themselves an appreciation of the breathtaking and glorious moments hidden inside the regular moments of family time.

Child development specialists remind us of the importance of routine schedules and predictability. Children need to feel safe, and part of that comes from knowing what is expected of them. This is especially significant for some children for whom predictability is central to their ability to have a nonanxious day. However, as veteran camp counselors and youth group advisors, we understand that for many children an element of surprise can contribute positively to their inner spiritual growth. Flexibility and buoyancy serve them well, as children will undoubtedly face many unpredictable moments in life. When they practice changing directions, they also exercise viewing the world as a journey packed with inherent possibility and joy.

The Many Different Kinds of Joy

Simcha (joy) is at the center of Jewish life. Or at least it is supposed to be. When Rabbi Nachman of Breslov declared *simcha* to be a great mitzvah, he derived his insight from the *Tanach* (Hebrew Bible). In the Torah, Moses chastised the Jewish people for not serving God with *simcha* when things were abundant, blaming their future problems on that lack of joy and gladness (Deuteronomy 28:47). King David called on Israel to "serve God with gladness; come before God's presence with *birnana* [a synonym for *simcha*]" (Psalm 100:2). In Chronicles, we are instructed, "Glory in God's holy name, let the hearts of those who seek God rejoice" (1 Chronicles 16:10). Rabbi Nachman explains that "the essential means of being connected to God is only through being in a consistent state of absolute joy, and to strengthen oneself to fully distance sadness and depression with all of one's strength."[1]

Being joyous when doing a mitzvah is as important as the mitzvah itself. Thirteenth-century Spanish rabbi Bachya ben Asher asserted, "A person is required to perform *mitzvot* with joy. The happiness that one experiences while performing a mitzvah is in itself a mitzvah."[2] Rabbi Isaac Luria once said that "all that he achieved—the fact that the gates of wisdom and divine inspiration were opened for him—was a reward for his observance of *mitzvot* with tremendous, limitless joy!"[3]

Avot D'Rabbi Natan, a minor tractate of the Talmud, lists ten words that are used to describe joy (*Avot D'Rabbi Natan* 34:9). But, according to our count, Judaism has at least four more. Each illuminates another facet of joy:

1. *Simcha*—considered the broadest word for joy, it also connotes complete happiness in its fullest sense
2. *Chedva*—pure and unfiltered, expressing the happiness of being with others
3. *Ditza*—awe-inspiring, related to dancing
4. *Gila*—a stronger sensation that bursts forth but is more transient and worldly (related to *gal*, meaning "wave")
5. *Hana'a*—enjoyment of something specific

6. *Nachas*—prideful joy brought on especially by our children
7. *Osher*—deeper, abiding, connected to a yearning for inner peace and a life of meaning
8. *Ora*—signifying both "light" and "joy," suggesting an interplay between awareness and uplift
9. *Pitzcha*—bursting into song
10. *Ranan*—being so overcome as to cry or shout out in joy
11. *Rina*—related to singing and shouting, often very revitalizing
12. *Sasson*—happiness coming on unexpectedly
13. *T'rua*—joy expressed in a shout or cheer
14. *Tzahala*—combining both happiness and dancing[4]

What can we learn from Judaism's overabundance of words for joy? Rabbi Yaakov Kranz, known as the Dubner Maggid, the famous storyteller of the eighteenth century, tells this parable:

> A jewelry merchant and a tool seller, traveling separately on business, checked into the same hotel in a certain town at the same time. The jewelry merchant had with him a small suitcase containing his diamonds, pearls, and other gems. The other merchant had a big, heavy trunk filled with hammers, saws, and other tools.
>
> The jewelry merchant asked a porter to take his suitcase up to his room. The porter came down soon afterward and presented himself for a tip, and the merchant gave him something. Instead of leaving, the porter coughed and shrugged, signifying his dissatisfaction with the tip amount. Finally, he mumbled that the suitcase was "terribly heavy" and extremely difficult to "drag up the stairs."
>
> The surprised merchant said to him, "If you're talking about a heavy suitcase and how hard it was to drag up the stairs, you have made a mistake. That was not my suitcase. My suitcase is very light. You took the wrong one!"[5]

The Dubner Maggid conveyed the essence of *simcha* in Judaism: if we find our involvement with Judaism—its rituals, celebrations, and customs—to be burdensome and heavy, we have made a mistake. If we find Judaism dull and deadening, we have picked up the wrong suitcase. Jewish life is meant to be an expression of joyous living.

Play the Jumping for Joy Game

With your child, point out recent experiences or moments that made each of you happy. Consider the following questions:

- How did that happiness feel in your heart?
- How did it affect your body?
- Did you smile broadly, smile internally, or laugh out loud?
- Was it a private joy, or did you want to share it with others?
- What did you—or someone else—do to make that joy happen?

Then choose which of the Jewish words for joy listed above best describes the feeling.

The next time one of you is happy, practice naming your joy and describing it. In this way, you highlight your happiness and name it as a spiritual practice. Soon you may find yourself seeking out joy in its many flavors. You may just end up jumping for joy!

Bringing *Simcha* into Our Celebrations

It is easy to say, "Be joyous!" It is far more complex to *live* joyously. Congregation Or Ami's vision statement records *simcha* as one of our synagogue's primary values. In our own lives and beside one another in the congregation, we aim to "celebrate life through word and song because we believe that life is filled with blessing."

Yet from the personal to the historical to the existential, we each face an army of forces arrayed against the impulse to be joyous. We live intensely cognizant of our own suffering, be it medical, familial, financial, psychological, or romantic. Such awareness itself conspires with the pain to keep us from our happiness and contentment.

Similarly, television news and online blogs are filled with reports of doom and gloom. Our jobs, our schools, and our daily lives are sometimes pressure-filled cauldrons of anxiety. Even Jewish history is easily reduced to a chronology of crisis—from slavery in Egypt through the Spanish Inquisition in 1492, from pogroms beginning in the 1820s through the Holocaust in the 1940s, to today's anti-Semitism. When the world pushes us in the other direction, how do we lead our families to continually embrace *simcha*?

At the same time, we get caught up in comparisons with others. Social media presents continual images of others enjoying themselves. When we compare our lives to the curated online lives of others, we sometimes wonder: Why we are not as happy?

Judaism as a religion, culture, and peoplehood is predisposed to joyfulness. *Simcha* permeates our Jewish calendar. The year begins with Rosh Hashanah and Yom Kippur, days often observed with solemnity but that lead us toward the kind of *osher* (contented joy) that comes from living meaningful lives. The calendar quickly moves to Sukkot, also called *z'man simchateinu* (season of our joy), when we celebrate in a sukkah with our family and friends. From there we dance into the holiday of Simchat Torah, literally "rejoicing with the Torah," a Jewish holiday that entices us with *ditza* to celebrate the centrality of Torah.

Chanukah, our Festival of Lights, rededicates us to Jewish living amid the fun and *ora* (bright joy) of candlelighting, dreidel spinning, presents, food, and family. Purim reminds us that the world can change from painful to hopeful and back again in the blink of an eye; we therefore don costumes and act silly as we celebrate our people's survival. Passover recalls a serious story but does so in the most child-friendly way: by letting us play with our symbolic foods and learn from the experience. Shavuot, celebrating the receiving of Torah at Mount Sinai, combines the *sasson*, the special joy of a wedding—between God and the Jewish people—with receiving the gift of Torah.

Shabbat: Our Weekly Respite of Joy

Of course, many other holidays in the Jewish calendar—Tu B'shvat, our Jewish arbor day; Yom Haatzmaut, Israel's independence day; and Lag BaOmer, a bonfire-filled festival—are joy-infused celebrations of the stories and values of our people. Yet all of these pale in comparison to Shabbat, the primary holy day of the Jewish year, arriving every seven days. Beginning Friday before sundown and continuing through Saturday night as three stars emerge in the sky, the Sabbath has beauty and uplift. Celebrated with *osher* (deep, meaningful joyfulness), Shabbat can bind parent to child and reinforce the holiness inherent in life. It becomes a touchstone each week, reminding everyone of the love in our hearts, the bonding in our families, and the joy in our world.

Cultural Zionist Ahad Ha'am taught that "more than the Jewish people kept Shabbat, Shabbat kept the Jewish people."[6] Week in and week out, this oasis of time provides Jewish families with the opportunity to create something special and celebratory apart from the rest of the week.

Shabbat is inextricably connected to *kedusha*. In Genesis at the end of the story of Creation: "And God blessed the seventh day and made it holy" (Genesis 2:3). Rabbi Abraham Joshua Heschel wrote, "One of the most distinguished words in the Bible is the word *kadosh*, holy; a word which more than any other is representative of the mystery and majesty of the divine. What was the first holy object in the history of the world?" Rabbi Heschel insightfully points out that this first holy thing—Shabbat—was neither a mountain nor an altar. It was a designated period of time. Heschel says, "There is no reference in the record of Creation to any object in space that would be endowed with the quality of holiness."[7]

Why should we parents prioritize Shabbat as a joyous Jewish practice? We might begin by exploring the power of Shabbat as a Jewish spiritual moment. Shabbat points us to six important holy experiences: awareness, Jewish identity, pleasure, family, spirituality, and the world to come.

- *Awareness*: Shabbat celebrates the creation of the world and our covenant with God. On Shabbat we remember that we are God's children, blessed to enjoy God's creations, and responsible for caring for our world and each other.
- *Jewish identity*: Shabbat rituals are our weekly opportunity to rise to new levels of holiness, helping us live our Jewishness in its fullness and pass it *l'dor vador* to our children.

- *Pleasure*: On Shabbat, we enjoy family time and holy time, as we share delicious food and restful moments filled with blessings, song, and celebration.
- *Family*: Setting aside family time to celebrate the holiness of Shabbat, we reaffirm the centrality of *mishpacha* (family) to our lives.
- *Spirituality*: Shabbat makes meaningful all we have done this past week and all that we strive to do in the week ahead. It provides us with a chance to pause, reflect on our blessings and accomplishments, and rejuvenate ourselves.
- *The world to come*: Shabbat is a taste of a future world, a better world. We are taught that if every Jewish family would celebrate two *Shabbatot* ("Shabbats") in a row, then the messianic age would be upon us.[8]

Some Jewish families observe the fullness of Shabbat with dinner on Friday night, a day at synagogue, a *seudat shlisheet* (third meal with friends), and a beautiful *Havdalah* ceremony to end Shabbat. Others do not. Many do some combination of these rituals, decided week by week.

We encourage parents to be intentional yet realistic in their expectations of self and family. Children create realities that do not always mesh with preconceived religious absolutes. Set goals for your family's Shabbat practice, but be compassionate and forgiving with yourselves. Neither set the bar unrealistically high nor reprimand yourself too harshly when you do not meet those goals. Let Shabbat be an opportunity for joy, not a burden to bear. As life changes—marital status, family size and structure, maturing children's temperaments, and our proximity to family and friends—so too may your Shabbat celebration evolve.

Our own Shabbat practice has evolved over time. When our children were little, we had Shabbat dinner together, often with grandparents and other friends. Occasionally, we would mix in a Tot Shabbat service—on Friday night or Saturday morning—at one of our local synagogues. As the kids grew, we took them regularly to temple services on the Friday nights when they seemed rested and able to enjoy them. As the children got older still, we invested them in Shabbat by giving them responsibility for setting the table with candles, challah, and *Kiddush* cups and for leading the blessings.

When they were in middle and high school, we encouraged our kids to invite their friends—and later girlfriends and boyfriends—to join us for dinner. They also attended youth group Shabbat gatherings to relish this holy time in the most socially rewarding way, among their peers.

Paul & Michelle: Shabbat Shalom from the Kitchen Floor

Noah was teething and not yet crawling; Rachel was five, and Daniel was three. It was Friday night, and after a full week of work, neither of us had the oomph for cooking or setting a special table, yet we relished the candlelight and wanted to keep our Shabbat family ritual.

Paul ordered a pizza and we slid to the kitchen floor for an impromptu picnic. Daniel grinned while sitting atop Paul's shoulders, and Noah snuggled into Michelle. Rachel swung her legs from her perch on the counter. We lit the candles, and the older kids led us in the ritual of closing our eyes and circling our hands three times. They explained proudly they learned in temple nursery school that we were bringing three rings of blessing—light, warmth, and love—toward our faces. Nestled close to one another we sang a boisterous *Kiddush* over the grape juice and *Hamotzi* over the challah. Daniel danced to the melodies, while Rachel belted out the words with confidence. Noah grinned and drooled. We blessed our children and each other with *Birkat Kohanim* (the Priestly Blessing), all the while struggling to keep from bursting out with laughter at the decidedly unorthodox setting. Pizza on paper plates with tomato sauce dripping everywhere made the moment especially delicious. We gave the kids a quick bath, slipped on their pajamas, put them in their beds, and collapsed beside each other on our bed.

We routinely welcomed Shabbat on Friday nights with the traditional rituals but on that particular night, Shabbat never seemed sweeter. The impromptu informality of the kitchen floor picnic felt just right for our young family.

Bless Candles, Grape Juice, Your Family, and Challah

Set aside Shabbat time on Friday night, even if you are going out later to the movies or to dinner. It takes but ten minutes to do the blessings. Only a modicum of planning is necessary to pick up a challah—available at most supermarkets and bakeries and even at some coffee or bagel shops—and to make sure you have candles and wine or grape juice at home. This short ritual marks this day as something special. In fact, this opening ritual for your night transforms a movie night into a spiritual practice of Shabbat *menucha* (rest).

Candlelighting

The lights in the room can be turned down or off. In nontraditional observance, any adult can light the matches, because both women and men are full participants in Jewish life. Allow a child to place a hand on the hand of the adult lighting the candles, emphasizing the trust and partnership we share in all spiritual matters. In time, the passage into maturity is actualized as a child is deemed responsible enough to light the candles alone. Ask everyone to cup their hands and make three small circles, bringing toward them "the light, the warmth, and the love." Covering your eyes, sing together the candle blessing. Opening your eyes, share smiles.

Rabbi Bruce Block explains the Ashkenazi custom of lighting Shabbat candles first, covering our eyes, reciting the blessing, and then uncovering our eyes to admire the candlelight. He asks, "What is the first command God utters?" Pointing to Genesis 1:3, "*Yehi or*—let there be light," Rabbi Block teaches that "God articulated words, commanding that there be light, and behold, there was light. If an element of Shabbat is the commemoration of Creation, then symbolically we imitate God's action by first saying words out loud and then opening our eyes to see that there is indeed light. This sequence reinforces our effort to be God's partners in the ongoing work of creation."[9]

Grape Juice: *Kiddush*

For the *Kiddush* (literally, "sanctification" or "making holy"), you might choose grape juice over wine, deciding that your children need not develop a taste for wine until they are older. Some people share one cup, passing it around the table after the blessing. We use a *Kiddush* fountain from Israel that uses one large cup to distribute its grape juice via spouts into eight smaller cups. The children love watching the juice pour into each cup and appreciate that they can each lift their own mini-*Kiddush* cup.

You might begin by saying, "Just as this grape juice is sweet, so may our days and our lives be sweet." The *Kiddush* has two parts, the first being a short blessing over the wine. The second longer paragraph ushers in Shabbat by recalling Creation, remembering the Exodus from Egypt, and naming this day as holy. Through words, we transform ordinary into holy.

Family Blessing: *Birkat Kohanim*

On Shabbat in many families, the father blesses the mother with the *Eshet Chayil* (Woman of Valor) blessing from Proverbs, and the mother blesses the father with a section from Psalms. Together, parents bless their children with *Birkat Kohanim* (the Priestly Blessing). In our home, this ritual morphed into a family blessing:

We hold hands in a circle around the table as everyone recites the blessing out loud—first in Hebrew, then in English—to bless one another. When guests are present, one person says the words aloud, inviting others to repeat them. In this way, everyone can participate in blessing each other. When older children are away at college, enjoy a quick Shabbat call to recite the family blessing together; on occasion, a text or voice-mail message will need to suffice. Kisses follow the blessing, as you wish each other *Shabbat shalom* (a Sabbath of peace) and seal with love the hope for peacefulness. In elementary school, our kids created a "Shabbat train," moving in a line around the table, sharing kisses with each person, reinforcing the values of *mishpacha* (family) and *ahava* (love).

Challah: *Hamotzi*

Nothing tastes better than a warm challah. Papa braided and baked challah for our holiday dinners. You might learn to bake challah, use pre-prepared challah dough, or buy challah for your Shabbat table.

Borrowing a tradition from Jewish summer camp, after removing the challah cover, invite everyone at your table to place a hand on the challah and sing a version of the *Hamotzi* prayer:

Baruch atah Adonai Eloheinu Melech ha'olam,
Hamotzi lechem min ha'aretz. Amen.
Blessed are You, Adonai our God, Guide of the universe,
Who brings forth bread from the earth.

The preschool version:

Hamotzi lechem min ha'aretz,
We give thanks to God for bread.
Our voices join in song together,
As our joyful prayer is said.
Baruch atah Adonai Eloheinu Melech ha'olam,
Hamotzi lechem min ha'aretz. Amen.

Or the longer URJ Camp Newman version:

Baruch El asher bara,
Mazon lakol l'tova v'livracha.
Va'anachnu, va'anachnu,
Bameh, bameh, nodeh lo
La la la la la la la la la la
Baruch hu u'varuch sh'mo.
Baruch atah Adonai Eloheinu Melech ha'olam,
Hamotzi lechem min ha'aretz. Amen.

Shabbat, more than anything, is a gift. As parents, we are continually running. Our children are often busy too. Shabbat gives us time to pause from our week and return to ourselves: physically (slowing down), emotionally (connecting to loved ones), and spiritually (grounding ourselves in the security of ritual). Observing Shabbat ensures that we make time for spiritual reflection and inspiration.

Creating Joyful Jewish Celebrations

We know how to bring *rina* and *gila* into a wedding, a bar or bat mitzvah, or a *brit milah* or *brit bat* (ceremonies welcoming a new baby son or daughter into the covenant with God). Most of us too know how to make a birthday celebration festive. But how do we transform other Jewish experiences into high points of family life? By employing the same techniques we use to create fun elsewhere, we can develop memorable Jewish celebrations.

Michelle: Tailoring the Celebration to Your Unique Child, Part 1

Create exciting celebrations by taking into account the personalities within your family. Tailoring experiences to your unique mix allows joy to burst forth from each holiday experience. How you celebrate is as key to success as what you celebrate.

Some of us love to be surprised while others do not. Our daughter, Rachel, was born an enthusiastic participant. From her earliest moments in the maternity ward, she engaged in the world. Rachel loves surprises; impromptu activities bring her immense delight. On her third birthday, as Rachel woke from her nap, I whispered in her ear, "How would you like to have a birthday party in the backyard?" Thank goodness, as we anticipated, Rachel's face lit up. Within minutes, she was barely able to contain her excitement. Our well-rested little girl (part of the plan!) relished her celebration alongside her friends on lawn blankets, with her cousin, "Annie the Clown," entertaining. Rachel then went on to savor every bite of birthday cake. I call Rachel a "citizen of the world" because to this day she unearths joy in new tastes, sights, cultures, and experiences. For Rachel, we fill holiday celebrations with spontaneity and imagination.

Try This Surprise the Child Who Loves Surprises

If your child loves surprises, build them into your holiday celebrations. Around Tu B'shvat in the early winter, plan a Family Mystery Day to plant trees. Around Shavuot, when we traditionally eat dairy, surprise your child with an ice-cream or cheesecake crawl, visiting ice-cream parlors and bakeries to taste and compare flavors. At Rosh Hashanah, serve a surprise birthday cake to celebrate the birthday of the world. If surprises bring your child joy, bring those surprises into Jewish living.

Michelle: Tailoring the Celebration to Your Unique Child, Part 2

When the boys were young, I brought Noah and Daniel to the school playground each morning for fifteen minutes of play before class began. Noah was three years old; Daniel was five and a half.

One day, the sandpit looked different. We noticed that a hole had been dug in anticipation of a new slide. A temporary but sturdy wood plank strategically bisected the pit, allowing children to cross safely from side to side. A quick glance at this new configuration and Daniel, without a moment's hesitation, raced across the plank. Physically uninhibited, Daniel was elated. Since Daniel experiences the world through movement and physicality, we include both in our holiday celebrations.

The wood plank remained in the sandpit for a week. With caution, Noah surveyed the makeshift bridge but on the first two days turned aside to go down the old slide. On day three, zooming across the plank, Daniel implored his brother, "Nooooaaah, you *have* to try this—it's grreat!" Noah chose to stick with what he knew. On day five, Noah approached the plank, tapping it lightly with his toe to examine it. Convinced that it was sturdy, he took a tentative first step and, with bolstered confidence, moved forward guardedly, gradually increasing his pace. Traversing that temporary bridge was a literal step out of his comfort zone.

Noah finds *hana'a* (enjoyment of something specific) in a new accomplishment, but he does so on his terms, in his time frame. He feels capable after having gathered the facts and doing his own observational research. Today, when planning holiday celebrations, we bear in mind how Noah is reassured by a reliable set of expectations.

The Joy of Infusing Time with Meaning and Awareness

When Joni Mitchell wrote "The Circle Game," she captured the continuous progression of time, the whimsical yet somber reality that we are getting older. She likened the passage of time to being on a carousel, always moving in one direction, leaving us in a position from which we can only look back. Acknowledging that we cannot stop time, her song imagined that we are captive to time's dictates, locked in by the loss of our youth. By contrast, Pete Seeger and the Limeliters sang in the 1950s, and the Byrds in the 1960s, "To everything turn, turn, turn, there is a season turn, turn, turn." They quoted the biblical sage in Ecclesiastes, who taught that there is always a time and a place for every emotion and experience we might have (Ecclesiastes 3:1–8).[10]

Mindful Jewish living brings timelessness into our lives. Judaism views time as a joyous cycle that—when approached with optimism and intentionality—provides seasons infused with meaningful celebration. The unceasing progression of time is insignificant in this cycle. With *kavannah*, we experience *kedusha* (holiness) and we elevate *simcha* to new heights.

We each have a choice. We can let the passing years make us bitter and grumpy, or we can celebrate with our family the holiness of life even as the days pass by.

Engage in Mindful Holy Days

Alone, and with your child:

- Make Rosh Hashanah a time to celebrate the birthday of the world. Take a walk together outside to appreciate nature. At the holiday table, count the blessings in your life. Purchase a shofar so that your child can learn to sound it. The unique sound of the ram's horn will linger in children's memories as an uplifting element of the Jewish New Year.
- Make an honest account of your life on Yom Kippur. Adults and children, especially teenagers, can imagine what their ideal self might be. Decide which steps each of you can take this month to bring you closer to your ideal you. ("I will be more patient with my sister." "I am going to volunteer at the local soup kitchen.")
- Build a sukkah with family and friends and eat meals together inside, reminding yourself what is precious. (Learn about sukkah building in the *L'dor vador* chapter.)

- Encircle your family with Torah's blessings and dance with *simcha* on Simchat Torah at your local synagogue. Or at home, intersperse Jewish dance music with secular party music and hold your own Simchat Torah family dance-a-thon.

Chanukah: An Opportunity for Meaningful Spiritual Connections

For parents intent on raising spiritually aware children, Chanukah is a gift. Beyond the candlelighting, the gift giving, and the dreidel spinning, Chanukah at its core is a spiritual holiday filled with *chedva* (happiness of togetherness) and *rina* (refreshing joy and song). Our children so anticipate the holiday that their minds and hearts are uniquely open to spiritual lessons. Even before the wrapping paper is ripped off, we have the chance to wrap our children in deep, joyful Jewish spirituality.

Rabbi Dan Ehrenkrantz, former president of the Reconstructionist Rabbinical College, illuminates the lesson of candlelighting at the heart of Chanukah. Traditional menorah lighting had three elements: fire, wick, and oil. The fire ignited the wick, and the oil (or, today, the wax candle) provided fuel for a continuous flame. Similarly, he suggests, our children may find spiritual connection in life by means of the same three elements: a creative spark (the holiness inside of us, like the flame) burns strongly within each child (who are like wicks) and continues to do so as long as the child provides it with sustenance through an intentional spiritual practice (the oil or candle).

Each element is essential for the development of our spiritual life. In fact, when we bring together the first letters of the Hebrew words for flame (*ner*), wick (*petil*), and oil (*shemen*)—*nun, pei, shin*—they form the Hebrew word *nefesh,* or soul. Each Chanukah candle is symbolic of our soul, a holy part within that allows us to live spiritually connected to each other, to the world, and to the Eternal Soul who energizes the universe. In that meaningful connection, *osher*—a deep, lasting happiness born by meaning and inner peace—can envelop us.[11]

How can we make Chanukah a joyous spiritual practice instead of merely a ritual justification for giving presents? We do so by intensifying our celebration of Chanukah, bringing together all the elements of meaningful holiday festivities. In the spirit of the Talmud, Paul once created this quasi-traditional rabbinic text:

> The Calabasas Rebbe teaches: One who does not do eight things during Chanukah ...
>
> Retell the story,
> Sing the songs,
> Sing the blessings, then place the lit menorah in a window,
> Eat latkes or *sufganiot* (jelly-filled donuts),
> Play dreidel,
> Give *tzedakah* to others,
> Give gifts to parents, and
> Celebrate with community
>
> ... is like one who stands at a beautiful sunrise with her eyes closed.[12]

Elevate Chanukah Eight Times

To make Chanukah—or any of our Jewish holidays—inspirational and infused with *simcha* requires that our preparations have the same level of forethought as any secular celebration, like a birthday or Thanksgiving. Special foods, fun activities, gift giving, storytelling, helping others, and singing songs—all of this needs to be part of our celebration.

Plan out each night of your Chanukah celebration to include a few of these rituals:

1. *Retell the story*: Chanukah celebrates the triumph of Jewish values over Greek pagan practice, when religious freedom prevailed over religious coercion. It reminds us to cherish our religious freedom. Chanukah gains meaning when its story and its lessons are made clear. Go online (www.reformjudaism.org) to find an age-appropriate version of the story. Let each participant read a

portion aloud. Conclude by inviting participants to share one lesson they learn from Chanukah.

2. *Sing Chanukah songs*: Counter King Antiochus's impulse to annihilate the Jews with *simcha*, the impulse to celebrate life and Jewish living. Singing is the glue that binds our Jewish soul with Jewish values in a way that we remember. Our favorite Chanukah songs, including original tunes by Cantor Doug Cotler, are collected at www.orami.org/Chanukah.[13]
3. *Sing the blessings and place the lit menorah in a window*: We celebrate the miracle of the oil and the continually burning creative spark within us by singing the blessings in Hebrew, then translating to English. By lighting the candles and placing the lit menorah in a front-facing window, we publicize the miracle of our existence as a Jewish family and the light that burns within.
4. *Eat latkes or* sufganiot *(jelly-filled donuts)*: *Latkes* are an Eastern European Ashkenazic tradition, while *sufganiot* are Middle Eastern Jewish delicacies. Both oil-cooked foods allow our children to symbolically ingest the Chanukah message: that oil enough for only one night lasted for eight nights. By consuming these foods, we become the oil, fortifying ourselves to hold on to our Jewish values.
5. *Play the dreidel game*: The dreidel game teaches that *nes gadol haya sham* (a great miracle happened there). Interweave explanations of the miracles of Chanukah around the competitive dreidel-spinning game. Play with chocolate candy (*gelt*), yogurt-covered raisins, or nuts, and the spoils are tasty too. (Kids always seem to have fun playing with their food.) Each player antes up into a common bank. The dreidel is spun. Winning or losing depends on which letter shows when the spinning stops. *Nun* stands for "nothing"; the player neither gives nor takes from the bank. *Gimel* stands for "get all"; the player takes the whole bank. *Hei* stands for "half"; the player takes half the bank. *Shin* stands for "put in"; the player adds two to the bank. (If the bank empties, each player antes up again.)
6. *Give* tzedakah *(charitable donations)*: Set aside at least one night for giving *tzedakah* to others instead of presents to each other. We emphasize the Jewish spiritual imperative that every moment of celebration is an opportunity for *tikkun olam*, to lift up others who

are in need. Everyone, including children, can contribute something; parents might multiply children's donations to make it a family donation. As a family, designate which causes and organizations you want to send your *tzedakah* to, including your local synagogue, often the gateway to Jewish life. Your children can go online with you and make the donation that very night after lighting candles.

7. *Give gifts to parents*: Set aside one night for children to give gifts to parent or other adults. On this night, children should not receive gifts, to teach our children the Jewish values of *kibud av v'em* (honoring one's father and mother), and that when we love another, we strive to give even more than we receive. Young children can make gifts using art supplies. A child's gift could also be cleaning the kitchen or folding a basket of clothes. Older children can choose gifts they think Mommy or Daddy might appreciate. A single parent can deputize friends or grandparents to help children prepare this night's present. Each child's heartfelt wishes can be written on a card they make or reflected by dictating the words to you. Let the child experience the memorable elation and *sasson* (sudden, unexpected happiness) of gift giving.
8. *Celebrate with community*: We enhance the meaning of the holiday when we gather with others. In larger groups, we can emphasize the power of Chanukah's spiritual message. Children can don costumes and act out the Chanukah story. Older children and adult relatives become the teachers of the tradition. Most synagogues host a family-friendly Chanukah celebration open to the community.

When we resist the urge to allow the holiday to simply be about gifts, we teach our children *osher*. Then we can rejoice in the meaning of the Festival of Lights for eight inspiring nights.

Shining the Light for Others: Prayers to Recite at Chanukah

Holidays become even more meaningful when we take time to think about and care for others. Gratitude and *simcha* go hand in hand. Just as Thanksgiving prompts many to serve food to the hungry, every Jewish holy day has some *tzedakah* activity associated with it. On Purim, we prepare *matanot l'evyonim* (gifts for the poor); on Shabbat we can place coins in the *tzedakah* box before lighting the candles.

On Chanukah, we turn our thoughts each night to a different group of people who could benefit from our prayers. Guests can suggest other individuals who need our love and care. In the midst of our own blessings, we want to remember that others are in need of blessings too.

Dedicate Each Chanukah Candle to Others

Dedicate a candle to those in need of blessing, healing, safety, shelter, or food by reciting one of these prayers before lighting the candles:[14]

- *For people in need*: May the light of the Chanukah candles remind us that there are always others who need our help. May the One who brings us light remind us that there are those in need of more help than ourselves.
- *For healing*: May the light of the Chanukah candles transform us into agents of healing. May the One who brings us light help us to find cures for illness, strengthen the caregivers, provide healing to the sick, and restore them to full health.
- *For American and Israeli soldiers*: May the light of the Chanukah candles bring aid in times of war. May the One who brings us light help the troops defending America and the State of Israel, stateside and abroad; may they return safely to their families.
- *For the poor*: May the light of the Chanukah candles bring warmth and brighten the lives of those who currently experience poverty. May the One who brings us light help humanity to provide for one another and to ensure that everyone has food to eat, clothes to wear, a warm bed to sleep on, and an education to enlighten.
- *For the State of Israel*: May the light of the Chanukah candles enable us to cherish Israel and hold her in our consciousness. May the One who brings us light create in us an everlasting feeling of oneness with Israel and her people.

- *For those living through tragedy*: May the light of the Chanukah candles bring light to those who have lost hope. May the One who brings us light enlighten the lives of those who are suffering from trauma.
- *For those who are bullied*: May the light of the Chanukah candles inspire us to stand up for others when they have been bullied or mistreated. May the One who brings us light give us strength and wisdom to always model kindness and respect.
- *For all of humanity*: May the light of the Chanukah candles be a reminder that God created humanity in God's image, man and woman alike. May the One who brings us light teach us that every individual is like an entire world, and each soul is a flame of the Holy One.

Smiling When You Don't Feel Like It

Every child and every family encounters bumps along life's path that challenge our ability to see blessing and goodness in spite of the problems. How much more difficult to find *simcha* in those life chapters!

The *Tikunei Zohar*, an appendix of seventy commentaries on the opening word of Torah, notes that the Hebrew word for "in happiness" (*b'simcha*) contains the same Hebrew letters as the word for "thought" (*machshava*), just in a different order. This teaches us that "the key to happiness is often found through our minds." Michael Green conveys the *Tikunei Zohar*'s lesson, suggesting that "we can train ourselves to weed out negative feelings" that prevent us from experiencing happiness.[15]

Our yoga instructor periodically reminds us to smile during our yoga practice, because smiling releases endorphins that make us feel happy. Similarly, the late twentieth-century rabbi Menachem Mendel Schneerson of Chabad counseled that by assuming the demeanor and mannerisms of one who is joyful, even if we do not feel happy, we will cultivate true feelings of happiness, because behaviors and actions impact the heart.[16]

This attitude helped us through difficult experiences. We learned that *simcha* is possible even during dark times. By pushing ourselves toward happiness, we were able to face some unpredictable moments.

One year, we had an unwelcome family surprise. In the middle of the night, a pipe burst silently in a bathroom and water seeped quietly down the hallways and into the rooms while we slept. We needed to move out of our home and into a rental to allow for the extensive repair. Our collective resilience was put to the test. Many items were destroyed—sentimental favorites (baseball cards, beloved hats and toys) and costly items (computers, furniture, a television). As we watched these objects relegated to the dumpster, we rediscovered as a family what matters most: each other and our health.

It was reassuring to learn that year, individually and as a family, that while our address and neighbors had changed, at its core we were still "us." While dwelling elsewhere temporarily, we relied on the reserve of our family's cohesiveness as a unit (so well that one of the kids wanted to stay in the rental home).

During those moments when we did not feel joy, we sometimes followed the advice of Rabbi Nachman of Breslov, who suggested that acting with a demeanor of happiness can lead us toward truly feeling happy.[17] This experience challenged us to review our priorities, to find comfort amid the dislocation. We concluded that our top priority was being together as a family, wherever that might be.

Singer Pharrell Williams's song "Happy" won a Grammy award and an Academy Award nomination. It became the best-selling song in 2014 in the United States, selling millions of copies.[18] Although one might attribute its success to the catchy tune, we believe the song's popularity reflects a universal impulse to be happy.

The blessings of parenthood are infinite. We place joy and happiness among our most important Jewish spiritual parenting goals. With our eyes, hearts, and arms wide open, we pursue *simcha* to guide ourselves and our families to reach for life's glorious possibilities.

Acknowledgments

We learn from our Eastern European Jewish ancestors that when goodness comes our way, we should be careful about speaking about it too loudly lest we attract *ayin hara* (the evil eye), which wants nothing more than to turn blessings into curses. Though we are not particularly superstitious, we feel that deeply embedded shtetl impulse to spit (*ptew, ptew, ptew*) at the evil eye after each mention of the goodness in our lives and in the lives of our children.

Like each of us, our children—Rachel, Daniel, and Noah—are works in progress. We are proud of who they are, and we know that they will face challenges and obstacles in life, which in the blink of an eye can transform blessing and hope into sadness and pain. We remain parents, concerned for our children's well-being and praying for continued blessing in their futures. We thank them for being inspiring human beings and for generously allowing us to share the stories in which they are featured.

We deeply appreciate the insights of many people highlighted in *Jewish Spiritual Parenting*. We are especially grateful for the closeness we share with each of our parents: Teri and Murray November and Linda and Ken Kipnes. They continue to inspire us as parents and grandparenting role models. We acknowledge a multitude of Jewish communities where we honed our skills guiding youth and parents, and where we raised our children: URJ Camps Newman (Santa Rosa, California), Swig (Saratoga, California), Kutz Teen Leadership Institute (Warwick, New York) and Camp Hess Kramer (Malibu, California); the Reform Movement's North American Federation of Temple Youth (NFTY); Southern California synagogues, including Congregation Or Ami (Calabasas), Temple Beth Hillel (Valley Village), Stephen Wise Temple (Los Angeles) and Wilshire Boulevard Temple (Los Angeles); and many educational institutions, including de Toledo High School (West Hills). We thank our colleagues, the directors, faculty, clergy, staff, leadership, congregants, students, and campers for being part of the village it took to train us and help us raise our children. We especially thank our dear friends who have journeyed along with us as we helped raise each other's children. (You know who you are.)

We are deeply appreciative that Stuart M. Matlins, founder and publisher of Jewish Lights, invited us to share our love of parenting in a book. We are indebted to the wonderful people at Jewish Lights—our editors Emily Wichland, Rachel Shields, and Debra Hirsch Corman, and also to Leah Brewer, Barbara Heise, and Tim Holtz—for guiding us with warmth and finesse to birth this, our first book; this book lives because of you.

The seed for *Jewish Spiritual Parenting* was born from Paul's blog (http://paulkipnes.com). We thank Scott Cooper for suggesting, "There's a book in there." We are grateful for the wisdom and primary source references of colleagues from CCAR (Central Conference of American Rabbis), JEDLAB (Jewish Education Lab), and ARJE (Association of Reform Jewish Educators, formerly National Association of Temple Educators), especially through their Facebook groups.

As *Jewish Spiritual Parenting* goes to print, we celebrate twenty-five years of marriage and almost as long of parenthood. Parenting is the most challenging, rewarding, exhausting, and wonderful thing we have ever done. So we thank each other—for waking up daily and reinvesting in each other, our family, and our future together. We are blessed.

Finally, we also honor our partnership with the Holy One. Somewhere out there and in here, there is a reality we call God, who infuses each moment with hope and blessing. Connected with *Ein Sof* (that which is "without end"), we continue on the lifelong journey of nurturing spiritually healthy children.

Notes

Introduction

1. Ronald H. Isaacs, "What Parents 'Owe' Their Children," in *Beginnings—Raising a Jewish Child: Early Years* (New York: United Synagogue of Conservative Judaism Commission on Jewish Education, 2000), accessible at www.uscj.org/JewishLivingandLearning/FamilyLife/RaisingJewishChildren/WhatParents_Owe_TheirChildren.aspx.

Chapter 1

1. These articles of faith are found in Moses Maimonides's commentary on *Mishnah Sanhedrin* 10. They are also referred to as the Thirteen Creeds.
2. Karyn D. Kedar, "*Va-era*: The Many Names of God," in *The Women's Torah Commentary: New Insights from Women Rabbis on the 54 Weekly Torah Portions*, ed. Elyse Goldstein (Woodstock, VT: Jewish Lights, 2008), 132.
3. Arthur Green, *Seek My Face: A Jewish Mystical Theology* (Woodstock, VT: Jewish Lights, 2012), 8.
4. *Midrash Tanchuma, Pekudei* 3, end.
5. Institute for Jewish Spirituality, www.jewishspirituality.org/about-us/common-questions/ (accessed February 16, 2015).
6. Micah D. Greenstein, "Jewish Spirituality: 10 Ways to Be a Spiritual Person," Explorefaith.org, www.explorefaith.org/livingspiritually/following_a_sacred_path/jewish_spirituality.php#one (accessed February 16, 2015).
7. Ibid.
8. Ibid.
9. See Stuart M. Matlins, ed., *The Jewish Lights Spirituality Handbook: A Guide to Understanding, Exploring & Living a Spiritual Life* (Woodstock, VT: Jewish Lights, 2001).
10. David Wolpe, "Taking to Children about God," *Huffington Post*, June 14, 2010, www.huffingtonpost.com/rabbi-david-wolpe/talking-to-children-about_b_611174.html.
11. Robert Fowler, *Stages of Faith: The Psychology of Human Development and the Quest for Meaning* (New York: Harper One, 1995).
12. Sarah Reines, "How to Talk about God," Kveller.com, www.kveller.com/article/how-to-talk-about-god/ (accessed March 5, 2015).

Chapter 2

1. Moses Maimonides, commentary on *Pirkei Avot* 2:6.
2. Maurice Lamm, "Marriage and Community," Myjewishlearning.com. www.myjewishlearning.com/life/Relationships/Spouses_and_Partners/About_Marriage/Marriage_and_Community.shtml (accessed February 23, 2015).
3. Ibid.
4. Rabbi Moses Nachmanides, commentary on Genesis 2:23–24.
5. "Jewish Husbands, Jewish Wives, and Jewish Partners," Myjewishlearning.com, www.myjewishlearning.com/life/Relationships/Spouses_and_Partners.shtml (accessed February 26, 2015).
6. Rashi, the eleventh-century biblical commentator from Provence, France, notes that God instructed Abraham to "take up" (*v'ha'aleihu*) his son to the top of the mountain, not to "sacrifice" (*sh'chateihu*) him. From this, Rashi suggests that God intended only that Abraham bring his son up to the mountaintop for a spiritual experience. Abraham seemed to misunderstand God's intention.
7. *Zohar* on *Lech Lecha*: "*And Abram took Sarai his wife*. The word 'took' signifies that he pleaded with her and persuaded her. For a man is not permitted to take his wife with him to another country without her consent."
8. Richard Ferber, *Solve Your Child's Sleep Problems* (New York: Touchstone, 2006).
9. Wendy Mogel, *The Blessing of a Skinned Knee: Using Jewish Teachings to Raise Self-Reliant Children* (New York: Charles Scribner, 2008); and *The Blessing of a B Minus: Using Jewish Teachings to Raise Resilient Teenagers* (New York: Charles Scribner, 2011).
10. "Jewish Parent/Child Relationships," Myjewishlearning.com, www.myjewishlearning.com/article/jewish-parentchild-relationships/ (accessed February 26, 2015).

Chapter 3

1. Yosef Eisen, *Miraculous Journey: A Complete History of the Jewish People from Creation to the Present*, rev. ed. (Southfield, MI: Targum/Feldheim, 2004), 213.
2. Lawrence Kushner, *I'm God; You're Not: Observations on Organized Religion & Other Disguises of the Ego* (Woodstock, VT: Jewish Lights, 2012), 188.
3. Eugene Borowitz, *Exploring Jewish Ethics: Papers on Covenant Responsibility* (Detroit: Wayne State University Press, 1990), 327.
4. Isa Aron, *The Self-Renewing Congregation: Organizational Strategies for Revitalizing Congregational Life* (Woodstock, VT: Jewish Lights, 2002), 92.

Chapter 4

1. Jewish tradition identifies Mount Horeb and Mount Sinai as the same mountain.
2. Jonathan Sacks, "Covenant and Conversation: The Blessings of Grandchildren." December 18, 2010, Orthodox Union, www.ou.org/torah/parsha/rabbi-sacks-on-parsha/the_blessings_of_grandchildren/.
3. Ibid.
4. Kay Pomerantz, "Jewish Grandparenting," MyJewishLearning.com, www.myjewishlearning.com/life/Relationships/Parents_and_Children/Grandparenting.shtml (accessed February 19, 2015).
5. Ibid.
6. See our chapter on *simcha* (joy) for a fuller exploration of this prayer.
7. Adapted from Micah Peltz, "In Through the Out Dor" (sermon, Temple Beth Sholom, Cherry Hill, NJ, 2011), www.tbsonline.org/site/files/833/105234/363003/573090/In_Through_the_Out_Dor_-_Final+-1.pdf.
8. "Sukkot," Temple Isaiah website, www.templeisaiah.com/sukkot (accessed March 8, 2015).
9. Lawrence Kushner, *Invisible Lines of Connection: Sacred Stories of the Ordinary* (Woodstock, VT: Jewish Lights, 1998), 41.
10. Sunie Levin, *Mingled Roots: A Guide for Grandparents of Interfaith Children* (New York: URJ Press, 2003), 7–9.
11. Ibid.
12. Find out more about URJ Camps at http://urjyouth.org/camps/.

Chapter 5

1. See, for example, Ira F. Stone, "Truthfulness: *Emet*," Mussar Leadership, www.mussarleadership.org/pdfs/Emet%20(truthfulness).pdf (accessed February 27, 2015).
2. Arthur Green, *These Are the Words: A Vocabulary of Jewish Spiritual Life* (Woodstock, VT: Jewish Lights, 1999), 12.
3. Rashi on Deuteronomy 6:6, *Sifrei* 6:6.
4. Jack Riemer and Nathaniel Stampfer, eds., *Ethical Wills and How to Prepare Them* (Woodstock, VT: Jewish Lights, 2015).
5. *Midrash Tanchuma, VaYakhel* 1: "A person is called by three names: one that parents give him, one that people call her, and one that he acquires himself. The best one is the one that you acquire yourself."
6. Moshe Hayyim Luzzatto, *Derech HaShem, The Way of God* (eighteenth century): "A person has the power of choice, and is able to choose either side, knowingly and willingly, and possess whichever one he wishes. Humans were therefore created with both a good urge [*yetzer hatov*] and an evil urge [*yetzer hara*]."

7. Adapted from the teachings of the Josephson Institute of Ethics (http://josephsoninstitute.org).

Chapter 6

1. Bernard Bamberger, "The Life of Holiness," in *The Torah: A Modern Commentary*, ed. Gunther Plaut (New York: Union of American Hebrew Congregations, 1981), 891–92.
2. Abraham Joshua Heschel, *Moral Grandeur and Spiritual Audacity: Essays* (New York: Farrar, Straus and Giroux, 1997), 342.
3. Samuel M. Stahl, "A Father Anticipates His Daughter's Marriage," in *Boundaries, Not Barriers: Some Uniquely Jewish Perspectives on Life* (Austin, TX: Eakin Press, 2005), 9–13. Originally a sermon given March 7, 1997, by Rabbi Samuel M. Stahl.
4. Ibid.
5. Nachman of Breslov, *Likkutei Moharan* I 65:2.
6. Tamar Frankiel and Judy Greenfeld, *Minding the Temple of the Soul: Balancing Body, Mind and Spirit Through Traditional Jewish Prayer, Movement, and Meditation* (Woodstock, VT: Jewish Lights, 1997), 26.
7. Aqua, "Good Morning Sunshine," on *Aquarium* (1997); Craig Taubman, "Boker Tov," on *How Good* (2010).
8. Abraham Joshua Heschel, *God in Search of Man: A Philosophy of Judaism* (New York: Farrar, Straus and Giroux, 1976), 49.
9. Thanks to educator Rachel Margolis and Rabbi Ari Margolis, Rabbi Kate Speizer, Rabbi Zoe Klein, Susan Kroll, Rabbi Seth Stander, and Rabbi Alex Shuval-Weiner for sharing their morning intention-setting words and rituals via Facebook.
10. Deborah Echt-Moxness, *Keeper of Traditions: Family Activities to Strengthen Connections and Celebrate Life Every Day* (CreateSpace Independent Publishing Platform, 2013), 43.
11. Adapted from *Hashkiveinu*, music by Mah Tovu (S. Brodsky and J. Zweibach, text Evening Liturgy ©1996. Music and text for *Shelter Us*, by Larry Jonas, in *The Complete Shireinu: 350 Fully Noted Jewish Songs*, ed. Joel N. Eglash (New York: URJ Transcontinental Music, 2001), 276. Used by permission.

Chapter 7

1. Moses Maimonides, *Mishneh Torah*, *Hilchot Teshuva* 3:6–8.
2. Arthur Green, *Radical Judaism: Rethinking God and Tradition* (New Haven, CT: Yale University Press, 2010), 121–22.
3. Jonathan Slater, commentary on *Mei Hashilo'ach*, *Bamidbar*, Institute for Jewish Spirituality, www.jewishspirituality.org/resources/past-text-studies/ (accessed March 9, 2015).

4. Ibid.
5. Shalom Freedman and Irving Greenberg, *Living in the Image of God: Jewish Teachings to Perfect the World: Conversations with Rabbi Irving Greenberg* (New York: Jason Aronson, 1998), 67.
6. Daniel Siegel, *And God Braided Eve's Hair* (New York: United Synagogue of America, 1976), 3, revised by the poet, and used with permission.
7. Freedman and Greenberg, *Living in the Image of God*, 68.
8. Based on a *metta* meditation by Rabbi Sheila Weinberg, Institute of Jewish Spirituality.

Chapter 8

1. Kasey Edwards, "When Your Mother Says She's Fat," *Huffington Post*, January 6, 2014, www.huffingtonpost.com/kasey-edwards/when-your-mother-says-shes-fat_b_4482899.html. Ms. Edwards also writes at www.kaseyedwards.com.
2. Philo Judaeus, *The Worse Attacks the Better*, section 10, cited in Francine Klagsbrun, *Voices of Wisdom: Jewish Ideals and Ethics for Everyday Living* (Middle Village, NY: Jonathan David, 1986), 210.
3. Moses Maimonides, *Mishneh Torah, Hilchot De'ot* 4:1.
4. Yirmiyahu Ullman, "Physical Health," www.asktherabbi.org/DisplayQuestion.asp?ID=9953#.VOKo5UK4ndQ (accessed March 23, 2015).
5. See *Mishkan T'filah: A Reform Siddur: Weekdays, Shabbat, Festivals, and Other Occasions of Public Worship* (New York: CCAR Press, 2007), 32–33. For a child-friendly interpretation, see *Gates of Prayer for Young People* (New York: CCAR Press, 1997), 50.
6. Carole B. Bailin, "Making Every Forkful Count: Reform Jews, Kashrut, and Mindful Eating, 1840–2010" in *The Sacred Table: Creating a Jewish Food Ethic*, ed. Mary L. Zamore (New York: CCAR Press, 2011), 5.
7. Adapted from Mary L. Zamore, "What Kosher Eating Can Teach Us about Healthy Eating," ReformJudaism.org, October 24, 2012, www.reformjudaism.org/blog/2012/10/24/what-kosher-eating-can-teach-us-about-healthy-eating. For more about food, eating, and Jewish values, see Mary L. Zamore, *The Sacred Table: Creating a Jewish Food Ethic* (New York: CCAR Press, 2011).
8. Translation by Rami Shapiro, *Ecclesiastes: Annotated & Explained* (Woodstock, VT: SkyLight Paths, 2010), 41.
9. "Embodied Practices," Institute of Jewish Spirituality, www.jewishspirituality.org/our-spiritual-practices/embodied-practices/ (accessed May 21, 2015).
10. Asher ben Yehiel, *Orchot Chaim*, thirteenth century.
11. Mordechai of Lechovitz, quoted in Joe Bobker, *Middos, Manners & Morals with a Twist of Humor* (Jerusalem: Gefen, 2008).

Chapter 9

1. Jan Katzew, "*Davar Acher*: What is a *Davar Acher*? One Jew, Two Opinions," *RJ.org* (blog), September 27, 2010, http://blogs.rj.org/blog/2010/09/27/davar_acher_what_is_a_davar_ac/. The F. Scott Fitzgerald quotation Katzew uses is from "The Crack-Up," *Esquire*, February–April 1936, www.esquire.com/news-politics/a4310/the-crack-up/.
2. Lawrence A. Hoffman, *Covenant of Blood: Circumcision and Gender in Rabbinic Judaism* (Chicago: University of Chicago Press, 1996), 98.
3. Fred Guttman, "Building a World of Love" (sermon, Temple Emanuel, 2013), https://tegreensboro.org/yom-kippur-morning-5774-sermon-building-world-love.
4. Ebn Leader, "The Service of Love," in *Jewish Mysticism and the Spiritual Life: Classical Texts, Contemporary Reflections*, eds. Lawrence Fine, Eitan Fishbane, and Or N. Rose (Woodstock, VT: Jewish Lights, 2010), 124–25.
5. Adapted from Joel Ben Izzy, *The Beggar King and the Secret of Happiness: A True Story* (Chapel Hill, NC: Algonquin Books, 2005), 11–12.
6. We thank friends and congregants—from both our online and offline communities—for their parenting insights here, including Rabbi Ruth Adler, Beth Bloom, Lisa Colton, Resa Davids, Jonathan Freund, Ed Kaz, Jessica Kramer, Rabbi Michael Latz, Daniel Oschin, Craig Pollack, Rabbi Lisa Rosenberg, Stephanie Schneider, Tamara Lawson Schuster, Dr. Ira Schweitzer, Rabbi Margie Slome, Rabbi Ronald Stern, Rabbi Don Weber, Alison Westermann, and Adrienne Wynner.
7. Based on a midrash, *Genesis Rabbah* 38.

Chapter 10

1. Rick Jacobs, "The Genesis of Our Future" (address, Union for Reform Judaism, San Diego Biennial, December 12, 2013), http://urj.org/about/union/leadership/rabbijacobs/?syspage=article&item_id=109240.
2. Rashi and Abraham ibn Ezra on Exodus 4:10. In his commentary on the Bible, ibn Ezra writes, "And whoever says that he [Moses] had forgotten the Egyptian tongue is mistaken.... He was not referring to that, but rather ... to being unable to produce all the sounds made with the tongue and the lips, only some of which he could articulate with difficulty."
3. This and other material throughout the chapter is drawn from source material that Paul contributed to Congregation Or Ami's website (http://orami.org/community/multi-cultural-multi-racial-multi-ethnic-families).
4. Diane Tobin, "Young, Black, Jewish and Profiled," *Huffington Post*, July 30, 2013, www.huffingtonpost.com/diane-tobin/young-black-jewish-profil_b_3674073.html, referring to the 2011 Jewish Community Study of New York (www.ujafedny.org/who-we-are/our-mission/jewish-community-study-of-new-york-2011/).
5. Jewish Inclusion Project, http://thejewishinclusionproject.org (accessed March 27, 2015).

6. Rick Jacobs, "The Genesis of Our Future," talk given at the URJ San Diego Biennial, December 12, 2013. Full text available at http://urj.org/about/union/leadership/rabbijacobs/?syspage=article&item_id=109240.
7. Rami Shapiro, *Amazing Chesed: Living a Grace-Filled Judaism* (Woodstock, VT: Jewish Lights, 2012), ix.
8. Tirzah Firestone, *The Receiving: Reclaiming Jewish Women's Wisdom* (New York: HarperOne, 2003), 167.
9. Daniel C. Matt, trans. and ed., *The Zohar: Pritzker Edition*, vol. 1 (Stanford, CA: Stanford University Press, 2003), xlix.
10. "Special Needs at Or Ami," Congregation Or Ami website, http://orami.org/community/special-needs (accessed May 25, 2015).
11. Our local Los Angeles Jewish community resources include HaMercaz (www.jewishla.org/pages/special-needs), a Los Angeles–based community of support for families raising children with special needs; and Vista del Mar's Julia Ann Singer Center (www.vistadelmar.org), an outpatient service of Vista Del Mar serving youngsters with special needs, including learning disabilities, emotional problems, behavior problems, and developmental delays.
12. Norman J. Cohen, *Hineini in Our Lives: Learning How to Respond to Others Using 14 Biblical Texts and Personal Stories* (Woodstock, VT: Jewish Lights, 2003), 11.
13. Elyse Frishman, "Who's Calling, Please?" in *Text Messages: A Torah Commentary for Teens*, ed. Jeffrey K. Salkin (Woodstock, VT: Jewish Lights, 2012), 114.
14. Adapted from letters sent by Rabbi Andy Bachman and Rabbi Alan Cook.
15. Adapted from Avi Katz Orlow, "Promises for My Gay Children: Reflections of an Orthodox Rabbi for Yom Kippur," *The Canteen* (blog), October 2, 2014, www.myjewishlearning.com/blog/the-canteen/2014/10/02/promises-for-my-gay-children-reflections-of-an-orthodox-rabbi-for-yom-kippur/.
16. Adapted from blessings by Rabbi Denise Eger of Los Angeles and Rabbi Janet Marder of Palo Alto, CA.

Chapter 11

1. Nachman of Breslov, *Likkutei Moharan* 2:24.
2. Bachya on *parasha Ki Tavo*.
3. *Introduction to Charedim*, Tnai Hamitzvot, Tnai 4.
4. See Shmuly Yanklowitz, "Judaism's Value of Happiness: Living with Gratitude and Idealism," *Bloggish* (blog), *Jewish Journal*, March 9, 2012 (www.jewishjournal.com/bloggish/item/judaisms_value_of_happiness_living_with_gratitude_and_idealism_20120309); and Rabbi Sonia Saltzman, "The Pursuit of Holiness" (sermon, Temple Ohabei Shalom, Rosh Hashanah 2013), www.ohabei.org/wp-content/uploads/2013/09/Pursuit-of-Holiness-RH-day-1.pdf.

5. Adapted from Yitzhak Buxbaum, *Jewish Tales of Mystic Joy* (San Francisco: Jossey-Bass, 2002), 15.
6. Ahad Ha'am, *Hashiloah* (a monthly periodical he founded in Berlin), 1898, iii, 6.
7. Abraham J. Heschel, *Between God and Man: An Interpretation of Judaism* (New York: Simon & Schuster, 1959), 217.
8. "Shabbat Is ...," Chabad.org, www.chabad.org/library/article_cdo/aid/258916/jewish/Shabbat-Is.htm (accessed March 23, 2015).
9. From a Facebook conversation with Rabbi Bruce Block.
10. "Turn! Turn! Turn! (to Everything There Is a Season)," written by Pete Seeger. Originally by the Limeliters as "To Everything There Is a Season" on their album *Folk Matinee* and then on Seeger's *The Bitter and the Sweet*. In late 1965, the Byrds released a recording of this song as well.
11. Adapted from Dan Ehrenkrantz, "Thoughts on Kindling the Chanukah Lights," Ritualwell, www.ritualwell.org/ritual/thoughts-kindling-chanukah-lights (accessed March 1, 2015).
12. Paul Kipnes, Congregation Or Ami, Calabasas, CA.
13. "Cantor Doug Cotler's Chanukah Songsheet," Congregation Or Ami website, http://orami.org/worship/holidays/chanukah/cantor-cottlers-chanukah-song-sheet (accessed June 3, 2015).
14. Gratitude for this blessing to the colleague who shared this years ago in a Facebook group.
15. Michael Green, *Five Ways to Increase Your Spirituality* (Lulu.com, 2005), 9.
16. Menachem Mendel Schneerson, *Igrot Kodesh* (New York: Kehot Publication Society, 1987), 324.
17. Nasan Maimon, "Rabbi Nachman's Secret of Happiness," Breslov!, www.breslov.com/en/index.php?title=Rabbi_Nachman%27s_Secret_of_Happiness (accessed March 9, 2015).
18. Paul Grein, "It's Official: Pharrell Has 2014's Best-Selling Song," Yahoo! Music, December 31, 2014, www.yahoo.com/music/its-official-pharrell-has-2014s-best-selling-106748836876.html.

Suggestions for Further Reading

Storybooks on Spirituality

Kushner, Lawrence, and Karen Kushner. *Because Nothing Looks Like God*. Illustrated by Dawn Majewski. Woodstock, VT: Jewish Lights, 2000.

Sasso, Sandy Eisenberg. *But God Remembered: Stories of Women from Creation to the Promised Land*. Illustrated by Bethanne Anderson. Woodstock, VT: Jewish Lights, 2008.

———. *In God's Name*. Illustrated by Phoebe Stone. Woodstock, VT: Jewish Lights, 2004.

———. *God's Paintbrush*. 10th anniversary edition. Illustrated by Annette Compton. Woodstock, VT: Jewish Lights, 2004.

Jewish Parenting

Dardashti, Danielle, and Roni Sarig. *The Jewish Family Fun Book: Holiday Projects, Everyday Activities, and Travel Ideas with Jewish Themes*. 2nd edition. Illustrated by Avi Katz. Woodstock, VT: Jewish Lights, 2008.

Doades, Joanne. *Parenting Jewish Teens: A Guide for the Perplexed*. Woodstock, VT: Jewish Lights, 2013.

Mogel, Wendy. *The Blessing of a B Minus: Using Jewish Teachings to Raise Resilient Teenagers*. New York: Charles Scribner, 2011.

———. *The Blessing of a Skinned Knee: Using Jewish Teachings to Raise Self-Reliant Children*. New York: Charles Scribner, 2008.

Prouser, Ora Horn. *Esau's Blessing: How the Bible Embraces Those with Special Needs*. Teaneck, NJ: Ben Yehuda Press, 2012.

God and Spirituality

Barkin, Josh. *God: Jewish Choices for Struggling with the Ultimate*. Los Angeles: Torah Aura, 2008.

Citrin, Paul, ed. *Lights in the Forest: Rabbis Respond to Twelve Essential Jewish Questions*. New York: CCAR Press, 2014.

Feinstein, Edward. *Tough Questions Jews Ask: A Young Adult's Guide to Building a Jewish Life*. 2nd edition. Woodstock, VT: Jewish Lights, 2012.

Green, Arthur. *Judaism's Ten Best Ideas: A Brief Guide for Seekers*. Woodstock, VT: Jewish Lights, 2014.

———. *These Are the Words: A Vocabulary of Jewish Spiritual Life*. 2nd edition. Woodstock, VT: Jewish Lights, 2012.

Korngold, Jamie S. *The God Upgrade: Finding Your Twenty-First-Century Spirituality in Judaism's 5,000-Year-Old Tradition*. Woodstock, VT: Jewish Lights, 2011.

Matlins, Stuart M., ed. *The Jewish Lights Spirituality Handbook: A Guide to Understanding, Exploring and Living a Spiritual Life*. Woodstock, VT: Jewish Lights, 2001.

Wolpe, David. *Teaching Your Children about God: A Modern Jewish Approach*. New York: Harper Perennial, 1994.

Holidays and Family Life

Cohen, Debra Nussbaum. *Celebrating Your New Jewish Daughter: Creating Jewish Ways to Welcome Baby Girls into the Covenant*. Woodstock, VT: Jewish Lights, 2001.

Suneby, Liz, and Diane Heiman. *The Mitzvah Project Book: Making Mitzvah Part of Your Bar/Bat Mitzvah ... and Your Life*. Woodstock, VT: Jewish Lights, 2011.

Wolfson, Ron. *Hanukkah: The Family Guide to Spiritual Celebration*. 2nd edition. Woodstock, VT: Jewish Lights, 2001.

———. *Passover: The Family Guide to Spiritual Celebration*. 2nd edition. Woodstock, VT: Jewish Lights, 2003.

———. *Shabbat: The Family Guide to Spiritual Celebration*. 2nd edition. Woodstock, VT: Jewish Lights, 2002.

Online Resources

G-dcast.com. High-quality videos to give every Jewish child and adult the chance to learn the basics about Torah and Jewish holidays.

Keshetonline.org. A national organization for families and communities to create support and connection and to work for the full inclusion of LGBTQI Jews in Jewish life.

Kveller.com. A website for those who want to add a Jewish twist to their parenting.

Pjlibrary.org. Pajama Library, a program that mails free, high-quality Jewish children's literature and music to families across the continent on a monthly basis.

ReformJudaism.org. A great source for learning about Judaism, especially for unaffiliated Jews and those wishing to learn more about Reform Judaism.

AVAILABLE FROM BETTER BOOKSTORES. TRY YOUR BOOKSTORE FIRST.

Bible Study / Midrash

Passing Life's Tests: Spiritual Reflections on the Trial of Abraham, the Binding of Isaac *By Rabbi Bradley Shavit Artson, DHL*
Invites us to use this powerful tale as a tool for our own soul wrestling, to confront our existential sacrifices and enable us to face—and surmount—life's tests.
6 x 9, 176 pp, Quality PB, 978-1-58023-631-7 **$18.99**

Speaking Torah: Spiritual Teachings from around the Maggid's Table—in Two Volumes *By Arthur Green, with Ebn Leader, Ariel Evan Mayse and Or N. Rose*
The most powerful Hasidic teachings made accessible—from some of the world's preeminent authorities on Jewish thought and spirituality.
Volume 1—6 x 9, 512 pp, HC, 978-1-58023-668-3 **$34.99**
Volume 2—6 x 9, 448 pp, HC, 978-1-58023-694-2 **$34.99**

A Partner in Holiness: Deepening Mindfulness, Practicing Compassion and Enriching Our Lives through the Wisdom of R. Levi Yitzhak of Berdichev's *Kedushat Levi*
By Rabbi Jonathan P. Slater, DMin; Foreword by Arthur Green; Preface by Rabby Nancy Flam
Contemporary mindfulness and classical Hasidic spirituality are brought together to inspire a satisfying spiritual life of practice.
Volume 1— 6 x 9, 336 pp, HC, 978-1-58023-794-9 **$35.00**
Volume 2— 6 x 9, 288 pp, HC, 978-1-58023-795-6 **$35.00**

The Genesis of Leadership: What the Bible Teaches Us about Vision, Values and Leading Change *By Rabbi Nathan Laufer; Foreword by Senator Joseph I. Lieberman*
6 x 9, 288 pp, Quality PB, 978-1-58023-352-1 **$18.99**

Hineini in Our Lives
Learning How to Respond to Others through 14 Biblical Texts and Personal Stories
By Dr. Norman J. Cohen 6 x 9, 240 pp, Quality PB, 978-1-58023-274-6 **$18.99**

Masking and Unmasking Ourselves: Interpreting Biblical Texts on Clothing & Identity *By Dr. Norman J. Cohen* 6 x 9, 224 pp, HC, 978-1-58023-461-0 **$24.99**

The Messiah and the Jews: Three Thousand Years of Tradition, Belief and Hope
By Rabbi Elaine Rose Glickman; Foreword by Rabbi Neil Gillman, PhD
Preface by Rabbi Judith Z. Abrams, PhD 6 x 9, 192 pp, Quality PB, 978-1-58023-690-4 **$16.99**

The Modern Men's Torah Commentary: New Insights from Jewish Men on the 54 Weekly Torah Portions *Edited by Rabbi Jeffrey K. Salkin*
6 x 9, 368 pp, HC, 978-1-58023-395-8 **$24.99**

Moses and the Journey to Leadership: Timeless Lessons of Effective Management from the Bible and Today's Leaders *By Dr. Norman J. Cohen*
6 x 9, 240 pp, Quality PB, 978-1-58023-351-4 **$18.99**; HC, 978-1-58023-227-2 **$21.99**

The Other Talmud—The *Yerushalmi*: Unlocking the Secrets of *The Talmud of Israel* for Judaism Today *By Rabbi Judith Z. Abrams, PhD*
6 x 9, 256 pp, HC, 978-1-58023-463-4 **$24.99**

Sage Tales: Wisdom and Wonder from the Rabbis of the Talmud
By Rabbi Burton L. Visotzky
6 x 9, 256 pp, Quality PB, 978-1-58023-791-8 **$19.99**; HC, 978-1-58023-456-6 **$24.99**

The Torah Revolution: Fourteen Truths That Changed the World
By Rabbi Reuven Hammer, PhD 6 x 9, 240 pp, Quality PB, 978-1-58023-789-5 **$18.99**
HC, 978-1-58023-457-3 **$24.99**

The Wisdom of Judaism: An Introduction to the Values of the Talmud
By Rabbi Dov Peretz Elkins 6 x 9, 192 pp, Quality PB, 978-1-58023-327-9 **$16.99**

Or phone, fax, mail or email to: **JEWISH LIGHTS Publishing**
Sunset Farm Offices, Route 4 • P.O. Box 237 • Woodstock, Vermont 05091
Tel: (802) 457-4000 • Fax: (802) 457-4004 • www.jewishlights.com
Credit card orders: **(800) 962-4544** (8:30AM–5:30PM EST Monday–Friday)
Generous discounts on quantity orders. SATISFACTION GUARANTEED. Prices subject to change.

Life Cycle

Marriage / Parenting / Family / Aging

Jewish Spiritual Parenting: Wisdom, Activities, Rituals and Prayers for Raising Children with Spiritual Balance and Emotional Wholeness
By Rabbi Paul Kipnes and Michelle November, MSSW
Offers parents, grandparents, teachers and anyone who interacts with children creative first steps and next steps to make the Jewish holidays and every day engaging and inspiring. 6 x 9, 224 pp, Quality PB, 978-1-58023-821-2 **$18.99**

Jewish Wisdom for Growing Older: Finding Your Grit & Grace Beyond Midlife *By Rabbi Dayle A. Friedman, MSW, MA, BCC* Mines ancient Jewish wisdom for values, tools and precedents to embrace new opportunities and beginnings, shifting family roles and experiences of illness and death.
6 x 9, 176 pp, Quality PB, 978-1-58023-819-9 **$16.99**

Ethical Wills & How to Prepare Them
A Guide to Sharing Your Values from Generation to Generation
Edited by Rabbi Jack Riemer and Dr. Nathaniel Stampfer; Foreword by Rabbi Harold S. Kushner
A unique combination of "what is" and "how to" with examples of ethical wills and a step-by-step process that shows you how to prepare your own.
6 x 9, 272 pp, Quality PB, 978-1-58023-827-4 **$18.99**

Secrets of a Soulful Marriage: Creating & Sustaining a Loving, Sacred Relationship *By Jim Sharon, EdD, and Ruth Sharon, MS*
Useful perspectives, tools and practices for cultivating a relationship; with insights from psychology, the wisdom of spiritual traditions and the experiences of many kinds of committed couples. 6 x 9, 192 pp, Quality PB, 978-1-59473-554-7 **$16.99***

Celebrating Your New Jewish Daughter: Creating Jewish Ways to Welcome Baby Girls into the Covenant—New and Traditional Ceremonies *By Debra Nussbaum Cohen Foreword by Rabbi Sandy Eisenberg Sasso* 6 x 9, 272 pp, Quality PB, 978-1-58023-090-2 **$18.95**

The Creative Jewish Wedding Book, 2nd Edition: A Hands-On Guide to New & Old Traditions, Ceremonies & Celebrations *By Gabrielle Kaplan-Mayer*
9 x 9, 288 pp, b/w photos, Quality PB, 978-1-58023-398-9 **$19.99**

Divorce Is a Mitzvah: A Practical Guide to Finding Wholeness and Holiness When Your Marriage Dies *By Rabbi Perry Netter; Afterword by Rabbi Laura Geller*
6 x 9, 224 pp, Quality PB, 978-1-58023-172-5 **$18.99**

Embracing the Covenant: Converts to Judaism Talk About Why & How
By Rabbi Allan Berkowitz and Patti Moskovitz 6 x 9, 192 pp, Quality PB, 978-1-879045-50-7 **$16.95**

The Jewish Pregnancy Book: A Resource for the Soul, Body & Mind during Pregnancy, Birth & the First Three Months
By Sandy Falk, MD, and Rabbi Daniel Judson, with Steven A. Rapp
7 x 10, 208 pp, b/w photos, Quality PB, 978-1-58023-178-7 **$16.95**

Jewish Visions for Aging: A Professional Guide for Fostering Wholeness
By Rabbi Dale A. Friedman, MSW, MAJCS, BCC; Foreword by Thomas R. Cole, PhD Preface by Dr. Eugene B. Borowitz 6 x 9, 272 pp, HC, 978-1-58023-348-4 **$24.99**

Making a Successful Jewish Interfaith Marriage: The Big Tent Judaism Guide to Opportunities, Challenges and Resources *By Rabbi Kerry M. Olitzky with Joan Peterson Littman*
6 x 9, 176 pp, Quality PB, 978-1-58023-170-1 **$18.99**

A Man's Responsibility: A Jewish Guide to Being a Son, a Partner in Marriage, a Father and a Community Leader *By Rabbi Joseph B. Meszler*
6 x 9, 192 pp, Quality PB, 978-1-58023-435-1 **$16.99**

The New Jewish Baby Album: Creating and Celebrating the Beginning of a Spiritual Life—A Jewish Lights Companion
By the Editors at Jewish Lights; Foreword by Anita Diamant; Preface by Rabbi Sandy Eisenberg Sasso
8 x 10, 64 pp, Deluxe Padded HC, Full-color illus., 978-1-58023-138-1 **$19.95**

The New Jewish Baby Book, 2nd Edition: Names, Ceremonies & Customs—A Guide for Today's Families *By Anita Diamant* 6 x 9, 320 pp, Quality PB, 978-1-58023-251-7 **$19.99**

Parenting Jewish Teens: A Guide for the Perplexed
By Joanne Doades 6 x 9, 176 pp, Quality PB, 978-1-58023-305-7 **$16.99**

**A book from SkyLight Paths, Jewish Lights' sister imprint*

Spirituality

Amazing *Chesed*: Living a Grace-Filled Judaism
By Rabbi Rami Shapiro Drawing from ancient and contemporary, traditional and non-traditional Jewish wisdom, reclaims the idea of grace in Judaism.
6 x 9, 176 pp, Quality PB, 978-1-58023-624-9 **$16.99**

Jewish with Feeling: A Guide to Meaningful Jewish Practice
By Rabbi Zalman Schachter-Shalomi (z"l) with Joel Segel
Takes off from basic questions like "Why be Jewish?" and whether the word *God* still speaks to us today and lays out a vision for a whole-person Judaism.
5½ x 8½, 288 pp, Quality PB, 978-1-58023-691-1 **$19.99**

Perennial Wisdom for the Spiritually Independent: Sacred Teachings—Annotated & Explained *Annotation by Rabbi Rami Shapiro; Foreword by Richard Rohr*
Weaves sacred texts and teachings from the world's major religions into a coherent exploration of the five core questions at the heart of every religion's search.
5½ x 8½, 336 pp, Quality PB, 978-1-59473-515-8 **$16.99***

A Book of Life: Embracing Judaism as a Spiritual Practice
By Rabbi Michael Strassfeld 6 x 9, 544 pp, Quality PB, 978-1-58023-247-0 **$24.99**

Bringing the Psalms to Life: How to Understand and Use the Book of Psalms
By Rabbi Daniel F. Polish, PhD 6 x 9, 208 pp, Quality PB, 978-1-58023-157-2 **$18.99**

Does the Soul Survive? 2nd Edition: A Jewish Journey to Belief in Afterlife, Past Lives & Living with Purpose *By Rabbi Elie Kaplan Spitz; Foreword by Brian L. Weiss, MD*
6 x 9, 288 pp, Quality PB, 978-1-58023-818-2 **$18.99**

Entering the Temple of Dreams: Jewish Prayers, Movements and Meditations for the End of the Day *By Tamar Frankiel, PhD, and Judy Greenfeld*
7 x 10, 192 pp, illus., Quality PB, 978-1-58023-079-7 **$16.95**

First Steps to a New Jewish Spirit: Reb Zalman's Guide to Recapturing the Intimacy & Ecstasy in Your Relationship with God *By Rabbi Zalman Schachter-Shalomi (z"l) with Donald Gropman*
6 x 9, 144 pp, Quality PB, 978-1-58023-182-4 **$16.95**

Foundations of Sephardic Spirituality: The Inner Life of Jews of the Ottoman Empire
By Rabbi Marc D. Angel, PhD 6 x 9, 224 pp, Quality PB, 978-1-58023-341-5 **$18.99**

God & the Big Bang: Discovering Harmony between Science & Spirituality
By Dr. Daniel C. Matt 6 x 9, 216 pp, Quality PB, 978-1-879045-89-7 **$18.99**

God in Our Relationships: Spirituality between People from the Teachings of Martin Buber
By Rabbi Dennis S. Ross 5½ x 8½, 160 pp, Quality PB, 978-1-58023-147-3 **$16.95**

The God Upgrade: Finding Your 21st-Century Spirituality in Judaism's 5,000-Year-Old Tradition *By Rabbi Jamie Korngold; Foreword by Rabbi Harold M. Schulweis*
6 x 9, 176 pp, Quality PB, 978-1-58023-443-6 **$15.99**

The Jewish Lights Spirituality Handbook: A Guide to Understanding, Exploring & Living a Spiritual Life *Edited by Stuart M. Matlins*
6 x 9, 456 pp, Quality PB, 978-1-58023-093-3 **$19.99**

Judaism, Physics and God: Searching for Sacred Metaphors in a Post-Einstein World
By Rabbi David W. Nelson
6 x 9, 352 pp, Quality PB, inc. reader's discussion guide, 978-1-58023-306-4 **$18.99**
HC, 352 pp, 978-1-58023-252-4 **$24.99**

Repentance: The Meaning and Practice of Teshuvah
By Dr. Louis E. Newman; Foreword by Rabbi Harold M. Schulweis; Preface by Rabbi Karyn D. Kedar
6 x 9, 256 pp, HC, 978-1-58023-426-9 **$24.99**; Quality PB, 978-1-58023-718-5 **$18.99**

The Sabbath Soul: Mystical Reflections on the Transformative Power of Holy Time
Selection, Translation and Commentary by Eitan Fishbane, PhD
6 x 9, 208 pp, Quality PB, 978-1-58023-459-7 **$18.99**

***Tanya*, the Masterpiece of Hasidic Wisdom:** Selections Annotated & Explained
Translation & Annotation by Rabbi Rami Shapiro; Foreword by Rabbi Zalman Schachter-Shalomi (z"l)
5½ x 8½, 240 pp, Quality PB, 978-1-59473-275-1 **$18.99***

These Are the Words, 2nd Edition: A Vocabulary of Jewish Spiritual Life
By Rabbi Arthur Green, PhD 6 x 9, 320 pp, Quality PB, 978-1-58023-494-8 **$19.99**

**A book from SkyLight Paths, Jewish Lights' sister imprint*

Inspiration

The Chutzpah Imperative: Empowering Today's Jews for a Life That Matters *By Rabbi Edward Feinstein; Foreword by Rabbi Laura Geller*
A new view of chutzpah as Jewish self-empowerment to be God's partner and repair the world. Reveals Judaism's ancient message, its deepest purpose and most precious treasures. 6 x 9, 192 pp, HC, 978-1-58023-792-5 **$21.99**

Judaism's Ten Best Ideas: A Brief Guide for Seekers
By Rabbi Arthur Green, PhD A highly accessible introduction to Judaism's greatest contributions to civilization, drawing on Jewish mystical tradition and the author's experience. 4½ x 6½, 112 pp, Quality PB, 978-1-58023-803-8 **$9.99**

Into the Fullness of the Void: A Spiritual Autobiography *By Dov Elbaum*
One of Israel's leading cultural figures provides insights and guidance for all of us. 6 x 9, 304 pp, Quality PB, 978-1-58023-715-4 **$18.99**

The Bridge to Forgiveness: Stories and Prayers for Finding God and Restoring Wholeness
By Rabbi Karyn D. Kedar 6 x 9, 176 pp, Quality PB, 978-1-58023-451-1 **$16.99**

The Empty Chair: Finding Hope and Joy—Timeless Wisdom from a Hasidic Master, Rebbe Nachman of Breslov *Adapted by Moshe Mykoff and the Breslov Research Institute*
4 x 6, 128 pp, Deluxe PB w/ flaps, 978-1-879045-67-5 **$9.99**

The Gentle Weapon: Prayers for Everyday and Not-So-Everyday Moments—Timeless Wisdom from the Teachings of the Hasidic Master Rebbe Nachman of Breslov
Adapted by Moshe Mykoff and S. C. Mizrahi, together with the Breslov Research Institute
4 x 6, 144 pp, Deluxe PB w/ flaps, 978-1-58023-022-3 **$9.99**

God Whispers: Stories of the Soul, Lessons of the Heart *By Rabbi Karyn D. Kedar*
6 x 9, 176 pp, Quality PB, 978-1-58023-088-9 **$16.99**

God's To-Do List: 103 Ways to Be an Angel and Do God's Work on Earth
By Dr. Ron Wolfson 6 x 9, 144 pp, Quality PB, 978-1-58023-301-9 **$16.99**

Happiness and the Human Spirit: The Spirituality of Becoming the Best You Can Be
By Rabbi Abraham J. Twerski, MD
6 x 9, 176 pp, Quality PB, 978-1-58023-404-7 **$16.99**; HC, 978-1-58023-343-9 **$19.99**

Life's Daily Blessings: Inspiring Reflections on Gratitude and Joy for Every Day, Based on Jewish Wisdom *By Rabbi Kerry M. Olitzky* 4½ x 6½, 368 pp, Quality PB, 978-1-58023-396-5 **$16.99**

Restful Reflections: Nighttime Inspiration to Calm the Soul, Based on Jewish Wisdom
By Rabbi Kerry M. Olitzky and Rabbi Lori Forman-Jacobi
4½ x 6½, 448 pp, Quality PB, 978-1-58023-091-9 **$16.99**

Sacred Intentions: Morning Inspiration to Strengthen the Spirit, Based on Jewish Wisdom
By Rabbi Kerry M. Olitzky and Rabbi Lori Forman-Jacobi
4½ x 6½, 448 pp, Quality PB, 978-1-58023-061-2 **$16.99**

Saying No and Letting Go: Jewish Wisdom on Making Room for What Matters Most
By Rabbi Edwin Goldberg, DHL; Foreword by Rabbi Naomi Levy
6 x 9, 192 pp, Quality PB, 978-1-58023-670-6 **$16.99**

The Seven Questions You're Asked in Heaven: Reviewing and Renewing Your Life on Earth *By Dr. Ron Wolfson* 6 x 9, 176 pp, Quality PB, 978-1-58023-407-8 **$16.99**

Kabbalah / Mysticism

Ehyeh: A Kabbalah for Tomorrow
By Rabbi Arthur Green, PhD 6 x 9, 224 pp, Quality PB, 978-1-58023-213-5 **$18.99**

The Gift of Kabbalah: Discovering the Secrets of Heaven, Renewing Your Life on Earth
By Tamar Frankiel, PhD 6 x 9, 256 pp, Quality PB, 978-1-58023-141-1 **$18.99**

Jewish Mysticism and the Spiritual Life: Classical Texts, Contemporary Reflections *Edited by Dr. Lawrence Fine, Dr. Eitan Fishbane and Rabbi Or N. Rose*
6 x 9, 256 pp, Quality PB, 978-1-58023-719-2 **$18.99**

Seek My Face: A Jewish Mystical Theology *By Rabbi Arthur Green, PhD*
6 x 9, 304 pp, Quality PB, 978-1-58023-130-5 **$19.95**

Zohar: Annotated & Explained *Translation & Annotation by Dr. Daniel C. Matt*
Foreword by Andrew Harvey 5½ x 8½, 176 pp, Quality PB, 978-1-893361-51-5 **$18.99**
(A book from SkyLight Paths, Jewish Lights' sister imprint)

Bar / Bat Mitzvah

The Mitzvah Project Book
Making Mitzvah Part of Your Bar/Bat Mitzvah ... and Your Life
By Liz Suneby and Diane Heiman; Foreword by Rabbi Jeffrey K. Salkin; Preface by Rabbi Sharon Brous
The go-to source for Jewish young adults and their families looking to make the world a better place through good deeds—big or small.
6 x 9, 224 pp, Quality PB, 978-1-58023-458-0 **$16.99** *For ages 11–13*
Workshop Leader's Guide: 8½ x 11, 9 pp, PB, 978-1-58023-530-3 **$8.99**

The Bar/Bat Mitzvah Memory Book, 2nd Edition: An Album for Treasuring the Spiritual Celebration *By Rabbi Jeffrey K. Salkin and Nina Salkin*
8 x 10, 48 pp, 2-color text, Deluxe HC, ribbon marker, 978-1-58023-263-0 **$19.99**

For Kids—Putting God on Your Guest List, 2nd Edition: How to Claim the Spiritual Meaning of Your Bar or Bat Mitzvah *By Rabbi Jeffrey K. Salkin*
6 x 9, 144 pp, Quality PB, 978-1-58023-308-8 **$16.99** *For ages 11–13*

The Jewish Prophet: Visionary Words from Moses and Miriam to Henrietta Szold and A. J. Heschel *By Rabbi Dr. Michael J. Shire*
6½ x 8½, 128 pp, 123 full-color illus., HC, 978-1-58023-168-8 **$14.95**

Putting God on the Guest List, 3rd Edition: How to Reclaim the Spiritual Meaning of Your Child's Bar or Bat Mitzvah *By Rabbi Jeffrey K. Salkin*
6 x 9, 224 pp, Quality PB, 978-1-58023-222-7 **$18.99**
Teacher's Guide: 8½ x 11, 48 pp, PB, 978-1-58023-226-5 **$8.99**

Teens / Young Adults

Text Messages: A Torah Commentary for Teens
Edited by Rabbi Jeffrey K. Salkin
Shows today's teens how each Torah portion contains worlds of meaning for them, for what they are going through in their lives, and how they can shape their Jewish identity as they enter adulthood.
6 x 9, 304 pp, HC, 978-1-58023-507-5 **$24.99**

Hannah Senesh: Her Life and Diary, the First Complete Edition
By Hannah Senesh; Foreword by Marge Piercy; Preface by Eitan Senesh; Afterword by Roberta Grossman
6 x 9, 368 pp, b/w photos, Quality PB, 978-1-58023-342-2 **$19.99**

I Am Jewish: Personal Reflections Inspired by the Last Words of Daniel Pearl
Edited by Judea and Ruth Pearl 6 x 9, 304 pp, Deluxe PB w/ flaps, 978-1-58023-259-3 **$19.99**
Download a free copy of the ***I Am Jewish Teacher's Guide*** at www.jewishlights.com.

The JGirl's Guide: The Young Jewish Woman's Handbook for Coming of Age
By Penina Adelman, Ali Feldman and Dr. Shulamit Reinharz
6 x 9, 240 pp, Quality PB, 978-1-58023-215-9 **$16.99** *For ages 11 & up*
Teacher's & Parent's Guide: 8½ x 11, 56 pp, PB, 978-1-58023-225-8 **$8.99**

The JGuy's Guide: The GPS for Jewish Teen Guys
By Rabbi Joseph B. Meszler, Dr. Shulamit Reinharz, Liz Suneby and Diane Heiman
6 x 9, 208 pp, Quality PB, 978-1-58023-721-5 **$16.99**
Teacher's Guide: 8½ x 11, 30pp, PB, 978-1-58023-773-4 **$8.99**

Tough Questions Jews Ask, 2nd Edition: A Young Adult's Guide to Building a Jewish Life *By Rabbi Edward Feinstein*
6 x 9, 160 pp, Quality PB, 978-1-58023-454-2 **$16.99** *For ages 11 & up*
Teacher's Guide: 8½ x 11, 72 pp, PB, 978-1-58023-187-9 **$8.95**

Pre-Teens

Be Like God: God's To-Do List for Kids
By Dr. Ron Wolfson
Encourages kids ages eight through twelve to use their God-given superpowers to find the many ways they can make a difference in the lives of others and find meaning and purpose for their own.
7 x 9, 144 pp, Quality PB, 978-1-58023-510-5 **$15.99** *For ages 8–12*

The Book of Miracles: A Young Person's Guide to Jewish Spiritual Awareness
By Lawrence Kushner, with all-new illustrations by the author
6 x 9, 96 pp, 2-color illus., HC, 978-1-879045-78-1 **$16.95** *For ages 9–13*

Children's Books

Lullaby

By Debbie Friedman; Full-color illus. by Lorraine Bubar

A charming adaptation of beloved singer-songwriter Debbie Friedman's best-selling song *Lullaby*, this timeless bedtime picture book will help children know that God will keep them safe throughout the night.

9 x 12, 32 pp, Full-color illus., w/ a CD of original music & lyrics by Debbie Friedman
HC, 978-1-58023-807-6 **$18.99** *For ages 3–6*

Around the World in One Shabbat

Jewish People Celebrate the Sabbath Together

By Durga Yael Bernhard

Takes your child on a colorful adventure to share the many ways Jewish people celebrate Shabbat around the world.

11 x 8½, 32 pp, Full-color illus., HC, 978-1-58023-433-7 **$18.99** *For ages 3–6*

It's a … It's a … It's a Mitzvah

By Liz Suneby and Diane Heiman; Full-color illus. by Laurel Molk

Join Mitzvah Meerkat and friends as they introduce children to the everyday kindnesses that mark the beginning of a Jewish journey and a lifetime commitment to *tikkun olam* (repairing the world).

9 x 12, 32 pp, Full-color illus., HC, 978-1-58023-509-9 **$18.99** *For ages 3–6*

Also Available as a Board Book: **That's a Mitzvah**
5 x 5, 24 pp, Full-color illus., Board Book, 978-1-58023-804-5 **$8.99** *For ages 1–4*

What You Will See Inside a Synagogue

By Rabbi Lawrence A. Hoffman, PhD, and Dr. Ron Wolfson; Full-color photos by Bill Aron

A colorful, fun-to-read introduction that explains the ways and whys of Jewish worship and religious life.

8½ x 10½, 32 pp, Full-color photos, Quality PB, 978-1-59473-256-0 **$8.99*** *For ages 6 & up*

Because Nothing Looks Like God

By Lawrence Kushner and Karen Kushner

Invites parents and children to explore, together, the questions we all have about God.

11 x 8½, 32 pp, Full-color illus., HC, 978-1-58023-092-6 **$18.99** *For ages 4 & up*

In God's Hands *By Lawrence Kushner and Gary Schmidt*

Each of us has the power to make the world a better place—working ordinary miracles with our everyday deeds.

9 x 12, 32 pp, Full-color illus., HC, 978-1-58023-224-1 **$16.99** *For ages 5 & up*

What Makes Someone a Jew? *By Lauren Seidman*

Reflects the changing face of American Judaism. Helps preschoolers and young readers understand that you don't have to look a certain way to be Jewish.

10 x 8½, 32 pp, Full-color photos, Quality PB, 978-1-58023-321-7 **$8.99** *For ages 3–6*

In Our Image: God's First Creatures

By Nancy Sohn Swartz God asks all of nature to offer gifts to humankind—with a promise that the humans would care for creation in return.

Full-color illus., eBook, 978-1-58023-520-4 **$16.95** *For ages 5 & up*

Animated app available on Apple App Store and the Google Play Marketplace **$9.99**

The Book of Miracles: A Young Person's Guide to Jewish Spiritual Awareness
Written and illus. by Lawrence Kushner
6 x 9, 96 pp, 2-color illus., HC, 978-1-879045-78-1 **$16.95** *For ages 9–13*

The Jewish Family Fun Book, 2nd Edition: Holiday Projects, Everyday Activities, and Travel Ideas with Jewish Themes *By Danielle Dardashti and Roni Sarig*
6 x 9, 304 pp, w/ 70+ b/w illus., Quality PB, 978-1-58023-333-0 **$18.99**

When a Grandparent Dies: A Kid's Own Remembering Workbook for Dealing with Shiva and the Year Beyond *By Nechama Liss-Levinson*
8 x 10, 48 pp, 2-color text, HC, 978-1-879045-44-6 **$15.95** *For ages 7–13*

**A book from SkyLight Paths, Jewish Lights' sister imprint*

Children's Books by Sandy Eisenberg Sasso

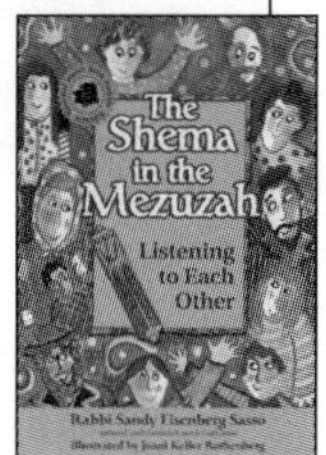

The *Shema* in the Mezuzah
Listening to Each Other
Introduces children ages 3 to 6 to the words of the *Shema* and the custom of putting up the mezuzah. Winner, National Jewish Book Award.
9 x 12, 32 pp, Full-color illus., HC, 978-1-58023-506-8 **$18.99** *For ages 3–6*

Adam & Eve's First Sunset
God's New Day
Explores fear and hope, faith and gratitude in ways that will delight kids and adults—inspiring us to bless each of God's days and nights.
9 x 12, 32 pp, Full-color illus., HC, 978-1-58023-177-0 **$17.95** *For ages 4 & up*
Also Available as a Board Book: **Adam and Eve's New Day**
5 x 5, 24 pp, Full-color illus., Board Book, 978-1-59473-205-8 **$7.99*** *For ages 1–4*

But God Remembered
Stories of Women from Creation to the Promised Land
Four different stories of women—Lilith, Serach, Bityah and the Daughters of Z—teach us important values through their faith and actions.
9 x 12, 32 pp, Full-color illus., Quality PB, 978-1-58023-372-9 **$8.99** *For ages 8 & up*

For Heaven's Sake
Heaven is often found where you least expect it.
9 x 12, 32 pp, Full-color illus., HC, 978-1-58023-054-4 **$16.95** *For ages 4 & up*

God Said Amen
An inspiring story about hearing the answers to our prayers.
9 x 12, 32 pp, Full-color illus., HC, 978-1-58023-080-3 **$16.95** *For ages 4 & up*

God's Paintbrush: Special 10th Anniversary Edition
Wonderfully interactive, invites children of all faiths and backgrounds to encounter God through moments in their own lives. Provides questions adult and child can explore together. 11 x 8½, 32 pp, Full-color illus., HC, 978-1-58023-195-4 **$18.99** *For ages 4 & up*
Also Available as a Board Book: **I Am God's Paintbrush**
5 x 5, 24 pp, Full-color illus., Board Book, 978-1-59473-265-2 **$7.99*** *For ages 1–4*
Also Available: **God's Paintbrush Teacher's Guide**
8½ x 11, 32 pp, PB, 978-1-879045-57-6 **$8.95**

God's Paintbrush Celebration Kit:
A Spiritual Activity Kit for Teachers and Students of All Faiths, All Backgrounds
9½ x 12, 40 Full-color Activity Sheets & Teacher Folder w/ complete instructions
HC, 978-1-58023-050-6 **$21.95**
8-Student Activity Sheet Pack (40 sheets/5 sessions), 978-1-58023-058-2 **$19.95**
Single-Student Activity Sheet Pack (5 sessions), 978-1-58023-059-9 **$3.95**

In God's Name
Like an ancient myth in its poetic text and vibrant illustrations, this award-winning modern fable about the search for God's name celebrates the diversity and, at the same time, the unity of all people.
9 x 12, 32 pp, Full-color illus., HC, 978-1-879045-26-2 **$18.99** *For ages 4 & up*
Also Available as a Board Book: **What Is God's Name?**
5 x 5, 24 pp, Full-color illus., Board Book, 978-1-893361-10-2 **$8.99*** *For ages 1–4*
Also Available in Spanish: **El nombre de Dios**
9 x 12, 32 pp, Full-color illus., HC, 978-1-893361-63-8 **$16.95** *For ages 4 & up*

Noah's Wife
The Story of Naamah
When God tells Noah to bring the animals of the world onto the ark, God also calls on Naamah, Noah's wife, to save each plant on earth.
9 x 12, 32 pp, Full-color illus., HC, 978-1-58023-134-3 **$16.95** *For ages 4 & up*
Also Available as a Board Book: **Naamah, Noah's Wife**
5 x 5, 24 pp, Full-color illus., Board Book, 978-1-893361-56-0 **$7.95*** *For ages 1–4*

**A book from SkyLight Paths, Jewish Lights' sister imprint*

About Jewish Lights

People of all faiths and backgrounds yearn for books that attract, engage, educate, and spiritually inspire.

Our principal goal is to stimulate thought and help all people learn about who the Jewish People are, where they come from, and what the future can be made to hold. While people of our diverse Jewish heritage are the primary audience, our books speak to people in the Christian world as well and will broaden their understanding of Judaism and the roots of their own faith.

We bring to you authors who are at the forefront of spiritual thought and experience. While each has something different to say, they all say it in a voice that you can hear.

Our books are designed to welcome you and then to engage, stimulate, and inspire. We judge our success not only by whether or not our books are beautiful and commercially successful, but by whether or not they make a difference in your life.

For your information and convenience, at the back of this book we have provided a list of other Jewish Lights books you might find interesting and useful. They cover all the categories of your life:

Bar/Bat Mitzvah
Bible Study / Midrash
Children's Books
Congregation Resources
Current Events / History
Ecology / Environment
Fiction: Mystery, Science Fiction
Grief / Healing
Holidays / Holy Days
Inspiration
Kabbalah / Mysticism / Enneagram
Life Cycle
Meditation
Men's Interest
Parenting
Prayer / Ritual / Sacred Practice
Social Justice
Spirituality
Theology / Philosophy
Travel
Twelve Steps
Women's Interest

Stuart M. Matlins, Publisher

Or phone, fax, mail or email to: **JEWISH LIGHTS Publishing**
Sunset Farm Offices, Route 4 • P.O. Box 237 • Woodstock, Vermont 05091
Tel: (802) 457-4000 • Fax: (802) 457-4004 • www.jewishlights.com
Credit card orders: **(800) 962-4544** (8:30AM–5:30PM EST Monday–Friday)